QUESTS SURD AND ABSURD

There are certain queer times and occasions in this strange mixed affair we call life when a man takes this whole universe for a vast practical joke, though the wit thereof he but dimly discerns, and more than suspects that the joke is at nobody's expense but his own. ISHMAEL

QUESTS SURD AND ABSURD

Essays in American Literature

JAMES E. MILLER, JR.

The University of Chicago Press
Chicago and London

Library of Congress Catalog Card Number: 67–25520
THE UNIVERSITY OF CHICAGO PRESS, CHICAGO 60637
The University of Chicago Press, Ltd., London W.C.1

For WALTER BLAIR
Teacher, Counselor, Critic, Friend

*I reckon that a body that ups and tells the truth
when he is in a tight place is taking considerable
many resks, though I ain't had no experience, and
can't say for certain; but it looks so to me, anyway;
and yet here's a case where I'm blest if it don't look
to me like the truth is better and actuly* safer *than
a lie.*   HUCK FINN

PREFACE

Quests Surd and Absurd is a volume of essays loosely related by their recurring concern with the quest theme in American literature. There have been so many books in recent times claiming to provide the *key* to American literature by tracing exhaustively through selected works a single theme or image that it is perhaps best to begin with a disclaimer. This book does *not* provide a key to American literature, and, indeed, is written out of the belief that no key exists, especially in the simplified form of a single image (the Garden) or character (Adam *or* Eve) or relationship (white and dark males). The reality and vitality of American literature are more complex and compelling than these oversimplifications admit; such a literature does not yield its mysteries and meanings so easily nor so quickly. *Quests Surd and Absurd*, then, makes no attempt to bend the whole of American literature to a fixed, predetermined pattern.

The essays brought together in this volume were written over a period of years, under a variety of circumstances, with no thought at the beginning of providing a single, unified work. It was only gradually to become clear that a theme was emerging—the theme of the quest. The surfacing of this theme, it should be said now, may probably be traced as much to the author's personal interests as to the inherent nature of American literature. But no one, I think, would deny the predominance of the quest in American literature, just as no one deeply immersed in that literature would want to oversimplify the nature of the recurring quest. *Quests Surd and Absurd* should be read as a series of related explorations, rather than the application and testing of a precisely defined thesis. The essays have not been revised to fit a pattern projected backward upon them, but have been allowed to stand largely as originally written, in the view that their value is as much individual as collective.

The quests of American literature are many and varied, and include and involve an astonishing range of characters: Young Goodman Brown, the protagonist of "Ulalume," the speaker of "Song of Myself," Ahab, Ishmael, Huck Finn, Jay Gatsby, Joe Christmas, Holden Caulfield, Haze Motes, Gordon Boyd, Augie March. These names are but a few that could be cited, and do not include the names of authors themselves whose entire work may be viewed as quest: Thoreau, Whitman, Dickinson, Cather, Wharton, Hemingway—and many more. As the title of this book suggests, all the quests in American literature are far from identical. *Quests Surd and Absurd* is, as a title, meant to point in two different directions, and at the same time to suggest a fundamental identity and continuity. The two directions are not mutually exclusive and are meant to suggest multiplicity rather than singularity.

The Quest Absurd, as it applies to the existential hero in contemporary literature, is perhaps self-explanatory, but the Quest Surd, as it applies to an earlier hero, needs a note of explanation. *Surd* in its root meaning is irrational, without reason; it is used today in mathematics, for example, to indicate an irrational number, such as the square root of three—a number which does not actually exist except as it is expressed symbolically $\sqrt{3}$. There is, then, irrationality in both the Quest Surd and the Quest Absurd. But in the Quest Surd the irrationality lies predominantly in the Seeker; in the Quest Absurd, the irrationality lies predominantly in the world where he wanders. Ahab's vision in *Moby Dick* was an irrational vision of a world purified of its evil; Whitman's vision in *Leaves of Grass* was an irrational (or mystical) vision of transcendent spirituality beyond the world of the physical. Both of these visions, however, posited a real and stable world which was in some sense rational, susceptible of comprehension through power of personal reason. It is this real world which has become irrational (unreal, a nightmare) in the Quest Absurd, as exemplified in such modern writers as William Faulkner, Wright Morris, or J. D. Salinger. And as the world of these recent novelists has become more irrational, their visions—the dreams of their searchers and seekers—have become more rational, humble, and human.

These distinctions, of course, have their limitations and should not be crystallized into formulas for mechanical application to writers of genius. The world of Melville's Bartleby or of Whitman's "The Sleepers" was in some sense irrational, just as the vision of Faulkner's Thomas Sutpen (in *Absalom, Absalom!*) is inhuman and (in some sense) insane. But nevertheless the distinctions may serve to point up a real shift in the direction and emphasis of our earlier literature in contrast with our more recent. In brief, the Quest Surd of the nineteenth century (and beyond) was the irrational quest in a rational world; the Quest Absurd in the later twentieth century is the rational quest in an irrational (or absurd) world.

But the structure of this book was not designed to support the weight of a thundering thesis. The essays follow their own bypaths into their own labyrinths of complexity. They range widely, from the early nineteenth century American romantics to the post–World War II new American novel, but they are arranged in inverted chronological order, to give emphasis to twentieth century developments in American literature. Essays venturing treatment and discussion of groups of writers alternate with essays dealing extensively with the total work of individual writers; included also are essays comparing two related or contrasting writers, as well as essays which analyze in depth single literary works. Critical judgments, some quite bold and perhaps eccentric, have been made without hesitation, in the view that it is the function of a critic to weigh and evaluate, as well as interpret and analyze. The very act of selection, in a literature as recent as ours, becomes by its very nature an act of evaluation.

In a way this book is in itself a quest in the American tradition. Whether it is a Quest Surd or a Quest Absurd, the reader must decide for himself.

A few of the pieces in this volume first appeared in journals or reviews. "J. D. Salinger: Some Crazy Cliff" was published in *Western Humanities Review*, Spring, 1956; "*My Ántonia*: A Frontier Drama of Time" in *American Quarterly*, Winter, 1958; "Walt Whitman: The Quest for Spirit" (in part) in *Emerson Society Quarterly*, 1961; "Whitman and Eliot: The Poetry of Mysticism" (in part) in *Southwest Review*, Spring, 1958; "Emily Dickinson's Bright Orthography" in *Hudson Review*, Summer, 1961; "Emily Dickinson: The Thunder's Tongue" in *Minnesota Review*, Spring, 1962; "Melville's Quest in Art and Life" (in part) in *The South Atlantic Quarterly*, Autumn, 1959; "Hawthorne and Melville: The Unpardonable Sin" in *PMLA*, March, 1955; "Poe's 'Ulalume' Resurrected" in *Philological Quarterly*, April, 1955; "Uncharted Interiors: The American Romantics Revisited" in *Emerson Society Quarterly*, 1964. I wish to express my thanks to the editors of these publications for permission to reprint these essays.

CONTENTS

CONTENTS

I

DEPARTURES, DISLOCATIONS, DESCENTS

. . . life is a phenomenon but not a novelty, the same frantic steeplechase toward nothing every- where and man stinks the same stink no matter where in time.   WILLIAM FAULKNER

The Quest Absurd:
The New American Novel

All of us, from time to time, have moments of insight that seem to go to the heart of our predicament, moments in which we see ourselves as we really are in all the inglorious and even ridiculous but inescapable terms of our existence. I wish to begin with such an experience that will perhaps suggest symbolically what I shall try to get at more specifically and literally in recent American fiction.

One wintry day not long ago I returned by jet from some place in the East (was it New York or Philadelphia or Washington?) to my hometown Chicago, landing at Chicago's O'Hare International Airport in late afternoon, when the dead light of day was on the verge of disappearing into the blackness of night. Briefcase in hand, I walked rapidly the long, people-thronged corridors of the airport and found my way to the vast area of the parking lot. Only the previous evening I had driven the hour's distance from my home to the airport and left the car in the lot, assuring my instant departure the moment of my return from my one-day conference in some distant yet immediately reachable city. As I emerged from the labyrinthine airport terminal into the bone-chilling winds of a Chicago winter, I fumbled in my pocket for my car check and turned it over in the leaden light to find the location of my car. Whenever I parked in the immense space of the O'Hare parking lot, it was my habit to jot down the location number on the back of the parking ticket; on this occasion, to my surprise, I found nothing—blankness. Jolted out of my half-conscious state, I began to scramble about frantically in my mind for the path I had taken from the car to the airport. I started out several times in several directions to retrace my steps from memory, but after many abortive attempts, in which everything looked familiar and yet everything looked strange, I discovered that I could not really sort out yesterday's arrival at the airport from all my other arrivals. Gradually, in a kind of strange terror, shot through simultaneously with a strong sense of the absurdity of my predicament, I had my moment of *inverted* illumination—a momentary vision not of unattainable heaven but of instant hell.

The sky was tinged with a yellowish-green color, the color of sickness, and seemed both near and far. As I rushed in minor panic up one endless parking corridor after another searching at random for my lost automobile, I stumbled over large, misshapen lumps and blocks of asphalt-blackened ice that in the unreal light took on the contours of prehistoric boulders blasted and tossed over the earth by some powerful, primitive, and diabolical energy bursting its way out of the earth's innards. I passed other people looking for automobiles, but they were intent on their missions, their eyes glazed over with abstract preoccupations or glittering with the barely submerged hysteria of panic. We were all strangers, or aliens in a foreign land—each of us seemed utterly alone on a vast Antarctica of concrete and cars, wrapped in densities of silence and muteness that were impenetrable. The streaming jet planes soaring into the space above us, the swooping, swirling, looping superhighways gigantically patterning the heights surrounding us, the glass-walled, multi-branched airport terminal itself looming like an endless and meaningless maze at our backs—all of these familiar sights became in the fading half-light sinister presences, mocking, hostile, and threatening.

I find it hard to define the feeling of loneliness, isolation, and remoteness that swept over me when I found myself in this situation. (At such moments you are left alone with your soul and you wonder if it is really there.) But at the same time, as I groped my way among the obsessed car-seekers and over the ice boulders, stumbling and staggering along the glass-glazed acres of concrete, I sensed the essential ridiculousness of my situation. I felt like a figure of tragedy (or perhaps melodrama) forced to play out a role in a semi-slapstick farce. I was not

Ahab, nor was meant to be. I was confronted with no immense moral issue nor was I engaged in some titanic struggle with some inexplicable force, within or without. My vision of hell had been precipitated by a minor lapse of memory, a lost automobile. I seemed caught in my feelings between a kind of panic and horror on the one side, and laughter and hysteria on the other. My vision of contemporary hell was both shocking and comic, horrible and hilarious.

This kind of experience, although it may not be much talked about at cocktail parties and social affairs, is, I would guess, not uncommon in today's world. I have described it in some detail because it seems to me to suggest the nature of the world in the new American novel—the American novel as it gradually evolved after World War II and as it now appears in the mid-1960's. America's machine-made, jet-propelled, plastic-comfortable world transfigured into nightmare, evoking feelings of horror mingled with a strong sense of the ridiculous—such is the nature in broad outline of novels written by such post–World War II novelists as J. D. Salinger, Wright Morris, John Updike, Reynolds Price, and Philip Roth; Norman Mailer, James Jones, Jack Kerouac, and J. P. Donleavy; William Styron, Truman Capote, Carson McCullers, and Flannery O'Connor; Saul Bellow, Bernard Malamud, Ralph Ellison, and James Baldwin; Joseph Heller, Ken Kesey, John Hawkes, and James Purdy; Thomas Pynchon, William Burroughs, Terry Southern, and John Barth. Now I would not claim that these semi-randomly selected twenty-five contemporary American novelists are all alike, or that they all equally emphasize the kind of nightmarish world or disoriented sensibility that I have been describing. Nor would I claim that these elements are radically new in literature. What I do want to suggest is that for the first time in our literature, after World War II, the world that dominated our fiction was sick, hostile, or treacherous, and that the recurring stance of the modern fictional hero reflected some mixture of horror, bewilderment, and sardonic humor—or, to use the popular term, alienation. The common pattern of action which recurred was the pattern of the quest, the quest absurd in a world gone insane or turned opaque and inexplicable, or become meaningless.

With this somewhat large and unwieldy generalization hovering over my remarks, I would like to reduce my amorphous and somewhat defiant subject to manageable proportions and order. I shall first take a look at the post–World War II period, to suggest some of the sources, in history and the times, of the materials and moods of the fiction. Next I shall glance at some of the literary currents of the past to suggest what streams seem to have flowed most vigorously into the present. Then I shall examine, with examples, what strike me as the dominant elements in our contemporary fiction. Finally I shall go out on a critical limb and name and characterize what I take to be the most significant novelists of the post-war period; and I shall sort through them rapidly, dropping tentative, and perhaps inflammable, critical judgments right and left.

The mushroom cloud that rose into the sky in 1945 was etched indelibly in men's minds forever after, separating the time before and after World War II with a gulf so wide and deep that the most agile imaginations could not leap it. The possible destruction of the world was no longer a madman's dream, but the sober reality of the so-called sane. That mushroom cloud has hung in the sky since its first creation with a somber tenacity, casting its ominous shadow over every man's least gesture, waking or sleeping. Subsequent events have ambushed the modern imagination—the explosion of the hydrogen bomb in 1953, the launching of the first manmade satellite in 1957, the landing of a space vehicle on the moon in 1966—but no one of these events, however important or ingenious scientifically, has dislodged that strangely domed pillar of fire and smoke that has burned its image into the deepest recesses of the mind.

The creation and use of the atom bomb in 1945 is, thus, one of those events, like the discoveries of Copernicus or Darwin, that radically changed man's image of himself and his possibilities. In a sense, it represented man's final takeover of power from God and Satan: from God in the discovery of the ultimate mysteries of the origin of energy; from Satan in use of the released energy for diabolical purposes. Like all such events or discoveries, the bomb would not necessarily lend itself in its own nature to the artistic imagination. But it would so alter the habits of thinking, so change the characteristic modes of perception, so pervade, however subtly, the usual ways of looking at the world, that no serious writer could fail to take it into account, even without the remotest reference to the bomb itself.

Although what the bomb did on the terrible occasions of its use was awful enough, its most profound consequence was not on the flesh but on the imagination. It set the tone and determined in subtle ways the very spirit and quality of life after World War II, changing it deeply and forever from the life of the prewar world. But there were, of course, other elements which contributed to the quality of mid-twentieth century American life. The war itself, with its casual destruction of human life on enormous scales—in the concentration camps and extermination centers or in the cities blasted by innumerable bombs or seared from the earth by the Bomb—the war itself forced a reconsideration of the nature of man and his capacity for evil and suffering, a reexamination of his proclaimed belief in the value and dignity of his own species. Who can calculate the effect on the imagination of those images out of Buchenwald of bulldozers shoveling the piles of entangled, nude, emaciated bodies, men, women and children, into huge trenches serving as common graves; or out of Hiroshima of the stunned, hurt creatures, blinded, half-burned, grotesquely disfigured or maimed. In fact the imagination reeled back from these images, incapable of comprehending at once the blinding truth of the mangled and destroyed flesh. It would take time—and it did—to absorb so much soul-staggering truth about man's inhumanity to man.

But though the shock to the collective American psyche of these events and images was profound and permanent, the surface of American life after World War II was placid and undisturbed. Instead of returning to the economic depression of the Thirties, as many expected, America moved forward into the age of affluence, an age in which organization men in gray flannel suits commuted quietly between their air-conditioned offices with the firm or corporation in the central city and their air-conditioned homes in a suburban world of manicured lawns and quiet desperation. The truth of the precarious human condition was not confronted, but it could not be entirely ignored. It was shoved into some dark corner of the unconscious, where it could fester and pain and occasionally erupt to the level of consciousness, disrupting the placidity of

7

life's empty surface. The grotesque incongruity between the tenuous spiritual plight of modern man and his fat, vacuous, unrippled life has been the source of much wonder and dismay, horror and burlesque in the modern novel.

A sequence of critical books, which could be called the "after" series, might be used for a moment to give us our bearings in literary history. In 1937, Malcolm Cowley edited a volume called *After the Genteel Tradition*, which announced the age of the lost generation. Some fourteen years later, in 1951, John W. Aldridge wrote a book called *After the Lost Generation*, proclaiming the advent of the age of alienation. About thirteen years later, in 1964, Marcus Klein published his book entitled *After Alienation*, announcing the arrival of the age of accommodation. As you can see by the shorter and shorter periods between these books, the ages announced have been coming and going with such rapidity that readers have hardly had time to become used to one before the arrival of another. Although *After Alienation* appeared as recently as 1964, it is possible that a sequel, *After Accommodation*, may appear before the decade is out. Fortunately, unless the nature of criticism changes radically, no critic can write this book until the new novelists have appeared to begin the new age with some new novels.

If we are to believe the "after" series in criticism, the Genteel Tradition was followed after World War I by the Lost Generation, followed in turn after World War II by the Age of Alienation, and bringing us currently in the 1960's to the Age of Accommodation. Although this sequence of terms has some value in enabling us to see in broad strokes some of the main currents in our fiction, we are all aware, I am sure, that such a sequence provides as much distortion as illumination. Ages are never that neat and clean and sharply delineated, particularly when expressed through novels that are by definition individualistic in attitude and vision. There is, I suspect, as much alienation now as there was when John Aldridge was discovering it in 1951—and, indeed, I imagine that it wouldn't be too hard to find in the Lost Generation, or, to go back a hundred years, in Melville's *Moby Dick* or *Bartleby the Scrivener*. In making these statements, I know that I am ignoring some of the finer discriminations that our critics have made—and that I shall want to make in trying to describe the new American novel. But since so much emphasis in recent criticism has been placed on the advent of the new, it is perhaps useful to turn for a moment to certain continuities that connect the past with the present in our fiction.

The persistence of the past may be noted in one way by looking at the writers strongly identified with a long-since faded period of the past who are still alive in the second half of the decade of the Sixties—for example, John Dos Passos and John Steinbeck. More important than these, however, were Ernest Hemingway, who killed himself so recently as 1961, and William Faulkner, who died even more recently in 1962. It is probable that Hemingway and Faulkner cast such long shadows beyond themselves that even in the latter part of their lives, when they were producing their weakest works, they were still keeping our contemporary age from seeing the genuine talent of its new writers. As long as Faulkner and Hemingway were alive, along with such poets as Robert Frost and William Carlos Williams, who lived into 1963, and T. S. Eliot, who lived into 1965, we seemed in America to have already at hand our contemporary literature. Any younger writer, when measured by these contemporary giants out of the past, fell woefully short.

But with the passing of all these giants in the first part of the present decade of the Sixties, our past as well as our present seemed to fall into better perspective. Our younger writers emerged from the wings and took center stage, and we began to see them and the older writers in a new light. As for the older American novelists, the three who seemed to have the greatest impact on contemporary fiction and to speak most deeply to the contemporary mood were Herman Melville, Henry James, and William Faulkner. These three major American novelists appeared to possess the metaphysical concerns, the psychological insights, or the fictional strategies that seemed most relevant to the new times. If these three novelists may be considered as constituting the major river running in full flood from the past to the present, we may then go on to identify a number of tributaries, streams and creeks, which also connect. Somewhere in these last categories must be placed Ernest Hemingway and F. Scott Fitzgerald, with Hemingway taking a much lesser place and Fitzgerald a greater place than most of us thought not long ago—the Fitzgerald not only of

The Great Gatsby but also and especially of *Tender Is the Night* and *The Crack-up*. And when we come to such names as Thomas Wolfe, John Dos Passos, James T. Farrell, or John Steinbeck, we are dealing with mere rivulets—or perhaps even with still or stagnant pools that have no outlets at all.

There are of course many other tributaries to the contemporary novel. I shall list a number, not to exhaust the possibilities, but to suggest the diversity. A list of names of European writers could probably be extended indefinitely, but would surely include Dostoevski, Kafka, Joyce, Proust, and Lawrence. Back in the 1950's, there were subterranean connections between France's Existentialism, England's Angry Young Men, and America's Beat Generation. Though the latter two categories or movements seem to have faded, Existentialism, although watered down and thinned out, seems still an inescapable philosophy or attitude. Whether or not there is universal agreement that substance precedes essence, existential terms such as *anguish, absurdity,* and *nausea* seem not only applicable but necessary for the description of much in contemporary fiction. But in absorbing elements from the French Existentialists, American writers may be more native than they at first seem. Just as Edgar Allan Poe and his American Gothic arrived in America in the twentieth century not by a direct route but via a French detour (imported by T. S. Eliot), so such writers as Dos Passos, Hemingway, and particularly Faulkner come home to us now, not only along native roads, but also from across the seas, as subtly transmuted by Sartre and Camus. The French have once again taught us to see with new eyes what we already have.

Two additional shaping influences on the contemporary novel need to be mentioned in passing. The first is a rivulet that may be traced back to the 1930's, but not in the proletarian novels of the depression. I refer to Henry Miller, and his *Tropic of Cancer* and *Tropic of Capricorn,* both of which works led subversive lives outside the country until their recent official admission. They must stand as forerunners of such contemporary works as Jean Genet's *Our Lady of the Flowers* in France and William Burroughs' *Naked Lunch* in America. Whether we consider Henry Miller a rivulet that is pure stream or a sewer leak, his mute presence in many dark corners of contemporary fiction must be admitted. The second influence, not so special yet difficult to trace, is the Theater of the Absurd. The post-World War II revival of an art form that had so many times been declared dead and buried came as something of a surprise to most critics. Such playwrights as Eugene Ionesco, Samuel Beckett, Harold Pinter, and America's own Edward Albee, with such plays as *The Bald Soprano, Waiting for Godot, The Caretaker,* or *The American Dream,* have had an impact on both the conception and the art of the contemporary novel. The mad or upside-down or forsaken world so often portrayed in the theater of the absurd is the kind of world the American novel has been tending toward ever since World War II. And the startling disjuncture between the thunderclap of events and the inanity of the response of the characters in the Theater of the Absurd is the kind of disjuncture that recent American fiction has tended to portray and explore. No doubt influence has traveled two ways, from drama to novel and back again. The compatibility of the Theater of the Absurd and the contemporary novel may be suggested symbolically by noting that Edward Albee has found suitable material for two of his full-length dramas in two important recent novels, Carson McCullers' *The Ballad of the Sad Cafe,* and James Purdy's *Malcolm.* And in his dramatizations, Albee did not find it necessary to change the worlds of the novels; his only problem was to discover how to realize those worlds dramatically.

By now I have thrown out some strong suggestions about the dominant characteristics which I find in contemporary fiction. But it should be useful to look at these characteristics systematically, with a few illustrative examples in each case. I have, more or less arbitrarily, identified four elements in the contemporary novel which seem to me distinctive and significant, and which, in combination, set the novel of our time off from the pre-World War II novel. First, there is what might be called the inverted or nightmare world of recent fiction. Second, there is the disoriented, disaffected, or alienated hero, suffering a severe sickness of the soul—or spiritual nausea. Third, there is, conversely, a quest for identity, a search for a self that is leaking away, disappearing, or lost, or—most horrible of all—non-existent. And fourth, there is in the actions of these novels a multitude of events compounded indiscriminately of horror and humor, a bizarre and even sick comedy that repels at the same time that it evokes guilty and perhaps sinister laughter. Let us briefly explore each of these elements in turn.

1. *The Nightmare World* Although the nightmare world is not peculiar to post–World War II fiction, as witness the Gothic novel and the example of Edgar Allan Poe—still the world of contemporary fiction seems to have its own special inversion of views and values, a kind of Gothic terror stalking main street in broad daylight. It was once thought that only Southern Gothic, in the tradition of Poe and Faulkner, created a misshapen and haunted world, peopled by grotesques and misfits, spooks of the spirit, deformed and warped in brain and body. And it is certainly true that in our own time such southerners as Carson McCullers, in *The Ballad of the Sad Cafe*, or Truman Capote, in *Other Voices, Other Rooms* or the recent *In Cold Blood*, or Flannery O'Connor, in *Wise Blood* or *The Violent Bear It Away*—such southerners have continued the tradition of the Gothic, putting it to use for their own special purposes. But it is also true that the Gothic has travelled north and turned up in the works of such novelists as James Purdy, in *Malcolm* or *The Nephew*, or John Hawkes, in *The Cannibal* or *Second Skin*. Of course the nightmare world has been a convention of the war novel for some time, and it was such a world that Norman Mailer created in *The Naked and the Dead*. But the nightmare achieves an extra dimension in a war novel like Joseph Heller's *Catch-22*, where the hostilities and brutalities are deepened by a hair-raising whimsicality, pettiness, and insanity. In one of the book's most frightening scenes, the "hero" Yossarian wanders at night in liberated Rome. Listen to just a few of the sentences: "The night was filled with horrors and he thought he knew how Christ must have felt as he walked through the world, like a psychiatrist through a ward full of nuts, like a victim through a prison full of thieves. What a welcome sight a leper must have been! At the next corner a man was beating a small boy brutally in the midst of an immobile crowd of adult spectators who made no effort to intervene. Yossarian recoiled with sickening recognition." Such images of senseless brutality as this abound not only in *Catch-22* but throughout contemporary fiction; the sinister lurks in the familiar, hatred hides in the package of love, and our fondest dreams explode in our hands as we look on in horror.

2. *Alienation and Nausea*   The term "hero" seems a misnomer, for there are no heroes in contemporary fiction. Everybody loses, nobody wins. "Anti-hero" seems too precious a term to substitute. Perhaps the best term is "antagonist," for the main character seems always in deadly conflict in contemporary fiction—in conflict with the world, which is out to crush or destroy him. The passage from *Catch-22* quoted above concludes: "Yossarian recoiled with sickening recognition." This recoil and this sickening recognition are the recurring responses to the world not only of Yossarian but of most contemporary protagonists. Saul Bellow's Henderson or Herzog survive their defeats, their heads both a bit bloodied and a bit bowed. James Baldwin's Rufus Scott in *Another Country,* on the other hand, commits suicide. Flannery O'Connor's Haze Motes in *Wise Blood* blinds himself and walks in his glass-filled shoes until he finds death. The suicidal impulse recurs in Norman Mailer's *An American Dream* and becomes the central theme and structural device in John Barth's *The Floating Opera.* Probably the most famous suicide in contemporary fiction is that of J. D. Salinger's Seymour Glass, which takes place in a short story called "A Perfect Day for Bananafish," and about which we have not yet heard the last. Although it turns out in Salinger's continuing retrospective accounts that Seymour Glass's capacity for understanding and forgiveness was boundless, still at the heart of his self-destruction was a profound vision of the world's insensitivity, heartlessness, and phoniness. His spirit suffering from shell-shock of the war, his marriage to the vulgar and shallow Muriel floundering into meaninglessness—he picks up a gun and puts a bullet through his brain. Such alienation seems to be the obsessive subject of Salinger, as character after character hovers on the brink of the total withdrawal, from Sergeant X and Holden Caulfield to Franny, Zooey, and Buddy Glass. Franny Glass seems to speak for them all when she cries out, "I'm just sick of ego, ego, ego. My own and everybody else's." Although suffering from acute spiritual nausea, all these characters (unlike Seymour Glass) make some kind of separate peace with themselves and with the world.

3. *Quest for Identity*   Although the search for the self runs deep in American literature, as might be expected in a country not at all sure of its own identity or soul, the quest takes on a new poignancy in the modern novel. The new hero usually

—but not always—has his literal identity, an address and a name, but in spirit he is Ishmael still, searching for a strayed, runaway, or uncreated self. He becomes an alien in his familiar land. James Baldwin gives a title to his book of essays, *Nobody Knows My Name*, which may stand for this recurring theme in contemporary fiction. The search for the heart of one's own nature runs all through Baldwin's novels, from *Go Tell It on the Mountain* to *Another Country*. And it runs, too, through Flannery O'Connor's *Wise Blood* and *The Violent Bear It Away*. Wright Morris' Gordon Boyd (in *The Field of Vision* and *Ceremony in Lone Tree*) digs deep in his past—to the time when as a kid he tried to walk on water—to discover the remnants of a long-squandered or never-discovered self. Bernard Malamud's Frank Alpine in *The Assistant* and S. Levin in *A New Life* both travel journeys into the interior being in search of an old and lost—or new and elusive—self. The protagonist of Ralph Ellison's *Invisible Man*, at one point on the downward spiral of his fortunes, after the explosion of the bubbling paint-vat in the white-paint factory, is swimming back to consciousness and sees the words looming above him: "Who . . . are . . . you?" He remembers: "Something inside me turned with a sluggish excitement. This phrasing of the question seemed to set off a series of weak and distant lights. . . . Who am I? I asked myself. But it was like trying to identify one particular cell that coursed through the torpid veins of my body. Maybe I was just this blackness and bewilderment and pain. . . ." The question, "Who are you?" resounds throughout *Invisible Man*, as it does through all contemporary fiction—and frequently remains, at the end of the road, unanswered and perhaps unanswerable.

4. *The Humor in the Horror* Though all the ingredients of modern fiction look like the ingredients of stark tragedy, they turn out most frequently, when mixed with heavy dashes of the modern ironic sensibility, to be the ingredients of a kind of comedy of outrage, often hilarious. Near the end of Salinger's *Catcher in the Rye*, after Holden Caulfield has seemingly tried and found locked all the doors that might lead him out of his terrible predicament, he attempts to preoccupy himself by reading a magazine he finds on a park bench: "But this damn article I started reading made me feel almost worse. It was all about hormones. It described how you should look, your face

14

and eyes and all, if your hormones were in good shape, and I didn't look that way at all. I looked exactly like the guy in the article with lousy hormones. So I started getting worried about my hormones. Then I read this other article about how you can tell if you have cancer or not. It said if you had any sores in your mouth that didn't heal pretty quickly, it was a sign that you probably had cancer. I'd had this sore on the inside of my lip for about *two weeks*. So I figured I was getting cancer. That magazine was some little cheerer upper." This is but one instance in a multitude in the book in which an episode of crucial seriousness is alleviated—or intensified—by a comic mode. Wright Morris repeatedly injects the absurd in his serious novels, as when in *The Field of Vision* he has Gordon Boyd shake a bottle of pop and squirt the supercharged liquid into the face of a bull in the middle of the bull fight, or when in *Ceremony in Lone Tree*, he portrays the mailman Bud Momeyer, arrayed in Indian feathers, shooting an arrow through Colonel Ewing's pet bulldog which has been insured for $10,000. The comic tone filters through all of the grotesqueries of Flannery O'Connor: near the end of *Wise Blood*, Haze Motes has blinded himself and begins to indulge in other means of self-torture, such as wrapping barbed wire around his chest in preparation for sleep; his landlady Mrs. Flood exclaims, "There's no reason for it. People have quit doing it"; he answers with stoic logic: "They ain't quit doing it as long as I'm doing it." Absurdity abounds everywhere in such surrealists and satirists as James Purdy (from *Malcolm* to *Cabot Wright Begins*) and Terry Southern (from *Candy* to *The Magic Christian*). And even in so sober a novelist as Saul Bellow, *Herzog* is structurally based on an essentially comic device, the protagonist's mad letter-writing to everyone ranging from his enemies to the classic philosophers and even to God—copiously quoted letters which are never sent anywhere, except to the reader.

As the comic doomsday vision has come to dominate the fiction of the post–World War II period, it has recently acquired the title of "black humor." And although it is not difficult to find pre–World War II examples (as in William Faulkner's *Sanctuary* or *As I Lay Dying*, or Herman Melville's *Bartleby* or *Confidence Man*), never before in our literature, perhaps, has the blackness been so bleak or the comedy so savage. Recent examples which loom largest, all novels of the 1960's, are Joseph Heller's *Catch-22*, Ken Kesey's *One Flew Over the Cuckoo's Nest,* and Thomas Pynchon's *V.* If, for example, we read Kesey's *Cuckoo's Nest* as a paradigm of the predicament of modern man, we find the entire world a nuthouse, with Big Nurse in her stiff, starched white, imposing her power through the use of all her gleaming, glittering, flashing machinery; and her power completes the degradation and dehumanization of her victims, who are efficiently divided into two groups: the "hopeful" Acutes, who "move around a lot. They tell jokes to each other and snicker in their fists . . . and they write letters with yellow, runty, chewed pencils"; and the hopeless Chronics, who are the culls of the Acutes—the "Chronics are in for good . . . [and] are divided into Walkers . . . and Wheelers and Vegetables." The great fear of the Acute is to become a Chronic, as has happened to one Ellis, who came back from the "brain-murdering room," or the "Shock Shop," "nailed against the wall in the same condition they lifted him off the table for the last time, in the same shape, arms out, palms cupped, with the same horror on his face. He's nailed like that on the wall, like a stuffed trophy. They pull the nails when it's time to eat. . . ." Ellis may be one version of modern man, hopeless, helpless, self-crucified, committed for life to a super-efficient asylum that destroys what it cannot dehumanize.

The nightmare world, alienation and nausea, the quest for identity, and the comic doomsday vision—these are the four elements that characterize recent American fiction. But a fifth element should be added, not as one of the central or dominant ingredients, but, as I place it here, as a kind of afterthought, or postscript. It is—

5. *A Thin, Frail Line of Hope* It would be misleading, if only slightly so, to imply that all is despair in the contemporary novel. There is, in fact, some measure of affirmation in nearly all of the contemporary novelists, slender in some, robust in others. In the novelists who are, in some complex sense, religious novelists, such as J. D. Salinger, Flannery O'Connor, or John Updike, the affirmation tends to be expressed in some kind of spiritually transcendental terms, however vague or faint. In such surrealistic novelists as James Purdy, John Hawkes, or William Burroughs, the hope, if it is there, appears

only occasionally and faintly in the tone of voice emerging from behind the pages of the novels. Perhaps most characteristic of the thin, frail line of hope in contemporary fiction is the kind of affirmation found in such novels as Heller's *Catch-22* and Kesey's *One Flew Over the Cuckoo's Nest*—the defiant assertion of one's humanity in the face of overwhelming forces that dehumanize and destroy.

If we may assume that these elements I have been trying to define are some of the most significant characteristics of contemporary fiction, there still remain the crucial critical questions. Who are the novelists most likely to endure? Where are our modern Melvilles, Jameses, and Faulkners? Measured by such high standards, it is difficult to see our age as running over with riches. There is now no talent, at least fully visible on the scene, of this high level. But it is sobering to recall that Melville, James, and Faulkner, each in his turn, had to wait for a delayed recognition of his genius. Who can say that we are not now overlooking our greatest writers?

With all the risks involved, I shall attempt to sort through some twenty-five post–World War II novelists (see the list, "Recent American Novelists," which gives their fiction and non-fiction, at the end of this essay). What I offer is far from a definitive critical statement. It is a personal account of my own reading blended with all the critical judgment I can summon to correct some of my more radical biases. Although I may seem harsh in my judgment of some of these writers, I should emphasize that I take them all seriously enough to read them with attention and care, and if I thought any of them hopelessly trivial, I would not have them on my list at all. And I should also emphasize that I have arbitrarily omitted a number of important writers from my list because they seem to me to belong to another, or previous, generation, even though they have published important books since World War II—such novelists as Robert Penn Warren (and his *All the King's Men*), Vladimir Nabokov (*Lolita*) and Katherine Anne Porter (and her *Ship of Fools*).

The novelists I group together first are all writers who at some point have inspired excitement—but have ended by disappointing. These novelists I conceive of now as traveling along some downward curve. I no longer look to them, as I might once have done, for innovation or important contribution to the American novel. They are James Jones, Norman Mailer, Carson McCullers, Truman Capote, Jack Kerouac, and James Baldwin. I shall never forget the time, shortly after many of us had just emerged from World War II, when Norman Mailer published *The Naked and the Dead* (1948) and James Jones *From Here to Eternity* (1951). These novels had a power and energy that appealed to us then, and I think we looked forward to the beginning of a creative renaissance similar to the one after World War I. As we watched over the years, however, these two immense talents seemed to leak away in a series of inferior works, manifesting time after time a simple lack of discipline in the craft of fiction. Of the two writers, Mailer maintained, and still maintains, a fairly vivid public image by sheer dramatic skill in playing the role of writer for the mass media. It is hard to know whether *An American Dream* (1965) was a cynical joke on its *Esquire* audience, or a serious effort of a genuinely deluded writer.

Not long after the initial powerful impact of Jones and Mailer, two frailer figures swam into our ken, Carson McCullers and Truman Capote, two writers usually listed in the Southern Gothic camp. Of course Carson McCullers had appeared before the war, with *The Heart Is a Lonely Hunter* (1940), but later, with *Ballad of the Sad Cafe* (1951), she took her place alongside Truman Capote and his exciting *Other Voices, Other Rooms* (1948), as one of the voices out of the South speaking up with precision of style and brilliance of form for the culls and rejects of society, for bypassed and forlorn areas in the hidden regions of the heart. But in their later work, both writers seemed to trail off into romantic regions of sentimentality. Capote's celebrated *In Cold Blood* (1966), a brilliant piece of reportage utilizing many of the techniques of fiction, is a remarkable feat both of memory and of imagination, but does not, I think, indicate a genuine resurgence of a fictional talent.

Jack Kerouac, king of the Beats, seemed to catch the restlessness of American life and the nervous energy of a generation in his *On the Road* (1957), but it turned out to be the kind of novel that did not really wear very well, and Kerouac's subsequent work, much of it written according to his weird theory of unconscious action-writing (analogous to action-painting) seemed more and more self-indulgent and undisciplined and less and less relevant to the very real problems of the real world. James Baldwin, on the other hand, focused in his fiction on the problems that filled the headlines of the 1960's. In dealing with race and deviant sex in a novel like *Another Country* (1962), Baldwin succeeded in being more sensational than significant—and ultimately sentimental. His first novel, *Go Tell It on the Mountain* (1953), written out of the searing experiences of his boyhood in Harlem, seems now likely to stand as his best and most powerful work.

Alongside these novelists in decline (and I hope that any one of them proves me wrong), I place another group that I arbitrarily designate as Cult writers. If I have ceased to look to the first group for major new work, I have never looked to the Cult writers for the startlingly important contributions to our fiction. Though they have written novels of some impact and interest, their work generally seems more experimental than significant, frequently marred by mere eccentricity and a kind of mannered superficiality. They are James Purdy, John Hawkes, William Burroughs, and Terry Southern. Each has a small group of devoted and articulate admirers.

James Purdy probably produced his most bizarre, semi-surrealistic effects in his early work, such as *63: Dream Palace* (1957) and *Malcolm* (1959), dealing repeatedly with the morbid seduction of innocence. His later novels, such as *Cabot Wright Begins* (1964), portraying a phenomenally successful rapist, seem a somewhat tired parody of earlier work. John Hawkes is, I think, a more serious worker than Purdy—but he is perhaps too serious. His fusion of the aftermaths of the two World Wars in his first novel, *The Cannibal* (1949), and his blurring of landscapes into unreality in his last novel, *Second Skin* (1964)—all seems highly mannered and not so much an advance on the techniques of Joyce or Faulkner as a working to exhaustion of the semi-stagnant backwaters of fictional craft. Hawkes appears in his tortured technique to have something significant to say, but his bleak wastelands and his blurred, dreamlike characters seem ultimately ends isolated in themselves, remarkable (but not vital) feats of a northern Gothic imagination. William Burroughs shook the scene with a minor earthquake, *Naked Lunch* (1962), a work that mixed violence and sex and dope-addiction in a kind of glorious or glorified incoherence. The book's surrealistic stream of consciousness seemed shallower and more self-consciously polluted than the streams of earlier fiction. Burroughs' *Nova Express* (1964) and *The Soft Machine* (1966) seem no advance, but more of the same. Terry Southern's *The Magic Christian* (1960) is the greatest collection of adolescent practical jokes to appear in a long time. And his notorious *Candy* (1959—written with Mason Hoffenberg) suggests a sense of humor permanently arrested in immaturity. I shall, of course, continue to follow all these Cult writers, even though I am unable to render them the homage and adulation demanded by their ardent coteries.

My four remaining clusters of novelists are less sharply defined than my Declining-Curve novelists and my Cult novelists. The four groups shade into one another so subtly and so imperceptibly that I have not entirely convinced myself that the categories are valid. The stable center of these clusters consists of novelists whose achievement is solid enough to warrant our attention regardless of future work. On this side of the center is a group of familiar novelists on whom I am waiting—with great expectations. On the far side is a group of newer, younger novelists whom I am watching, with considerable hope.

There are, I think, three novelists who belong in any discussion of contemporary fiction, but about whom there hovers a feeling of somewhat anxious expectancy. These novelists are not young enough to be called simply promising, but neither has their work, though substantial, reached a level of equilibrium. These novelists are poised on the threshold still, and hesitancy hangs in the air. They are Ralph Ellison, William Styron, and Bernard Malamud. Ralph Ellison's remarkable novel, *Invisible Man*, appeared as long ago as 1952, and has gradually established itself as *the* American Negro novel. Although it appears to far outrank the work of Richard Wright and James Baldwin, and although the protagonist has elicited comparison with Dostoevski's underground man and Melville's Ishmael, there persist still a few critical doubts about some of the lengthy, dreary passages (in the latter half of the novel) which suggest a flagging of the imagination. Ellison's next novel, long awaited, will perhaps clear up the doubts and tell us whether *Invisible Man* is the beginning or the climax of an important fictional talent. William Styron produced a remarkable first novel, *Lie Down in Darkness*, in 1951, and although many of the elements of plot and technique bore strong resemblance to the Faulkner of *The Sound and the Fury* (note, for example, the suicide of time-conscious Peyton Loftis and the suicide of clock-conscious Quentin Compson), Styron seemed on the verge of finding his own voice. But with *Set This House on Fire*, in 1960, he seemed to fall back rather than advance, mixing weak F. Scott Fitzgerald with watered-down existential philosophy. Bernard Malamud seemed to hit his stride with his second novel, *The Assistant* (1957). Although it had the quaint odor of the Depression-Thirties about it, the ex-Catholic protagonist's ultimate recognition that he must become a Jew seemed to be a direct confrontation with the anguished and suffering present. But Malamud's next novel, *A New Life* (1962), deflated high expectations with shock and dismay; his personal vision seemed replaced by personal vindictiveness against his academic enemies in an obscure college of the Pacific Northwest, a region clearly uncongenial to Malamud's imagination. And his new novel, *The Fixer* (1966), is a fictional reworking of historical materials and appears to represent not so much an advance as a retreat of imagination.

The novelists who, in my view, have crossed the threshold and have made serious claims for some kind of permanent recognition are four in number: J. D. Salinger, Flannery O'Connor (who died in 1964), Saul Bellow, and Wright Morris. It would be difficult to assemble four more radically differing talents. In terms of sheer bulk of productivity, Salinger and O'Connor belong on the thin side, Bellow and Morris on the heavy side of the ledger. My crystal ball tells me Salinger and O'Connor belong with that select group of American novelists whose slender novels have supported amazingly powerful reputations—such novelists as Nathaniel Hawthorne (with *The Scarlet Letter*), Stephen Crane (with *The Red Badge of Courage*), or F. Scott Fitzgerald (with *The Great Gatsby*). Salinger's *Catcher in the Rye* (1951) and O'Connor's *Wise Blood* (1952) have tough surface appeal as well as depths and profundities that reward re-exploration. These are the kinds of small novels that have big reverberations, in the individual and the culture.

On the other hand, it seems significant that when we think of Bellow and Morris, we think not so much of single works but of all half-dozen of Bellow's novels and all dozen of Morris'.

What we recognize in them is a sustained feat of the imagination, the prolonged and repeated exploration of a coherent and persuasive fictional world of their own brilliant creation. Single novels do not tend to stand out because the individual works seem to be part of a larger whole—as with the work of Dickens or James. This is more true of Morris than of Bellow, especially since Morris carries over his strange Nebraska characters from one novel to another, in the manner of Faulkner and his Yoknapatawpha County folk (or, indeed, in the manner of Salinger in his history of the Glass family). In spite of this characteristic of their work, however, it is possible to select novels that may serve best as initial entries into the fictive worlds of Bellow and Morris. For Bellow it may be an early novel, *The Victim* (1947), and for Morris two novels that form a single unit, *The Field of Vision* (1956) and *Ceremony in Lone Tree* (1960).

Do these four important contemporary novelists share, in spite of their marked differences, anything in common? Although their worlds are different, and sometimes even exotic in their differences, they are the recognizable worlds of here and now, the U.S.A. in mid-twentieth century in all its authentic multiplicity. J. D. Salinger creates the eastern city-world of rebelling wise kids and of humdrum existence occasionally redeemed by intense moments of mystical insight. Flannery O'Connor transports the reader to the rural Bible-belt South and a world of illiterate, religiously (or atheistically) obsessed grotesques, who turn out in her religious imagination to be more human in their grotesqueness than the comfort-seekers who surround and tempt them. Saul Bellow's world is the Jewish urban world of New York and Chicago in which anguish and terror predominate, the big questions are posed—and suffering man endures. Wright Morris holds up for scrutiny the small-town America of the midwest Great Plains—Willa Cather's pioneer world come to full dark flower—and searches through the bewildering flux of time present for the reverberating events of time past. East or West, North or South, the protagonists of all these novelists share a geography of the soul, a surrealistic landscape of brutally impersonal city streets, of gigantic superhighways sweeping meaninglessly, aimlessly across the land, of violence erupting like an enflamed boil and pouring its corruption over town and countryside, of death's skulls shining forth a grinning light out of the prevailing blackness, of the Bomb quietly ticking away in some obscure corner. This landscape is, of course, a montage, but it would not be foreign to Salinger's Holden Caulfield or Seymour Glass, O'Connor's Haze Motes or Francis Tarwater, Bellow's Asa Leventhal or Moses Herzog, or Morris' Gordon Boyd or Walter McKee. But in spite of their portrayal of experience as menacing and hostile, none of these novelists is a novelist of despair, each of them is in search of some affirmative thread to follow through the maze of contemporary life's nightmare world.

Of the eight novelists of promise—novelists worth watching—that I will mention in my last two clusters, one must be singled out for a special category and tribute—John Updike. Born in 1932, Updike has already outstripped many of his older fellow-novelists in productivity, having published four novels, four volumes of short stories, and two volumes of poetry. And in my view the quality has matched the quantity: Updike belongs at the very top of the new young novelists. From his first novel, *The Poorhouse Fair* (1959), to his most recent, *Of the Farm* (1965), Updike has dealt with plain subjects in simple settings: the old people at a poorhouse of the future plan their annual fair; a young man brings his second wife and her son to visit his mother on the family farm. Out of such homely situations Updike spins his stories—but the web he spins is frequently magic, and the depths he sounds often profound. Those who charge that Updike is a dazzling stylist caught without a subject—that nothing significant happens in his novels—have confused subtlety with superficiality, and have forgotten that the same confused charge was lodged against one of the greatest of our novelists, Henry James.

Two other novelists of promise are astonishing in their dissimilarities, especially in the material they treat. Reynolds Price seems at first glance to be an anachronism, discovering his material in bypassed rural areas of the South. But in his two lyrical novels (*A Long and Happy Life*, 1962, and *A Generous Man*, 1966) dealing with the Mustian family, he succeeds in investing simple, unsophisticated country folk with a significance and a dignity rare in contemporary fiction: his comedy is always gentle, his sympathies always engaged. Philip Roth, on the other hand, has difficulty in persuading his reader of the significance of the more sophisticated, more urbanized material he treats. His first work, *Goodbye, Columbus* (1959), displayed an immense talent that appeared under full control and in full power. But the ponderously realistic *Letting Go* (1962) seemed flaccid, undisciplined, and verging always on the pretentious or pompous. But both Price and Roth are young, and are seriously engaged with their craft.

The remaining five novelists I have gathered together under the now fashionable, perhaps faddish, term, black humor. This term is much too simplistic, if not simple-minded, but it will serve to join loosely together J. P. Donleavy, John Barth, Joseph Heller, Ken Kesey, and Thomas Pynchon. There is laughter in all these novelists, but it is a laughter slightly off key, a laughter shot through with needling pain, a laughter that shades off on one side into the hysterical, on the other into the moronic. Frequently the hero is a rogue, and a rogue hell-bent on his own pleasure, the world be damned—for, after all, the world is insane. Thomas Pynchon, with the parodistic allegory *V.* (1963), presents a fireworks display of immense talent, but too many of the firecrackers fizzle, and excessive length leads to tediousness and the death of humor, black, white, or gray. Even his shorter *The Crying of Lot 49* (1966) seems to fizzle more than it fires. J. P. Donleavy and John Barth have both produced a more substantial body of work than the relatively young Pynchon. But Donleavy's heroes, such as Sebastian Dangerfield in *The Ginger Man* (1958), or Samuel S in *The Saddest Summer of Samuel S* (1966), tend to lose their charm as they become anarchistic sadists, or sadistic anarchists, with a fatal tinge of self-pity. And John Barth's heroes, such as Todd Andrews in *The Floating Opera* (1956), Jacob Horner in *End of the Road* (1958), Ebenezer Cooke in *The Sotweed Factor* (1960), or George Giles in *Giles Goat Boy* (1966), tend too often to lose their cleverness and become philosophical abstractions debating relativism vs. absolutism in manners and morals—all too easily manipulated by an ingenious author. Of all these writers, Joseph Heller and Ken Kesey appear to hold the greatest promise of major work that will have a permanent impact on American fiction. Joseph Heller's *Catch-22* (1961) creates a paradigm of the modern world in the madness and violence of the U.S. Air Force in World War II; Ken Kesey's *One Flew Over the Cuckoo's Nest* (1962) creates its paradigm of the contemporary situation in the dehumanization and lunacy of an actual insane asylum. The worlds of these novels have been turned inside out. The ordered world of institutions is exposed as maniacal. The colonels and generals, doctors and nurses, are revealed as insane; the cowards and rebels of the Air Force, the Chronics and Acutes of the asylum are portrayed as the sane and the human. (It should be noted parenthetically that Kesey's second novel, *Sometimes a Great Notion* [1964], seems to represent not so much an advance in his talent but a marking of time.) All five of these novelists—Donleavy, Barth, Heller, Kesey, and Pynchon—have the kind of energy and zeal, vigor and force that will bear watching in the future. They are all capable of further surprises. And the novel-form itself seems resuscitated and revitalized by the live, warm blood they have sent coursing through its veins.

One concluding note of caution should be sounded. The more things change, the more they remain the same. It is possible to find the elements I have tried to identify in recent American fiction in other places, other times. In a sense, much of what I have said is summed up in a Charles Addams cartoon many will remember: a sinister little character, sitting in a movie house, is surrounded by an audience weeping copiously at the drama unfolding on the screen—while he, with a moronic grin, snickers behind his hand. Sometimes, I think, we identify uncomfortably with this little man as we laugh at the horrors in the contemporary novel. Or, if we go back several hundred years in time, to the macabre landscapes of the Dutch painter Hieronymus Bosch, we find in his doomsday world, with its mixture of lust, violence, horror, and humor, its people-eating monsters and its torture-machines, its tiny, limp people draped on huge keys, its enormous ears sliced by a monstrous knife blade—we find in this doomsday world a reminder of the kind of nightmare world of the grotesque and comic created by our modern novelists. We feel the shock of recognition. Or, finally, if we go back some one hundred years to that American epic novel, Melville's *Moby Dick*, we find the wanderer Ishmael meditating on the human predicament in terms that seem to be the credo of the contemporary novelist: "There are certain queer times and occasions in this strange mixed affair we call life when a man takes this whole universe for a vast practical joke, though the wit thereof he but dimly discerns, and more than suspects that the joke is at nobody's expense but his own." Not just at times and not just on occasion, but rather steadily and without relief, our recent writers portray the universe as a "vast practical joke"—and the joke is on everybody, novelist, characters, and readers alike. In such a universe, any quest at all is the quest absurd.

RECENT AMERICAN NOVELISTS
Downward Curve

1. JAMES JONES (1921–   )
   From Here to Eternity (1951)
   Some Came Running (1958)
   The Pistol (1959)
   The Thin Red Line (1962)
   Go to the Widow-Maker (1967)
2. NORMAN MAILER (1923–   )
   The Naked and the Dead (1948)
   Barbary Shore (1951)
   The Deer Park (1955)
   Advertisements for Myself (1959)
   The Presidential Papers (1963)
   An American Dream (1965)
   Cannibals and Christians (1966)
   Why Are We in Vietnam? (1967)
3. CARSON McCULLERS (1917–1967)
   The Heart Is a Lonely Hunter (1940)
   Reflections in a Golden Eye (1941)
   The Member of the Wedding (1946)
   The Ballad of the Sad Cafe (1951)
   Clock without Hands (1961)
4. TRUMAN CAPOTE (1924–   )
   Other Voices, Other Rooms (1948)
   A Tree of Night (1949) SS
   Local Color (1950)
   The Grass Harp (1951)
   The Muses Are Heard (1956)
   Breakfast at Tiffany's (1958)
   In Cold Blood (1966)
5. JACK KEROUAC (1922–   )
   Town and the City (1950)
   On the Road (1957)
   The Dharma Bums (1958)

* indicates non-fiction
SS indicates short stories

Downward Curve (*continued*)

The Subterraneans
(1958)
Doctor Sax (1959)
Maggie Cassidy (1959)
Tristessa (1960)
Visions of Cody (1960)
**Lonesome Traveler*
(1960)
*Book of Dreams
(1961)
Big Sur (1962)
Visions of Gerard
(1963)
Desolation Angels
(1965)
Satori in Paris (1966)

6. JAMES BALDWIN
(1924–   )
*Go Tell It on the
Mountain* (1953)
**Notes of a Native Son*
(1955)
Giovanni's Room
(1956)
**Nobody Knows My
Name* (1961)
Another Country
(1962)
**The Fire Next Time*
(1963)
Going to Meet the Man
(1965) SS

Cult

7. JAMES PURDY
(1923–   )
Color of Darkness (includes *63: Dream
Palace*) (1957) SS
Malcolm (1959)
The Nephew (1960)
Children Is All (1962)
SS
Cabot Wright Begins
(1964)
*Eustace Chisholm and
the Works* (1967)
8. JOHN HAWKES
(1925–   )
The Cannibal (1949)
The Beetle Leg (1951)
*The Goose on the
Grave & The Owl*
(1954)
The Lime Twig (1961)
Second Skin (1964)

The Innocent Party
(1967) Plays
9. TERRY SOUTHERN
(1924–   )
Flash and Filigree
(1958)
Candy (1959; with
Mason Hoffenberg)
The Magic Christian
(1960)
10. WILLIAM BURROUGHS
(1914–   )
Naked Lunch (1962)
(Olympia, 1959)
Nova Express (1964)
The Soft Machine
(1966) (Olympia,
1961)
The Ticket That Exploded (1967)
(Olympia, 1961)

Threshold (Permanent?)

11. RALPH ELLISON
(1914–   )
Invisible Man (1952)
*Shadow and Act
(1964)

12. WILLIAM STYRON
(1925–   )
Lie Down in Darkness
(1951)
The Long March
(1952)
Set This House on Fire
(1960)

*The Confessions of Nat
Turner* (1967)

13. BERNARD MALAMUD
(1914–   )
The Natural (1952)
The Assistant (1957)
The Magic Barrel
(1958) SS
A New Life (1961)
Idiot's First (1963) SS
The Fixer (1966)

Achievement (More or Less)

14. J. D. SALINGER
(1919–   )
*The Catcher in the
Rye* (1951)
Nine Stories (1953) SS
Franny & Zooey
(1961)
*Raise High the Roof
Beams, Carpenter and
Seymour: An Intro-
duction* (1963)

15. FLANNERY O'CONNOR
(1925–1964)
Wise Blood (1952)
*A Good Man Is Hard to
Find* (1955) SS
*The Violent Bear It
Away* (1960)
*Everything That Rises
Must Converge*
(1965) SS

16. SAUL BELLOW
(1915–   )

Dangling Man (1944)
The Victim (1947)
*The Adventures of
Augie March* (1953)
Seize the Day (1957)
*Henderson the Rain
King* (1959)
Herzog (1964)
The Last Analysis
(1965) Play

17. WRIGHT MORRIS
(1910–   )
My Uncle Dudley
(1942)
*The Man Who Was
There* (1945)
*The Inhabitants
(1946)
*The Home Place
(1948)
The World in the Attic
(1949)
Man and Boy (1951)

Achievement (More or Less) (*continued*)

The Works of Love (1952)
The Deep Sleep (1953)
The Huge Season (1954)
The Field of Vision (1956)
Love among the Cannibals (1957)
*The Territory Ahead (1958)

Ceremony in Lone Tree (1960)
What a Way to Go (1962)
Cause for Wonder (1963)
One Day (1965)
In Orbit (1967)

Promise . . . Achievement

18. JOHN UPDIKE (1932–   )
The Poorhouse Fair (1959)
The Same Door (1959) SS
Rabbit, Run (1960)
Pigeon Feathers (1962) SS
The Centaur (1963)
Olinger Stories (1964) SS
Of the Farm (1965)
The Music School (1966) SS

19. REYNOLDS PRICE (1933–   )
A Long and Happy Life (1962)
The Names and Faces of Heroes (1963) SS
A Generous Man (1966)

20. PHILIP ROTH (1933–   )
Goodbye, Columbus (1959) SS
Letting Go (1962)
When She Was Good (1967)

Black Comedy (Novelists to Watch)

21. J. P. DONLEAVY (1926–   )
The Ginger Man (1958)
A Singular Man (1963)
Meet My Maker the

Mad Molecule (1964) SS
The Saddest Summer of Samuel S (1966)

22. JOHN BARTH (1930–   )

Black Comedy (Novelists to Watch) (*continued*)

The Floating Opera (1956)
End of the Road (1958)
The Sotweed Factor (1960)
Giles Goat-Boy (1966)

23. JOSEPH HELLER (1923–   )
Catch-22 (1961)

24. KEN KESEY (1935–   )
One Flew Over the Cuckoo's Nest (1962)
Sometimes a Great Notion (1964)

25. THOMAS PYNCHON (1936–   )
V. (1963)
The Crying of Lot 49 (1966)

2

J. D. Salinger:
Some Crazy Cliff

Written with Arthur Heiserman

I

It is clear that J. D. Salinger's *The Catcher in the Rye* belongs to an ancient and honorable narrative tradition, perhaps the most profound in western fiction. The tradition is the central pattern of the epic and has been enriched by every tongue; for not only is it in itself exciting but also it provides the artist a framework upon which he may hang almost any fabric of events and characters.

It is, of course, the tradition of the Quest. We use the medieval term because it signifies a seeking after what is tremendous, greater than the love of a woman. The love of woman may be part of the seeking, part even of the object sought, for we have been told that the Grail has gender and Penelope did wait in Ithaca. But if the love of woman is essential to the seeking or to the object sought, we must call the search a romance. These two terms (quest and romance) distinguish thematic patterns, and have nothing to do with tragic or comic effects. Furthermore, the same plots, characters, and idioms might be employed inside either pattern. But somewhere upon the arc of the Quest, the love of woman must be eschewed or absorbed: the hero must bind himself to the mast, or must seek his Ducalinda because she is Virtue, not because she is Female.

There are at least two sorts of quests, depending upon the object sought. Stephen Dedalus sought a reality uncontaminated by home, country, church; for like Eugene Gant and Natty Bumppo he knew that social institutions tend to force what is ingenious in a man into their own channels. He sought the opposite of security, for security was a cataract of the eye. Bloom, on the other hand, was already an outcast and sought acceptance by an Ithaca and a Penelope which despised him. And, tragically enough, he also sought an Icarian son who had fled the very maze which he, Bloom, desired to enter. So the two kinds of quests, the one seeking acceptance and stability, the other precisely the opposite, differ significantly, and can cross only briefly to the drunken wonder of both heroes. Bloom, the protagonist of *The Waste Land*, the Joads, Alyosha Karamazov, Aeneas, Ulysses, Gatsby—these heroes seek acceptance, stability, a life embosomed upon what is known and can be trusted. Dedalus, Huck Finn, Ishmael, Hans Castorp, Huxley's heroes, Dostoevski's Idiot—these protagonists place themselves outside the bounds of what is known and seek not stability but a Truth which is unwarped by stability.

American literature seems fascinated with the outcast, the person who defies traditions in order to arrive at some pristine knowledge, some personal integrity. Natto Bumppo maintains his integrity out-of-doors only, for upon the frontier a man must be a man or perish. For Huck Finn both sides of the Mississippi are lined with fraud and hatred; and because the great brown river acts as a kind of sewer, you're liable to find murderers and thieves afloat on it—even the father whom you fled might turn up dead in it, as though the river were a dream. But in the middle of the great natural river, when you're naked of civilization and in company with an outcast more untarnished and childlike than yourself—*there* is peace. And in northern Mississippi, in the ante-Snopes era, frontiersmen conquer the wilderness using only their courage and their fury; and they behave, even when civilization has almost extinguished them, with the kind of insane honor that drives Quentin Compson outside of society and into suicide. And the hunter, as he tracks the great mythic bear or the incredible whale, must leave behind whatever is unnatural or convenient. Similarly, when the bull charges, you are faced with the same compulsion for integrity as is required by the wilderness, the whale, the bear, the river; and very often, the world so botches things that you must "make a separate peace" in order to maintain your moral entity intact.

All the virtues of these American heroes are personal ones:

they most often, as a matter of fact, are in conflict with home, family, church. The typical American hero must flee these institutions, become a tramp in the earth, cut himself off from Chicago, Winesburg, Hannibal, Cooperstown, New York, Asheville, Minneapolis. For only by flight can he find knowledge of what is real. And if he does not flee, he at least defies.

The protagonist of *The Catcher in the Rye*, Holden Caulfield, is one of these American heroes, but with a significant difference. He seems to be engaged in both sorts of quests at once; he needs to go home and he needs to leave it. Unlike the other American knight errants, Holden seeks Virtue second to Love. He wants to be good. When the little children are playing in the rye-field on the clifftop, Holden wants to be the one who catches them before they fall off the cliff. He is not driven toward honor or courage. He is not driven toward love of woman. Holden is driven toward love of his fellow man, charity—virtues which were perhaps not quite virile enough for Natty Bumppo, Ishmael, Huck Finn, or Nick Adams. Holden is actually frightened by a frontier code of masculinity—a code which sometimes requires its adherents to behave in sentimental and bumptious fashions. But like these American heroes, Holden is a wanderer, for in order to be good he has to be more of a bad boy than the puritanical Huck could have imagined. Holden has had enough of both Hannibal, Missouri, *and* the Mississippi; and his tragedy is that when he starts back up the river, he has no place to go—save, of course, a California psychiatrist's couch.

So Salinger translates the old tradition into contemporary terms. The phoniness of society forces Holden Caulfield to leave it, but he is seeking nothing less than stability and love. He would like nothing better than a home, a life embosomed upon what is known and can be trusted; he is a very wise sheep forced into lone wolf's clothing; he is Stephen Dedalus and Leopold Bloom rolled into one crazy kid. And here is the point; for poor Holden, there is no Ithaca. Ithaca has not merely been defiled by a horde of suitors: it has sunk beneath waves of phoniness. He does, of course, have a Penelope who is still intact. She is his little sister Phoebe whom he must protect at all costs from the phantoms of lust, hypocrisy, conceit and fear—all of the attributes which Holden sees in society and which Huck Finn saw on the banks of the Mississippi and

Dedalus saw in Dublin. So at the end, like the hero of *Antic Hay*, Holden delights in circles—a comforting, bounded figure which yet connotes hopelessness. He breaks down as he watches his beloved little Phoebe going round and round on a carousel; she is so *damned* happy. From that lunatic delight in a circle, he is shipped off to the psychiatrist. For Holden loves the world more than the world can bear.

Holden's Quest takes him outside society; yet the grail he seeks is the world and the grail is full of love. To be a catcher in the rye in this world is possible only at the price of leaving it. To be good is to be a "case," a "bad boy" who confounds the society of men. So Holden seeks the one role which would allow him to be a catcher, and that role is the role of the child. As a child, he would be condoned, for a child is a sort of savage and a pariah because he is innocent and good. But it is Holden's tragedy that he is sixteen, and like Wordsworth he can never be less. In childhood he had what he is now seeking— non-phoniness, truth, innocence. He can find it now only in Phoebe and in his dead brother Allie's baseball mitt, in a red hunting cap and the tender little nuns. Still, unlike all of us, Holden refuses to compromise with adulthood and its necessary adulteries; and his heroism drives him berserk. Huck Finn had the Mississippi and at the end of the Mississippi he had the wild west beyond Arkansas. The hero of *The Waste Land* had Shantih, the peace which passes human understanding. Bloom had Molly and his own ignorance; Dedalus had Paris and Zurich. But for Holden, there is no place to go.

II

The central theme of Salinger's work is stated explicitly in one of his best short stories, "For Esme—with Love and Squalor." Salinger quotes a passage from Dostoevski: "Fathers and teachers, I ponder 'What is Hell?' I maintain that it is the suffering of being unable to love."

The hero of "For Esme" is an American soldier who, driven too near psychosis by five campaigns of World War II and a moronic jeepmate, is saved in an act of childish love by two remarkable English children. Just as surely as war and neurosis are both manifestations of the lack of love, the soldier discovers peace and happiness are manifestations of love's presence. This

Love must be spelled with a capital; for it is not the alienated, romantic love of the courtly romances and "Dover Beach"—a love which is tragic because it is founded upon Eros; but rather it is the expansive, yea-saying love of all Creation which we find in the saints and which is never tragic because it is founded upon Agape. This love is the dominant trait of all Salinger's heroes, and when it is thwarted the hero either shoots himself, as does the veteran with "battle fatigue" in "A Perfect Day for Bananafish," or goes berserk or melancholic as do the heroes of *The Catcher in the Rye* and "Uncle Wiggly in Connecticut." But when, on the other hand, a person finds a way to love the world, then that person is saved from madness and suicide as is the soldier in "For Esme." Salinger thus diagnoses the neurosis and fatigue of the world in one simple way: if we cannot love, we cannot live.

Childhood and the loss of innocence have obsessed much of western literature at least since the Enlightenment, when man was declared innately good, corrupted only by his institutions. If we could return to childhood, or to noble savagery; or if we could retain the spontaneity of childhood, our social and personal problems would disappear. Emile, Candide, the young Wordsworth, Huck Finn, Holden Caulfield—all lament or seek a return to a lost childhood for precisely the same reasons that one is forced to make peace with one's childhood on the analyst's couch, or that the Marxist must look with a sigh upon Eden, where the fruits of production were consumed entirely by their tenders. Each of us does indeed carry an Adam inside us, whether he be Original Sin or Innocence: and the modern world has for the most part judged him innocent. Yet the clouds of glory which we trailed dwindle and turn back in adulthood; for when the world was new, before the pimples appeared, it was with us not too much but utterly and we could love it innocently, without fear. Of course, what Wordsworth remembered above Tintern Abbey, what Clemens recalled in New York, what Rousseau attempted to breed in France, what modern art attempted to recreate from Negro and Oriental models, never really existed in pure form in the first place. How horrified Wordsworth would have been had he learned what romanticism's dank blossom, Freud, discovered in the dictum that "the child is father of the man"! Nevertheless, as Freud made Childism clinical he also made it rampant; and the initiation story, the fable of Innocence Lost, has developed into a dominant motif in contemporary fiction.

The flight out of the world, out of the ordinary, and into an Eden of innocence or childhood is a common flight indeed, and it is one which Salinger's heroes are constantly attempting. But Salinger's childism is consubstantial with his concern for love and neurosis. Adultism is precisely "the suffering of being unable to love," and it is that which produces neurosis. Everyone able to love in Salinger's stories is either a child or a man influenced by a child. All the adults not informed by love and innocence are by definition phonies and prostitutes. "You take adults, they always look lousy when they're asleep with their mouths open, but kids don't . . . They look all right." Kids like Phoebe shut up when they haven't anything to say. They even say "thank you" when you tighten their skates, and they don't go behind a post to button their pants. The nuns expect no swanky lunches after standing on a corner to collect money. Young James Castle would not go back on his word even though he had to jump from a window to keep it.

Holden is the kind of person who feels sorry for the teachers who have to flunk him. He fears for the ducks when the lagoon freezes over, for he is a duck himself with no place to go. He must enter his own home like a crook, lying to elevator boys and tiptoeing past bedrooms. His dad "will kill" him and his mother will weep for his incorrigible "laziness." He wants only to pretend he is a deaf-mute and live as a hermit filling-station operator in Colorado, but he winds up where the frontier ends, California, in an institution for sick rich kids. And we can see, on the final note of irony in the book, that that frontier west which represented escape from "sivilization" for Huck Finn has ended by becoming the symbol for depravity and phoniness in our national shrine at Hollywood.

III

The most distinctive aspect of Salinger's humor is its invariable effect of intensifying poignance and even horror. At the end of "A Perfect Day for Bananafish," Seymour Glass, the sensitive young protagonist, is unable to reconcile himself to the evil adult world into which he has been thrust, with its brutal wars and sordid and even hateful relationships with a shallow-headed wife and her self-centered family. Even the steadying influence of the genuine innocence of little Sybil Carpenter is not sufficient to deter Seymour from his will to self-destruction. As he is on his way to his room at the end of the story, he boards the hotel elevator and believes that one of his fellow passengers is scrutinizing him. "I see you're looking at my feet," he says, and the startled woman with zinc salve on her nose replies, "I *beg* your pardon?" But the young man has become acutely sensitive: "If you want to look at my feet, say so. . . . But don't be a God-damned sneak about it."

The story at this point is simultaneously at its funniest and its most poignant. In less than one brief page the young man is dead: "Then he went over and sat down on the unoccupied twin bed, looked at the girl, aimed the pistol, and fired a bullet through his right temple." The close juxtaposition of these two passages, the one a height in comic incongruity, the other a depth in tragic action, works a unique effect. The comic element intensifies rather than relieves the tragic. As we observe the young man raise the pistol to his head, we are horrified that we have just been laughing at his extreme sensitivity about his feet. Perhaps we even have the guilty feeling of having ridiculed a deformity—a deformity of the spirit. In any event we are stunned into a keen realization of the tragic human plight.

It is this poignance which characterizes all of Salinger's humor, this catch in the throat that accompanies all of the laughs. Holden Caulfield is no clown nor is he a tragic hero; he is a sixteen-year-old lad whose vivid encounter with everyday life is tragically humorous—or humorously tragic. At the end of the novel, as we leave Holden in the psychiatric ward of the California hospital, we come to the realization that the abundant and richly varied humor of the novel has reenforced the serious intensity of Holden's frantic flight from Adultism and his frenzied search for the genuine in a terrifyingly phony world.

Holden Caulfield, like Huckleberry Finn, tells his own story and it is in the language of the telling in both books that a great part of the humor lies. In the nineteenth century, Huck began, "You don't know about me without you have read a book by the name of *The Adventures of Tom Sawyer;* but that ain't no matter." The English of Huck's twentieth-century counterpart, Holden Caulfield, is perhaps more correct but nonetheless distinctive: "If you really want to hear about it, the first thing you'll probably want to know is where I was born, and what my lousy childhood was like, and how my parents were occupied and all before they had me, and all that David Copperfield kind of crap, but I don't feel like going into it, if you want to know the truth."

The skepticism inherent in that casual phrase, "if you want to know the truth," suggesting that as a matter of fact in the world of Holden Caulfield very few people do, characterizes this sixteen-year-old "crazy mixed up kid" more sharply and vividly than pages of character "analysis" possibly could. In a similar manner Huck's "that ain't no matter" speaks volumes for his relationship to the alien adult world in which he finds himself a sojourner. But if these two boys lay their souls bare by their own voices, in doing so they provoke smiles at their mishandling and sometimes downright mangling of the English language.

Huck's spelling of *sivilization* gives the word a look which makes what it stands for understandably distasteful. Holden's incorrectness frequently appears to be a straining after correctness ("She'd give Allie or I a push. . . .") which suggests a subconscious will to non-conformity. But the similarities of language of Huck and Holden are balanced by marked differences. Both boys are fugitives from education, but Holden has suffered more of the evil than Huck. Holden's best subject in the several schools he has tolerated briefly is English. And, too, Holden is a child of the twentieth century. Mark Twain himself would probably be startled not at the frankness of Holden's language but at the daring of J. D. Salinger in copying it so faithfully.

But of course neither J. D. Salinger nor Mark Twain really "copied" anything. Their books would be unreadable had they merely recorded intact the language of a real-life Huck and a real-life Holden. Their genius lies in their mastery of the technique of first-person narration which, through meticulous selection, creates vividly the illusion of life: gradually and subtly their narrators emerge and stand revealed, stripped to their innermost beings. It is a mark of their creators' mastery that Huck and Holden appear to reveal themselves.

It is not the least surprising aspect of *The Catcher in the Rye* that trite expressions and metaphors with which we are all familiar and even bored turn out, when emerging from the mouth of a sixteen-year-old, to be funny. The unimaginative repetition of identical expressions in countless situations intensifies the humor. The things in Holden's world are always jumping up and down or bouncing or scattering "like madmen." Holden always lets us know when he has insight into the absurdity of the endless absurd situations which make up the life of a sixteen-year-old by exclaming, "It killed me." In a phony world Holden feels compelled to reenforce his sincerity and truthfulness constantly with, "It really is" or "It really did." Incongruously the adjective "old" serves as a term of endearment, from "old" Thomas Hardy to "old" Phoebe. And many of the things Holden does, he does, ambiguously, "like a bastard."

Holden is a master of the ludicrous irrelevancy. Indeed, a large part of *The Catcher in the Rye* consists of the relevantly irrelevant. On the opening page, Holden says, "I'm not going to tell you my whole goddam autobiography or anything. I'll just tell you about this madman stuff that happened to me around last Christmas. . . ." By the time we have finished *Catcher* we feel that we know Holden as thoroughly as any biography could reveal him, and one of the reasons is that he has not hesitated to follow in his tale wherever whim and fancy lead him. For example, in the early part of the novel, Holden goes at some length into the history of the Ossenburger Memorial Wing of the new dorms, his place of residence. Ossenburger, we are told, was the Pencey alumnus who made a "pot of dough" in the undertaking business, and who, after giving money to Pencey, gave a speech in chapel "that lasted about ten hours." "He told us we should always pray to God—talk to Him and all—wherever we were. He told us we ought to think of Jesus as our buddy and all. He said *he* talked to Jesus all of the time. Even when he was driving his car. That killed me. I can just see the big phony bastard shifting into first gear and asking Jesus to send him a few more stiffs." Ossenburger, of course, has nothing to do, directly, with the "madman stuff" that happened to Holden around Christmas; but Holden's value judgment of the phony Ossenburger is certainly relevant to Salinger's purpose, the revelation of Holden's character.

When Holden refuses to express aggressive dislike of the

repulsive Ackley, the pimply boy whose teeth "looked mossy and awful," he is not being facetious nor is he lying. He is simply expressing an innocence incapable of genuine hatred. Holden does not suffer from the inability to love, but he does despair of finding a place to bestow his love. The depth of Holden's capacity for love is revealed in his final words, as he sits in the psychiatric ward musing over his nightmarish adventures: "If you want to know the truth, I don't *know* what I think about it. I'm sorry I told so many people about it. About all I know is, I sort of miss everybody I told about. Even old Stradlater and Ackley, for instance. I think I even miss that goddam Maurice. It's funny. Don't ever tell anybody anything. If you do, you start missing everybody." We agree with Holden that it is funny, but it is funny in a pathetic kind of way. As we leave Holden alone in his room in the psychiatric ward, we are aware of the book's last ironic incongruity. It is not Holden who should be examined for a sickness of the mind, but the world in which he has sojourned and found himself an alien. To "cure" Holden, he must be given the contagious, almost universal disease of phony adultism; he must be pushed over that "crazy cliff."

3

William Faulkner:
Descent into the Vortex

Like all men of genius, William Faulkner has been transfigured so thoroughly from fact into legend that it is difficult to know whether we have grasped anything of the real Faulkner or not. The various books that have attempted to represent a view of Faulkner have projected images that seem strangely discordant, that do not seem to deal with the same man. We know now that Robert Coughlan's book, *The Private World of William Faulkner* (1954), did not really penetrate Faulkner's private world but did incur Faulkner's personal hostility. It is nevertheless a useful compendium of Faulkner stories, true or not. For example, when Faulkner as a young man was forced, through his general incompetence, to give up his postmastership at Ole Miss, he is reported to have said, "Now I won't be at the beck and call of every son of a bitch who happens to have two cents." Or later, during the Depression, after one of Faulkner's stints of working in Hollywood to make ends meet, the only signs of his presence discovered when his office was cleaned were—an empty bottle and a single sheet of paper on which appeared, repeated five hundred times, "Boy meets girl."[1]

We might expect that the privileged position of John Faulkner within the true "private world" of his brother William

[1] Robert Coughlan, *The Private World of William Faulkner* (New York: Harper & Bros., 1954); paperback reprint (Avon, G-1144), pp. 47, 88.

would give his book *My Brother Bill* (1963) a kind of authenticity that no other could have. But from time to time throughout this book, sentences flash out to signal a warning to the reader. For example, John Faulkner writes: "A great many people, I think, try to read too much into Bill's writings. It simply is not there nor was it intended to be. If they would read him for the stories he was telling they would realize what a good storyteller Bill was." Even when we allow for the measure of truth in the statement, the remaining naïveté and simplistic view of "storytelling" are likely to numb if not stun us.

But the shocking revelation comes when John Faulkner writes about the difficulties brother Bill created for the family when he began to write and talk about integration. "It did not set well with the rest of us," John Faulkner writes; "he became subject to anonymous phone calls at odd hours. Mysterious voices cursed him, and his mail was filled with abusive anonymous letters. Since none of us agreed with Bill's views we said, 'It serves him right.' " John Faulkner concludes his treatment of this difficult subject by noting that during the last two or three years of his life, when William ceased promoting his pro-integrationist stand, "We were all relieved, glad that it was over."[2] Such statements as these, from a brother presumably close in intimacy, shock us by suggesting the appalling isolation of Faulkner, not only in Mississippi but even in the bosom of his family.

But if we turn from these two portraits to Faulkner's own informal self-portraits—that is, his tape-recorded conversations with students or his letters to Malcolm Cowley—we find that we are still unable to discover, among all the contradictions, the real Faulkner. *Faulkner in the University* (1959), edited by Frederick L. Gwynn and Joseph L. Blotner out of the taped class sessions Faulkner had with students at the University of Virginia, is an invaluable and monumental asset to Faulkner scholarship and criticism. But it can be misleading unless used with care, and it projects, in its entirety, an image of Faulkner that is simply unbelievable. For example, when a student asks his opinion of Henry Miller, Faulkner replies: "Sorry, I don't

[2] John Faulkner, *My Brother Bill* (New York: Trident Press, 1963); paperback reprint (Pocket Books, 50018), pp. 219, 241.

know him. Should I? You must believe me, I do live in the country and I don't keep up with literary things, I ain't a literary man. So if I should know Henry Miller I'll find out about him."[3] This most profoundly impressive "literary man" of America's twentieth century, carrying on the traditional myth of the primitive genius in American letters, insists over and over again—"I ain't a literary man."

The pose assumed in such declarations runs counter to the view of Faulkner we get from Malcolm Cowley in *The Faulkner-Cowley File: Letters and Memories, 1944–1962* (1966). This correspondence is primarily concerned with Cowley's preparation of the Viking *Portable Faulkner* back in 1944–45, published in 1946, and responsible in large part for a revival of interest in Faulkner then largely out of print and critically ignored. But it was a correspondence that almost ended before it began: Faulkner's first letter arrived some three months after Cowley's first query. Faulkner explained: "My mail consists of two sorts: from people who don't write, asking me for something, usually money, which being a serious writer trying to be an artist, I naturally dont have; and from people who do write, telling me I cant. So, since I have already agreed to answer No to the first and All right to the second, I open the envelopes to get the return postage stamps (if any) and dump the letters into a desk drawer, to be read when (usually twice a year) the drawer overflows."[4] Fortunately Faulkner did get around to answering Cowley's letters and the total *File* of correspondence provides another image of Faulkner that is fascinating but by no means conclusive: a Faulkner who is both literate and literary, so determined to be a serious novelist that he is willing to spend six months out of the year writing for Hollywood in order to earn time to spend the other six months writing his novels—which do not sell. The one overruling passion in Faulkner that emerges from these letters is a passion for privacy, and a deep and cold hostility to those who invade it.

Even after his death, *especially* after his death, that privacy will be invaded, and the biographies will be written. But I am willing to venture the guess now that, after they are written

[3] Frederick L. Gwynn and Joseph L. Blotner, eds., *Faulkner in the University* (Charlottesville: Univ. of Virginia Press, 1959), p. 282.
[4] Malcolm Cowley, *The Faulkner-Cowley File: Letters and Memories, 1944–1962* (New York: Viking Press, 1966), pp. 6–7.

and published, the enigmas of Faulkner's genius will persist. Clearly he assumed pose after pose to throw the people around him, and the biographical bloodhounds, off the genuine scent. I think we know enough now to see that Faulkner lived his life, his real life, the deep life of the imagination, so carefully preserved from public exposure, or even from family exposure, that the external facts of his life will, as they multiply and accumulate, seem more and more irrelevant to his great achievement in fiction. If we are somehow to come to know the real Faulkner, we must follow his advice and take seriously what he left in the public domain—his work. There we may discover what Walt Whitman called "a few hints, a few diffused faint clews and indirections." In the deepest sense, Faulkner's life and wisdom are in his books.

Faulkner's writing career is full of a number of paradoxes. He began as a writer of the Twenties, but he escaped the era of the Lost Generation and survived into the Thirties as few novelists did. His novels, in their concern with poor, rural folk, have the look of the Thirties about them, but they defy classification as proletarian or class novels, and escape far beyond the concerns of the Depression decade. Off and on in Faulkner criticism there has been an attempt to assign Faulkner the title of Southern Writer or even Southern Regionalist. But the novels in their profundity and universality tend to show up such titles as woefully superficial. Faulkner accurately pointed out in a letter to Cowley: "I'm inclined to think that my material, the South, is not very important to me. I just happen to know it, and don't have time in one life to learn another one and write at the same time."[5]

Faulkner's total achievement in his sixty-five years (1897–1962) gives the impression of a man who was able, against the greatest of odds, to preserve his life and his precious time for writing. In addition to his nineteen novels, he published some fifty short stories. There is no prolonged silence in his career, as in the case of Melville; he continued to produce important work up to the time of his death in 1962. But as in the case of any great writer, the work is uneven, and each critic must initially establish, by critical sorting, the basis for his view of the work. In order to conserve space for getting

---

[5] *Ibid.,* pp. 14–15.

at Faulkner's central techniques and themes, I shall not pause to justify the judgments that I make here; I simply present them as views slowly crystalized over a period of time of reading, rereading, and discussing Faulkner's books. It is a mistake, I think, to accept as great all the Yoknapatawpha County volumes and to reject as inferior all the remaining work. And I think that it is equally erroneous to make other such arbitrary critical divisions—humorous and serious, experimental and traditional, Southern and non-Southern.

My own critical views are at once both simpler and more complex. Although Faulkner wrote a number of brilliant short stories, his genius found its most congenial form in the novel. In his first three novels (*Soldier's Pay*, 1926; *Mosquitoes*, 1927; *Sartoris*, 1929), he was in process of discovering his material, his voice, and his technique. What he was discovering in essence was that the super-sophisticated, world-weary novel of disillusionment and despair—the lost generation novel—was not something that came naturally within his range: when he tried it, he became imitative—of Fitzgerald or Hemingway. As Faulkner himself has indicated, he found himself as a writer in the middle of *Sartoris*, and began with the very next novel to hit his stride—and, indeed, a gigantic stride it turned out to be.

Faulkner's period of awe-inspiring creativity extends from 1929 to 1936 and includes five novels of the very first rank: *The Sound and the Fury*, 1929; *As I Lay Dying*, 1930; *Sanctuary*, 1931; *Light in August*, 1932; and *Absalom, Absalom!*, 1936. Faulkner's reputation solidly rests on these five great novels, which fuse brilliance of technique and profundity of theme in ways and at depths simply not reached by any other of his books. There are some works of about this period that are frankly lesser efforts but interesting experiments: *Pylon*, 1935; *The Unvanquished*, 1938; and *The Wild Palms*, 1939. But the only works of Faulkner's remaining career that approach in substance and achievement the work of his greatest period are *The Hamlet*, 1940, and *Go Down, Moses*, 1942, both of which incorporate short stories of an earlier period and, like *The Unvanquished*, fall into that hybrid category which is a cross between a volume of short stories and a novel.

Faulkner's remaining work, though of a high order by any kind of measurement, simply does not rank with his five great novels. There is a flagging of the imagination, a decrease in complex thematic exploration along with an increase in simple didacticism (especially through the garrulous old Gavin Stevens), and mannerism or eccentricity in technique rather than brilliance and boldness of innovation—all suggesting that the creative juices were running thin in Faulkner's later career, and also, perhaps, that he had listened too closely to the critics and was trying to produce consciously (and rather mechanically) what he had produced naturally in the earlier work out of the depths of his unconscious. *Intruder in the Dust*, 1948, and *Requiem for a Nun*, 1951, are surface, perhaps even superficial, treatments of moral and racial themes handled much more profoundly in earlier works. *The Fable* (1954) looks like the answer to a critic's prayer, making visible and pompously prominent all of those parallels and allusions to the Christian myth that previously had remained deep within the complexity of the novels where they were subtly operative by suggestive echo or ironic reverberation. *The Town* (1957) and *The Mansion* (1959) complete the Snopes trilogy begun in *The Hamlet* (1940), but suffer in comparison with the brilliance of the earlier volume. And the last novel, *The Reivers* (1962), appears to be a comic capitulation to nostalgia. All of these works of Faulkner's later period could serve as the foundation of a lesser novelist's reputation. They represent a considerable achievement, especially in humor of the native American variety. But when measured by the works of Faulkner's great period —those five novels of solid achievement—these later works clearly fall short of a higher possibility and are genuinely disappointing.

If my critical estimate is right, a sustained exploration of Faulkner's five great novels should reveal something of the nature of his genius in both the theme and technique of his fiction. I shall attempt to get at and assess the nature of Faulkner's total achievement, but by using as my primary examples those five novels from his early career. It will be useful first to attempt definitions of his central theme and of his recurring technique. These definitions will lead to an examination of three groups of characters that reappear in each of the novels: characters of perception and futility; characters of hatred and villainy; and characters of dedication and redemption. And this examination should help to reveal the complexity and to round out the totality of Faulkner's vision of the human situation and condition. It should be acknowledged from the beginning, however, that to stress similarities in these five great novels is to distort or neglect their individuality. Awareness of this at the outset should help to dispel the impression sometimes conveyed that these books have yielded all the secrets of their separate souls by the comparative critical treatment used here.

In 1944, Faulkner wrote to Malcolm Cowley: "Art is simpler than people think because there is so little to write about. All the moving things are eternal in man's history and have been written before, and if a man writes hard enough, sincerely enough, humbly enough, and with the unalterable determination never never never to be quite satisfied with it, he will repeat them, because art like poverty takes care of its own, shares its bread." As this is one of the few serious statements on art ever articulated by Faulkner, we should treasure it and try to discover what it means. And what it means he makes relatively clear in this same letter to Cowley, in a statement which may stand at the beginning of an attempt to formulate Faulkner's central theme in his greatest work. He wrote: "life is a phenomenon but not a novelty, the same frantic steeplechase toward nothing everywhere and man stinks the same stink no matter where in time."[6]

This statement is so remarkably succinct and revealing that it bears repetition and contemplation. The statement appears in the passage in which Faulkner is countering Cowley's classification of him as a Southern writer, denying, in effect, that he is a regionalist or local colorist but rather a writer interested in universal themes, the eternal human condition, north, south, east, or west. In this view, his "material, the South" is not "important" to him, but "probably as good as another"—for "life is a phenomenon but not a novelty, the same frantic steeplechase toward nothing everywhere and man stinks the same stink no matter where in time." If we take this statement as a serious and meaningful statement of Faulkner's belief, it may serve as his own formulation of the *absurdity* of the human condition portrayed vividly and repeatedly in his greatest novels.

The use of the term *absurd* renders necessary and inevitable a brief glance at Faulkner's relationship to the French Existen-

[6] *Ibid.,* pp. 15, 16.

tialists, for whom the term was a guiding principle. Jean-Paul Sartre's admiration for Hemingway, Dos Passos, and especially for Faulkner has long been known. To understand Sartre's engagement with Faulkner's imagination, we need but glance at his two brief essays, first published in 1938 and 1939, on *Sartoris* and *The Sound and the Fury*. In the first, we encounter in the midst of his running quarrel with the book the sentence: "Faulkner's humanism is probably the only acceptable kind." In the second essay, we find Sartre saying: "I am afraid that the absurdity that Faulkner finds in a human life is one that he himself has put there. Not that life is not absurd, but there is another kind of absurdity."[7] The interesting thing is Sartre's use of the key term, absurdity, in reference to Faulkner. But it must be pointed out (and it has been noted before) that Sartre's gross misreading of Quentin's views in *The Sound and the Fury* as Faulkner's own views, and his neglect of Dilsey's role in the novel, render his statement on the novel's absurdity ironic: inasmuch as Dilsey represents the hope that Sartre missed and demands, his statement must be reversed. The absurdity Faulkner finds in human life is precisely the kind that Sartre finds—and to some extent discovered through Faulkner.

Faulkner himself saw a relationship between his own work and that of Albert Camus. In *Faulkner in the University*, when asked about his views of the European writers, Faulkner answered: "Yes I know Camus best and I think highest of him. He is one man that . . . is doing what I have tried to do, which is to search, demand, ask always of one's own soul. . . . Camus has stuck to his principles, which was always to search the soul, which I think is the writer's first job. To search his own soul, and to give a proper, moving picture of man in the human dilemma."[8] This quick and intense identification of Faulkner with Camus may be viewed as one more piece of evidence that will contribute one day to the history, yet to be written, of Faulkner's important links with and profound influence on the French novelists, and thus his indirect influence on the contemporary fiction of his own country through the French Existen-

[7] Jean-Paul Sartre, *Literary Essays* (New York: Philosophical Library, 1957), pp. 78, 87.
[8] *Faulkner in the University*, pp. 281–282.

tialists (like Poe before him coming into modern American poetry via the French Symbolistes).

All of this is meant to suggest that to use the term *absurdity* in describing the universe of Faulkner's novels is not simply to pick up the current fashionable term but rather to follow it back to its root and its source. Or to use Faulkner's own 1944 definition, life in his novels is portrayed as a "frantic steeple-chase toward nothing everywhere." In the five novels we have chosen to explore, life may not be precisely "a tale, told by an idiot, full of sound and fury, signifying nothing," but to the most sensitive of Faulkner's characters (such as Quentin) it certainly seems so at moments of their most intense insight; and the characters who endure (like Dilsey) do so not by relying on an order inherent in life, but rather by creating and impos-ing on the chaos of life a meaning and significance out of a deeply personal and instinctively human vision. The spectacle of life—the "frantic steeplechase"—in Faulkner's novels ranges all the way from tragedy to comedy, eliciting responses from characters (and readers) also ranging widely from horror, to nausea, to laughter. The response at any one moment is most likely to be determined not by the nature of an event in itself, but rather the distance from or the perspective on the event. And Faulkner is constantly and swiftly shifting that perspec-tive, as much as to say to the reader—now that you think you understand both intellectually and emotionally this event, I'll show you how from another angle or deeper knowledge you'll sympathize rather than hate, or you'll laugh rather than pity, or your horror will melt into stunned self-awareness.

Faulkner's ingenious and unique combination of the comic and the serious deserves special note because it lies at the heart of his meaning, of his conception of an absurd universe. Three major examples may suffice to suggest the pervasiveness of this technique of forcing the same material to serve both humorous and somber ends. The central action of *As I Lay Dying*, involving as it does the prolonged struggle of a family to follow the wishes of the dying mother to be buried in the distant town, appears in the face of floods and fires to take on the dimension of an epic and heroic act. But as the reader is drawn into this view, Faulkner forces him (in a sense simulta-neously) to see the family in its traipse across country with a putrefying corpse in obedience to a senseless and meaningless request as essentially absurd, as foolish as well as selfishly and sordidly rather than nobly motivated. It is a rare reader who does not find himself—at one and the same time—sympathetically pitying and exasperatedly chuckling. Similarly in the very middle of the violence and rape and murder that make up the horrifying plot of *Sanctuary*, Virgil and Fonzo Snopes enter innocently and unaware the Memphis brothel (Miss Reba's) where the shallow little flapper Temple Drake has been held captive; but in spite of all the women running around in kimonos, the two country boys do not figure out what is going on in the "hotel," and they have their initiation into brothels in a rival establishment, to which they are directed by a barber. They disagree on the value of the experience, which cost three dollars. "Wasn't it worth it?" asks Fonzo. And Virgil Snopes replies: "Ain't nothing worth three dollars you caint tote off with you" (Chapter XXI).[9] In *Light in August* the comic is structurally intermingled with the tragic, as the opening and closing humorous episodes involving the pagan earth goddess, Lena Grove, act as a thematic frame of contrasting affirmation for the essentially negative story of Joe Christmas, his violent struggles against the world, and his final castration and death. By introducing at the end of the novel the furniture dealer who picks up Lena, her baby, and the pursuing Byron Bunch on their way to Tennessee, Faulkner introduces a comic perspective on an episode that the reader by now is inclined to see in mythic terms, especially in the context of the horrifying events that have gone before. The reader is persuaded to spice the myth with reality when he hears the furniture dealer, relating his funny adventures to his wife, describe Lena in his own earthy terms: "Here's another gal that thought she could learn on Saturday night what her mammy waited until Sunday to ask the minister" (XXI).

With all the nauseous, the horrible, the grotesque, and the wildly comic that are blended into the absurdity of Faulkner's world, there is a pervasive, profoundly engaged, and deeply *human* sympathy that flows through his work to all the characters of whatever stripe or kind. We feel this when we read the novels. And we find out directly the broad sweep of Faulkner's

[9] Quotations from Faulkner's novels are located in the text by chapter, in order that any of the various editions may be used.

sympathies when he answers questions about his characters in *Faulkner in the University*. Is Popeye in *Sanctuary* "emblematic of evil"? "No, he was to me another lost human being." Is Sutpen in *Absalom, Absalom!* "meant to be a completely depraved character"? "To me he is to be pitied, as anyone who ignores man is to be pitied, who does not believe that he belongs as a member . . . of the human family." Why is "such a sort of bad man as Joe Christmas" suggested as a Christ figure? "Well, Joe Christmas—I think that you can't say that any man is good or bad. I grant you there are some exceptions, but man is the victim of himself, or his fellows, or his own nature, or his environment, but no man is good or bad either. He tries to do the best he can within his rights. Now with Christmas, for instance, he didn't know what he was."[10]

The questions imply the youthful impatience to see the world in terms of black and white, of villainy and virtue, and Faulkner's answers indicate the complexity of his vision, the patience and wisdom to see the terrible entanglements of the souls of poor, lost human beings. In an absurd world, shot through with the irrational, where cause and effect have only tortured and subterranean relationships, where every human act or gesture has a series of obscure but influential antecedents that reach back into the dim reaches of the past—in such a world the terms *good* and *bad*, hero and villain, tend to lose their meaning. It is in just such a world that Gail Hightower, the defrocked and discredited minister in *Light in August*, has his vision of the apotheosis of all those people with whom he has shared experiences—those who have befriended as well as those who have betrayed. As his "wheel of thinking" (Chapter XX) frees itself of its burden upon his confession to himself of his shared guilt in his failures both as minister and as husband, the wheel becomes a glowing halo full of the faces of his brothers in the human family, including all the actors that have played parts, large or small, in the sordid drama that has unfolded before his very eyes. As Hightower looks on in fascination, he notices that one of the obscure faces seems struggling to divide into two, and as the two separate and become distinct, he sees that one is Joe Christmas, both victim and victimizer of the community, and the other is Percy

---

[10] *Faulkner in the University*, pp. 74, 80–81, 117–18.

Grimm, the young boy who acted out the fantasies of the community in mutilating Christmas's sex in death, acting in a way as the community's priest in the ritualistic sacrifice of the scapegoat. In Hightower's vision, he recognizes Christmas and Grimm as his brothers in guilt—all members of the common human family in all its frailty. Hightower's all-embracing whirling wheel or halo appears to be one of Faulkner's finest devices to suggest the depth of understanding and the breadth of sympathy requisite for anyone who would genuinely comprehend the human condition and the dilemma of man.

Another circular image, from *Absalom, Absalom!*, is the most illuminating I have discovered in all of Faulkner in revealing the central technical or organizing device of his fiction. The passage comes from one of Quentin's meditations: "Maybe nothing ever happens once and is finished. Maybe happen is never once but like ripples maybe on water after the pebble sinks, the ripples moving on, spreading, the pool attached by a narrow umbilical water-cord to the next pool which the first pool feeds, has fed, did feed, let this second pool contain a different temperature of water, a different molecularity of having seen, felt, remembered, reflect in a different tone the infinite unchanging sky, it doesn't matter: that pebble's watery echo whose fall it did not even see moves across its surface too at the original ripple-space, to the old ineradicable rhythm" (Chapter VII). In actuality, this passage suggests the close relationship between technique and theme in Faulkner's fiction. Central to Faulkner's vision is the impingement of past on the present, and his technique is designed specifically for explorations in depth of the layers of time that lie below a particular and usually startling event of the present. Both theme and technique are suggested in the image of the series of mountain pools, connected by the narrow "umbilical water-cords," with a pebble splash (an action, event) on one imparting the ripples that move over pool, through water-cord, to another pool and another water-cord—and so on through levels of time to be felt in the present event that has baffled participants and observers alike as to its cause or origins.

To get at Faulkner's basic technique more precisely, I would like to invert or reverse this image, and substitute for the pebble a much larger object (a gigantic tree), which creates as it sinks an irresistible vortex along with huge waves that wash out in every direction. The object (or tree) is some major or even (for the community) cataclysmic event that Faulkner simultaneously traces forward through its consequences (the waves) and backward to its obscure and distant causes (through the vortex, up the umbilical water-cords to other pools and pebbles of the past). Faulkner's famous tortured, convoluted style is to a certain extent more understandable when it is seen as the major instrument used for the probing of time, backwards and forwards, in the search for the complex mysteries of both causes and consequences invariably intertwined in one vital and enigmatic and frequently tragic event. The language of his fiction itself seems to take on the movement of a whirlpool as it delves deep into the vortex of the event, sucking the reader into the descent into the past, or washing him out to the edges on the waves of the present and future.

In a sense, then, each one of Faulkner's novels represents a descent into the vortex of time, a vortex created by an event that disturbs, upsets, alarms, or frightens the family or community. In moving frantically back and forth in the search for the causes and consequences of this key and singular event, Faulkner creates the structure of his novels: a whirlpool or circular structure suggesting that the secret of time (or life) is not to be found in the simple, straight chronology of one event following another, but rather in hidden corners (or pools) of the past, with only remote or oblique or subterranean (umbilical water-cord) connections with the event of the present being probed. If we are to understand why or how things happen, Faulkner seems to be saying, we must look at time, and the past, in all its infinite complexity, and even then (as in *Absalom, Absalom!*), after meticulous investigation and imaginative speculation—we cannot be certain that we are right.

Each of the five novels of Faulkner's great period is structured about a key or precipitating event around which the author and his language revolve in exploration. In *The Sound and the Fury*, the precipitating event is the girl Quentin's theft of Jason's cache of money (most of which came from Caddy, the girl's mother). The theft takes place in the first (or Benjy's) book, entitled "April 7, 1928," and is witnessed but not understood by the idiot. Book II ("June 2, 1910") is an exploration of the distant past—the day of the boy Quentin's suicide at Harvard—for the remote or hidden causes of the theft. Book III ("April 6, 1928") is an exploration of the immediate past, the events of the day before the theft, from the perspective of the thief's apparent victim (but really the victimizer), Jason Compson. And the final Book IV ("April 8, 1928") is a tracing out of the consequences of the theft on the day after its occurrence, primarily from the perspective of Dilsey, the one person in the novel with the instinctive wisdom to understand the complexities that lay behind and that lie ahead of this singular event: "I seed de beginnin, en now I sees de endin."

The other four novels of this period are similarly structured. In *As I Lay Dying*, the precipitating event is Addie Bundren's death, and although major interest centers on the fantastic and appalling consequences of the death, complex consequences for each member of the numerous family, as they laboriously carry the body to town for burial—still the events that lie behind the death (via the umbilical water-cords to past pools), such as Addie's father's old saying ("the reason for living was to get ready to stay dead a long time") or Addie's adultery with the preacher Whitfield, such events are isolated and examined as they have flowed into and flow on beyond the event of Addie's death. Faulkner's use of a rotating consciousness in the novel, moving quickly from one interior monologue to another, emphasizes the suggestion of a whirlpool movement of circular motion around and around the key event: an entire family flung into the spinning vortex. In the remaining three novels, *Sanctuary, Light in August,* and *Absalom, Absalom!* the central structuring event is a murder. In *Sanctuary* it is the murder of the feebleminded Tommy by the dehumanized robot Popeye—an event whose causes may be obscurely traced to Popeye's birth as well as to Temple Drake's sluttish desires, and whose consequences in an absurd world are the lynching of an innocent man. In *Light in August* the event that shapes the rushing vortex is the murder of the New England spinster Joanna Burden by the rootless, homeless Joe Christmas, an event that has its umbilical water-cords running deep into the past and whose giant ripples move out to involve the entire community. From the opening view of the distant smoke that arises from the burning Burden mansion to the final communal castration of Joe Christmas, Faulkner structures his novel circularly around this precipitating event of the murder, exploring it alternately and repeatedly from the past that led up to it, the present that witnessed it, and the future that will be shaped by it. In *Absalom, Absalom!* the event is the murder of Sutpen's discarded son from his first marriage, Charles Bon, by his own half-brother, Henry Sutpen, during the Civil War. In this novel, Faulkner turns over to Quentin Compson and his roommate at Harvard, the northerner Shreve McCannon, the main job of narrating this tale of the past, and the method they use is indeed circular, as they repeatedly examine, by scrutinizing the aftermath and disentangling the consequences, a variety of possible causes for the murder—and finally (by such repeated circling) at the end of the book hit upon the discovery that Charles Bon was not only Henry's half-brother, making his marriage to Henry's sister incestuous, but also a mulatto, the issue of old Sutpen's first unwitting marriage to a part Negress: only this carefully veiled and hidden secret out of the past can explain the murder of brother by brother.

Although the charge has frequently been made, especially against such a novel as *Sanctuary*, that Faulkner deliberately seizes on sensational events of sex, crime, violence, or murder to make a cheap appeal to the reader, it must be clear that he makes no concessions for a cheap appeal in his technique of descending with his reader into the vortex of these sensational events to explore the complexities of their antecedents and the reverberations into the future. Although it would be difficult to find two more radically different writers than Faulkner and Henry James, they do share some common concerns and approaches. Apparently James's super-refined sensibility did not appeal to Faulkner. When asked if he had read James, he replied: "Yes, without much pleasure. Henry James to me was a prig. . . ." And Faulkner said on another occasion, "Henry James probably was quite happy to lie detached from life, to write Henry James." But it is important to note that Faulkner, on still another occasion, listed James alongside Melville, Hawthorne, and Twain (among others, including Conrad) as one of the masters from whom the writers of his generation learned their craft.[11] Both James and Faulkner use a convolute, entangled and entangling style to probe deep into the complex-

[11] *Ibid.*, pp. 16, 169, 243.

ities of reality. And both understand the enigmas and ambiguities that surround any human gesture or any act, large or small. They both eschew plot in the conventional sense, and turn instead to the exploration in depth of a single reverberating event, small, subtle, and sophisticated in the case of James, large, gross, and sensational in the case of Faulkner. But both aim at the same end—an illumination of some dark corner of human behavior and human life.

In exploring his major theme of absurdity through his basic technique of descent into the vortex, Faulkner created a great roster of characters by exploiting and inverting novelistic convention: he created heroes who turned out to be unheroic and defeatist; he created villains who turned out to be if not sympathetic at least pitiful; and he created outcasts and derelicts, "low-life" characters who turned out to be both durable and noble. Perhaps the one major reason for Faulkner's prolonged unpopularity and for his continuing misinterpretation is his refusal to fulfill the conventionally aroused expectations, his defiance of the conventional values, and his slyly encouraging and then undermining the usual easy judgments about virtue and vice, good and evil.

The reader accustomed to the theme of world-weary futility and the alienated hero in the literature of the 1920's must do a double take when he comes to this theme and hero in Faulkner, or he is likely to conclude, as Jean-Paul Sartre erroneously concluded of *The Sound and the Fury*, that they constitute the center and extent of Faulkner's meaning and vision. The characters most likely to thus seduce the reader are Quentin Compson in *The Sound and the Fury*, Darl Bundren in *As I Lay Dying*, Horace Benbow in *Sanctuary*, Gail Hightower in *Light in August*, and Henry Sutpen in *Absalom, Absalom!* All of these characters are to some extent indebted to the young Bayard Sartoris (in *Sartoris*), the young veteran whose twin brother John was killed in the war and who seeks death and finally finds it in the crash of an airplane he is test-piloting. They all share a deep sense of the meaninglessness of existence, they have a kind of superior insight into the absurdity of life, they generally are acute sensibilities, frequently educated at college, they often have fixations on the past, they tend to effeminacy, narcissism, and incest, and they all have a crippling inability to act except against their own being. There is, of course, much of Faulkner's vision projected through these characters, but the reader who remains imprisoned within their paralyzed sensibilities does not follow Faulkner's vision of the human condition to the end of its labyrinthine way.

Quentin Compson is the most celebrated of these figures of futility, and he is caught in the trap of his own narcissistic soul, his unpassionate love for his sister Caddy and his obsessive concern for her honor being merely (or mainly) a projection of his own self-absorption and his fixation on the past and the Compson fate. His real passion is his identification with his father's philosophy of life's utter meaninglessness. The ancestral watch Quentin carries was given him by his father with the admonition that it was "the mausoleum of all hope and desire." And his father has taught him that "all men are just accumulations dolls stuffed with sawdust swept up from the trash heaps where all previous dolls had been thrown away the sawdust flowing from what wound in what side that not for me died not." These morbid memories are the possessions and heirlooms that Quentin carries with him on the fated day at Harvard (described in Book II of *The Sound and the Fury*) when he commits suicide. The point is not that these views of life's futility are basically wrong (though we—and Faulkner—might want to express it in different terms and more tentatively), but rather that Quentin has been blinded by the morbidity of his obsessions to the potentiality of human relationships in the face of death and defeat; he has been cut off by his narcissistic concern for Caddy from human communion. His only escape from his prison of the self is suicide.

Darl Bundren in *As I Lay Dying* is the one member of the country family endowed with supersight, and it is his knowing too much precisely that undoes him and leads ultimately to his incarceration in the Jackson insane asylum. He is the one member of the family who has discovered intuitively all its sordid secrets: he knows that his mother has conceived his brother Jewel not from his father but from the preacher Whitfield; he knows that his sister Dewey Dell is pregnant from having lain in the cotton fields with Lafe; and he understands Jewel's confused infatuation with his wild horse and his mother. It is, therefore, natural that Darl is the one member of the family who sees the utter ridiculousness of their carrying a putrefying corpse for days over the countryside to honor a burial-request made in spite and contempt. His knowledge proving too much for him, Darl attempts to destroy his mother's corpse by burning down the barn where it is temporarily placed, thereby unwittingly giving his family the chance it has been seeking to have him committed. When last seen, Darl has become double, and can even see the absurdity of his own incarceration. One Darl stands aside in hysterical laughter and says of the other: "Darl is our brother, our brother Darl. Our brother Darl in a cage in Jackson where, his grimed hands lying light in the quiet interstices, looking out he foams." It is a chilling self-image, intermingling the tragic and the absurd, and shows the terrible fate of so much terrible knowledge, unalleviated by sufficient human sympathy.

Horace Benbow of *Sanctuary* was first introduced as a sensitive young veteran in *Sartoris,* where, half in love with his aptly named sister Narcissa Benbow, he follows his whim and marries the vulgar divorcée Belle Mitchell. In *Sanctuary* Horace, now disillusioned in his marriage, is in flight from his wife and life—and stumbles into the middle of the bizarre events of the novel. His marriage has come to be symbolized by the box of shrimp which he carried home dripping every Friday noon for his wife. He has come to think: "Here lies Horace Benbow in a fading series of small stinking spots on a Mississippi sidewalk." Like other sensitive creatures of his kind in Faulkner, Benbow hangs suspended in agony between paralysis and action. His personal image of despair is transfigured into a cosmic vision one evening when he is overcome by the highly sexualized odor of honeysuckle: "The voice of the night . . . followed him into the house; he knew suddenly that it was the friction of the earth on its axis, approaching that moment when it must decide to turn on or to remain forever still: a motionless ball in cooling space, across which a thick smell of honeysuckle writhed like cold smoke" (Chapter XXIII). Benbow is defeated at every turn, even in his attempt to defend the innocent Lee Goodwin for the murder of Tommy, and his ineffectuality finally leads him to capitulate and return to his marriage and his life of quiet despair. His rebellion like his gesture for justice has been without passion, and he is doomed to live on as life's disengaged and emasculated man.

Gail Hightower in *Light in August* and Henry Sutpen in *Absalom, Absalom!* are variations of this Faulkner type. We have already seen how Hightower, through acknowledgement of his own guilt, finally wins his way to the human community through his "wheel of thinking" transfigured into halo. Through most of his life, however, he has lived removed from life, genuinely engaged only with his ancestral past; and it is only as Byron Bunch gradually draws him into involvement with the Joe Christmas drama, in an incomplete and abortive defense of the hounded Christmas, that Hightower is prepared for his final transcendent vision of human communion, the guilty joined in union with the innocent. But by this time life has passed Hightower by, and his return to it cannot be with much force of passion for deep involvement. In *Absalom, Absalom!* Henry Sutpen offers to the narrator Quentin Compson (now at Harvard, shortly before his suicide) a terrible reflection of his own dilemma. Henry has a "fierce provincial's pride in his sister's virginity," and it is he that, seduced by Charles Bon ("Yes, he loved Bon"), in turn seduces his sister *for* Bon ("it was Henry who seduced Judith; not Bon"); and it is he who, on discovery that his half-brother is part Negro, kills him to protect his sister's honor. Thus Henry acts out the drama which Quentin, years later, can relive only in fantasy. Quentin's fate leads him to suicide; Henry's fate leads to a prolonged life in death, cut off from the human community, doomed to linger on among ghosts of the haunted past.

In contrast with these sensitive, ineffectual characters are the desensitized, often dehumanized individuals in Faulkner who are capable of action, even action of large moment—but inevitably destructive action. The roster contains some of Faulkner's most memorable characters: Jason Compson in *The Sound and the Fury*, Addie Bundren in *As I Lay Dying*, Popeye in *Sanctuary*, Joe Christmas in *Light in August*, and Thomas Sutpen in *Absalom, Absalom!* The characters have sometimes been called villains, and certainly their behavior in most cases suggests the term, but for the careful reader the term simply does not ring true with the sympathy and understanding ultimately elicited for these human beings.

Of all these characters, Jason Compson and Addie Bundren are perhaps the least redeemed by Faulkner's usual method of probing deep within the past to reveal the events that bring understanding if not pity. But even Jason, given all his despicable traits (the stealing of the girl Quentin's money, the burning of the ticket to the tent show before Luster's eyes), is a much put-upon man. Faulkner tells us (in his "Appendix"): ". . . following his dipsomaniac father's death, he assumed the entire burden of the rotting family in the rotting house, supporting his idiot brother because of their mother, sacrificing what pleasures might have been the right and just due and even the necessity of a thirty-year old bachelor." Even before this, the family money had gone to finance his sister Caddy's wedding and his brother Quentin's education at Harvard. The one had become a prostitute, the other a suicide. Jason's sourness and meanness have been shaped by his battering by fate, and though we cannot condone them, we can come to understand them. Addie Bundren in *As I Lay Dying*, the cause of all her family's travail and suffering in dragging her corpse through flood and fire for a senseless burial in town, has reached from beyond death to wreak the revenge on Anse she vowed. But like Jason she has been buffeted by a mean fate. The advice of her father ("the reason for living was to get ready to stay dead a long time") has led her to the realization of the emptiness of most human relationships, and the universal substitution of words for feelings or things. Her loveless marriage and her unwanted children have led her to her adultery with Whitfield, in obedience to the "bitter blood boiling through the land." Her attempt to find life among the living dead is understandable, even though her strange actions are devoid of human insight and sympathy.

Popeye in *Sanctuary* is perhaps the most horrible character in all of Faulkner. Repeatedly characterized in mechanistic terms (his eyes are "two knobs of soft black rubber," his hands "doll-like," he has the "vicious depthless quality of stamped tin"), he is impotent but violates Temple Drake with a corn cob, murders first the "feeb" Tommy and then the stud Red whom he has brought to service Temple in the Memphis brothel while he looked on drooling and whinnying. But after the reader has settled back comfortably in his hatred of Popeye as Evil, Faulkner turns in his last chapter to Popeye's origins: he was born on Christmas day the son of a diseased, roving father and the daughter of a boardinghouse keeper; at first he appeared to be blind, he did not learn to walk and talk until four, and he had no hair until five, at which age his mother was told that alcohol would kill him and that he would

never advance mentally beyond his present level. His grandmother tried to get rid of him first by burning the boardinghouse down, and then by abandoning him in a rich limou-
sine—but she succeeded only in destroying herself. Left alone
with the child, the invalid mother was unable to cope with the
boy's hostilities expressed on one occasion in his cutting up
alive two lovebirds and, on another, in his dismemberment of a
half-grown kitten. His final preparation for life was five years
spent in a home for incorrigible children. All of this background coming, as it does, at the end of *Sanctuary* neatly and
swiftly undermines the reader's certainty about Popeye's evil
nature. And the final irony comes when Popeye, free of punishment for the crimes we have watched him commit, is executed for a crime he could not have committed, with his last
words to the sheriff: "Fix my hair, Jack." Popeye is clearly
non-human more than inhuman, and as much a victim of fate
(or society) as the people he has victimized. The words "bad"
or "evil" do not seem relevant to his essentially psychotic,
dehumanized nature.

Like Popeye, Joe Christmas in *Light in August* and Thomas
Sutpen in *Absalom, Absalom!* stand revealed to us at first as
ruthless, brutal men, unscrupulous and criminal. But as we
descend into the vortex—or follow along the tortured path
into the past relentlessly cleared by Faulkner, we discover that
there are circumstances that, if they do not justify, certainly
clarify the terrible actions of these two men, and which render
the use of the term "evil" rather simplistic and hollow. First we
find out about the murderer Joe Christmas's early impression-
able years at an orphanage, and later his life with his foster
parents who are religious fanatics. In his unending flight over a
"thousand savage and lonely streets," he is pursued by the
rumor that he is part Negro—and it is his tragic fate never to
know who he is. Even near the end of the novel, when the
circumstances of his conception and illegitimate birth are presented through his grotesque and obsessed grandparents, the
mystery of his blood remains. And he finally stands exposed
before us a victim of a world he never made, of a fate he could
hardly avoid. And similarly the brutalized Thomas Sutpen's
complex background is gradually revealed to us, until we are
carried back to that single moment in his youth when his moral
destiny was determined. A poor-white mountaineer, he had

gone to carry a message to a Virginia plantation house, and had been ordered by a liveried Negro to go around to the back door. This traumatic experience, his first revelation of his own social worthlessness, was the shock that gave birth to the vision of a Sutpen dynasty and the dream of a Sutpen mansion at whose front door the world could be ordered to go around to the back. Sutpen's ruthlessness represents no violation of moral principles, for Sutpen's "innocence" (derived from the front door that rejected him) recognizes not good and evil but only achievement or failure: he was determined, at whatever human cost, to achieve his vision.

This tendency to undermine the simplistic moral judgment of his readers runs through all of Faulkner, and manifests itself dramatically in the moral regeneration of characters in subsequent books. It is as though Faulkner did not want any one character to bear too much blame. He provides, for example, for the moral regeneration of the tawdry Temple Drake in *Sanctuary* some twenty years later in *Requiem for a Nun*. And even his treatment of the Snopeses in *The Hamlet* mellows later, as in the last two volumes of the Snopes trilogy, *The Town* and *The Mansion*, both Mink Snopes and Flem Snopes, victims of each other's crafty ruthlessness and unflinching determination, are each embraced in Faulkner's refrain that is a sigh for the tortured human condition—"the poor son-of-a-bitch." This does not mean that all characters in Faulkner are absolved from moral responsibility, but rather that the actual responsibility does not always rest where it superficially appears to rest, and that it is sometimes difficult, perhaps impossible, to discover enough of reality to pass judgment. Frequently it is the community itself (including the reader, as he identifies with the community) which must be called to judgment in Faulkner: the community, for example, in *Sanctuary* that refuses the unmarried Ruby and her child a home, a sanctuary in her troubles. And even Percy Grimm in *Light in August* is acting out the wishes (and sexual fantasies) of the community when he castrates and kills the cornered Joe Christmas. If the reader searches too deeply in Faulkner for a villain, he may well find himself finally looking into his own heart.

As no man appears without some good in Faulkner's universe, so no individual is without blemish. But there are characters who seem in their endurance and their human sympathies to elicit our strong admiration. Among these are Dilsey in *The Sound and the Fury*, Cash in *As I Lay Dying*, Ruby La Marr in *Sanctuary*, Lena Grove in *Light in August*, and Clytemnestra in *Absalom, Absalom!* All of these characters share an unsophisticated, even primitive and simple approach to life, a deep instinct for human values, human responsibility, and the human community, a profound sympathy for the agony (however morally complex) arising from the human condition, and a dedication to endurance in the face of the most discouraging of obstacles.

Those who read to the end of *The Sound and the Fury* (as Jean-Paul Sartre apparently did not) cannot miss the important moral position that Dilsey assumes in the last book. It is Dilsey who has held the family together, protected the weak, admonished the wicked, sympathized with the hurt and wounded. It is she who instinctively knows, and it is above all she who invariably cares. In *As I Lay Dying* Cash is the only character who is not obsessively absorbed in himself and his own furtive desires and dreams. He is concerned with his craft of carpentry and (like Dilsey) with the job to be done. He meditates: "Folks seems to get away from the olden right teaching that says to drive the nails down and trim the edges well." And he is the only member of the family to regret sending Darl off to the insane asylum: "Sometimes I ain't so sho who's got ere a right to say when a man is crazy and when he ain't. Sometimes I think it ain't none of us pure crazy and ain't none of us pure sane until the balance of us talks him that-a-way." Ruby La Marr in *Sanctuary* is the long-suffering common-law wife of the bootlegger, Lee Goodwin; she has once before given herself as a fee to help her man get out of prison, and she is prepared again to pay the price to Horace Benbow. She represents, in her discredited position, all of the female virtues of courage, faithfulness, and endurance that the "respectable" Temple Drake lacks, and she lives to see her innocent man the victim of a guilty community's wrath.

Lena Grove opens and closes *Light in August*, and, on the birth of her illegitimate baby is drawn briefly into the orbit of Joe Christmas' tragedy; but her openness to human beings, her instinctive affirmation of human worth, her durability and loyalty to life in the face of adversity—all run counter to the grim story that dominates the center of the book. And Sutpen's

63

mulatto daughter Clytemnestra in *Absalom, Absalom!* is the one
character in the book who not only endures through the
shattering of Sutpen's dynasty, but shares her strength with the
left-over mutilated and maimed. It is Clytie who cares for her
father's issue, both white and Negro, both legitimate and illegitimate, both sane and feeble-minded, and it is she who shelters
the murderer Henry Sutpen from the law and finally gives her
own life in the fire she sets to save him (as she thinks) from
going to prison for the forgotten deed committed many decades before. It would be a mistake to see a moral superiority in
all of these humble characters: they have no sense of moral
righteousness. But they all have a sense of duty, a sense of
dedication, a commitment to life. And they have an unconscious insight into the nature of the human condition in all its
absurdity that calls forth from the depths of their being their
pity, their love, their very selves in the service of suffering
fellow beings.

In his later years Faulkner seldom mentioned the new American writers, but one novel he did mention (as the "best one"
he had read) was J. D. Salinger's *Catcher in the Rye.* It was, he
said in *Faulkner in the University*, the best expression he knew
of the writer's contemporary dilemma—how to function "in
isolation . . . to exist alone inside a vacuum of facts which he
did not choose and cannot cope with and cannot escape from
like a fly inside an inverted tumbler." Salinger's Holden Caulfield, said Faulkner, "loved man and wished to be a part of
mankind, humanity, . . . tried to join the human race and
failed. . . . His tragedy was that when he attempted to enter
the human race, there was no human race there."[12] In an absurd
universe, where "life is a phenomenon but not a novelty, the
same frantic steeplechase toward nothing everywhere and man
stinks the same stink no matter where in time," Faulkner's
repeated and powerful and even heroic descents into the vortex
of time and humanity have resulted in his discovery of a few
simple but terribly important truths. They are the truths of a
Dilsey or a Cash that confirm symbolically the "olden right
teaching that says to drive the nails down and trim the edges
well." Or, as Faulkner put them another way once (in *Faulkner in the University*), they are "such simple things as honesty

[12] *Ibid.*, p. 244.

with oneself and responsibility toward others and protection for the weak and compassion and pity for all." His total body of work may be read as these truths writ large, with especial emphasis on "compassion and pity for *all*." In describing to a group of young writers in 1958 the problem they all confronted, Faulkner offered one of the best dedications extant of his own work: "to save mankind from being desouled as the stallion or boar or bull is gelded; to save the individual from anonymity before it is too late and humanity has vanished from the animal called man."[13]

It is clear now, some forty years after the appearance of his first novel, that Faulkner's peer is not the writer of the Twenties whose name is usually ranked with his—Ernest Hemingway. Nor, for that matter, can Hemingway any longer be considered a serious challenger for the premium position. Indeed, as time has passed, Hemingway's initially huge reputation has tended to shrink, and especially has it declined since his work has had to stand by itself out from under the protective shadow of that powerfully dramatic presence of the live author, recreating the life of the books. Faulkner's passion for anonymity and privacy forced his own books to stand on their intrinsic merits from the beginning, and that beginning was indeed small, all of his works going out of print shortly after publication, disappearing into the out-of-print past by the time of World War II. After this inauspicious beginning and the post–World War II revival, Faulkner's reputation has steadily risen, overtaking and distancing all his rivals of the Twenties.

We are only now beginning to take the full measure of Faulkner's total imaginative achievement, and it is indeed awe-inspiring. He is one of our great American imaginations, ranking easily with Hawthorne, Melville, Twain, and James. But he also transcends national boundaries, and he is the one American modern that we may without question rank with such continental giants as Kafka, Mann, Proust, Lawrence, and Joyce. But he reaches beyond these early twentieth-century figures to our own time and day, either directly or via Sartre and Camus, and is a vital presence in the contemporary imagination, alongside J. D. Salinger, Wright Morris, Flannery O'Connor, Saul Bellow. We might say of him what he once said of his character Dilsey: he has endured.

[13] *Ibid.*, pp. 242, 245.

4

My Ántonia: A Frontier Drama of Time

Critics of Willa Cather have long been confronted with the baffling persistence in popularity of a novel apparently defective in structure. *My Ántonia* may well turn out to be Willa Cather's most fondly remembered and best-loved novel, while the perfectly shaped, brilliantly executed *A Lost Lady* continues unread. It does seem strange that one who wanted to unclutter the novel by throwing the furniture out the window should have bungled so badly the structure of one of her most important works.

René Rapin blames Cather for transplanting Ántonia from the country to Black Hawk: "only in her own natural habitat can she hold our attention and capture our emotion." And Rapin censures Cather severely for losing sight of Ántonia completely in the closing books of the novel.[1] David Daiches discovers the source of the defect in Cather's point of view. The "narrator's sensibility," he says, "takes control; and this raises problems which Willa Cather is never quite able to solve."[2] Like Daiches, E. K. Brown is disturbed by the disappearance of Ántonia for pages at a time, and says in the novel's defense: "Everything in the book is there to convey a feeling, not to tell a story, not to establish a social philosophy, not even to animate a group of characters."[3]

[1] René Rapin, *Willa Cather* (New York: R. M. McBride Co., 1930), p. 49.

[2] David Daiches, *Willa Cather: A Critical Introduction* (Ithaca, N.Y.: Cornell Univ. Press, 1951), p. 45.

[3] Edward K. Brown, completed by Leon Edel, *Willa Cather: A Critical Biography* (New York: Alfred A. Knopf, 1953), p. 206.

"My Ántonia": A Frontier Drama of Time

Most critics, like Brown, have felt the unified emotional impact of *My Ántonia* and have grappled with the puzzling problem of the book's actual lack of consistent central action or unbroken character portrayal. It is indeed a fine creative achievement to give the effect of unity when there apparently is none, and there are those who would claim that the nature of Cather's accomplishment is beyond the critic's understanding, an inscrutable mystery of the artist's miraculous creative process.

The action in *My Ántonia* is episodic, lacks focus and abounds in irrelevancies (consider the inserted wolf-story of Pavel and Peter, for example). Indeed, there is in the novel no plot in the accepted sense of the word. And further, there is not, as there usually is in the plotless story, a character who remains consistently on stage to dominate the obscurely related events. In the second and third books, entitled respectively "The Hired Girls" and "Lena Lingard," Ántonia fades gradually but completely from view, and the reader becomes engrossed, finally, in the excitingly sensual but abortive relationship of the narrator, Jim Burden, and the voluptuous hired girl turned seamstress, Lena Lingard.

But there is that quality of evoked feeling which penetrates the pages of the book, inhering even in the scenes omitting Ántonia, and which gathers finally to a profound and singular focus which constitutes the emotional unity of the book. We sense what we cannot detect—structural elements subtly at work reinforcing and sharpening the aroused feeling.

Jim Burden's assertion in the "Introduction" that he supposes the manuscript he has written "hasn't any form" should not deceive the reader too readily. He also states of Ántonia, "I simply wrote down pretty much all that her name recalls to me." If these confessions reveal that neither action nor character gives unity to the novel, they also suggest, indirectly, that a feeling—the emotion attached to Ántonia's name—informs the novel structurally. When Jim Burden, dissatisfied with "Ántonia" as his title, prefixes the "My," he is informing the reader in advance that the book is *not* about the real Ántonia, but rather about Ántonia as personal and poignant symbol. For Jim, Ántonia becomes symbolic of the undeviating cyclic nature of all life: Ántonia is the insistent reminder that it is the tragic nature of time to bring life to fruition through hardship and struggle only to precipitate the decline and, ultimately, death, but not without first making significant provision for new life to follow, flower and fall. The poignancy lies in the inability of the frail human being to rescue and retain any stage, no matter how beautiful or blissful, of his precious cycle. When Jim Burden asserts at the close of *My Ántonia* that he and Ántonia "possess" the "incommunicable past," he does not convince even himself. It is precisely this emotional conviction that neither they nor anyone else can possess the past, that the past is absolutely and irrevocably "incommunicable" even to those who lived it—which constitutes the novel's unity.

The "feeling" of *My Ántonia* is not the divorced and remote and discomforting "feeling" of the author, nor the displayed or dramatized "feeling" of a character, but the evoked feeling of the reader. And the element in the novel which produces and controls this feeling exists in the sensibility of the narrator, Jim Burden. It is in the drama of his awakening consciousness, of his growing awareness, that the emotional structure of the novel may be discovered.

It is Jim Burden's sensibility which imposes form on *My Ántonia* and, by that form, shapes in the reader a sharpened awareness of cyclic fate that is the human destiny. The sense of cyclic fate finds expression first in an obsessive engagement with the colorful, somber and varied seasons of the year, next in an unfolding realization of the immutable and successive phases of human life, and, finally, in an engrossing but bewildering encounter with the hierarchic stages of civilization, from the primitive culture to the sophisticated.

"The Shimerdas," the first book of *My Ántonia*, introduces from the start the drama of time in the vivid accounts of the shifting seasons. The book encompasses one year, beginning with the arrival in Autumn of the Shimerdas and Jim Burden on the endless Nebraska prairie, portraying the terrible struggle for mere existence in the bleakness of the plains' Winter, dramatizing the return of life with the arrival of Spring, and concluding with the promise of rich harvest in the intense heat of the prairie's Summer. This is Jim Burden's remembered year, and it is his obsession with the cycle of time that has caused him to recall Ántonia in a setting of the changing seasons.

Almost every detail in "The Shimerdas" is calculated to shrink the significance of the human drama in contrast with the drama of the seasons, the drama of nature, the drama of the land and sky. The struggle becomes, then, not merely a struggle for a minimum subsistence from the stubborn, foreign soil, but also even more a struggle to re-create and assert existence in a seemingly hostile or indifferent land. No doubt all of the Nebraska pioneers experienced Jim Burden's sensation on arriving on the prairie: "Between that earth and that sky I felt erased, blotted out."

The drama of "The Shimerdas" is the drama of the human being at the mercy of the cyclic nature of the universe. The "glorious autumn" of their arrival on the treeless prairie contributes to that acute sense that "the world was left behind" and that they "had got over the edge of it." The autumn is not the autumn of bountiful nature but the autumn of vast distances and approaching death. The descent of the winter snows heightens the vast primitive beauty of the undisturbed plains: "The sky was brilliantly blue, and the sunlight on the glittering white stretches of prairie was almost blinding." But ever innate to the sharp-colored beauty is an apparent hostility. The whiteness not only blinds but brings in its wake despair and death. When, after the first primitive struggle is over, Ántonia cries out to Jim in the midst of summer, "I wish my papa live to see this summer. I wish no winter ever come again," she displays intuitive insight into the relation of her father's suicide to the cosmic order of time which decrees that the death of winter must unfailingly follow the ripening autumn.

Like autumn, spring when it comes to the prairie is not so much manifest in visible nature as it is a hovering presence compellingly alive and dominant: "There was only—spring itself; the throb of it, the light restlessness, the vital essence of it everywhere: in the sky, in the swift clouds, in the pale sunshine, and in the warm, high wind." It is only with the arrival of spring, at its appointed time, that the Shimerdas and the Burdens, Ántonia and Jim, can emerge from the enforced retreat of winter to look forward to some benevolence from the enduring land. But as the winter shaped, and even took, the life of the prairie pioneer, so the spring imposes a cruelly exacting ritual of tilling and tending the virgin land. Life is hard and the soil close and unyielding without its due. And the "breathless, brilliant heat" of summer, when it descends with fiery fury on the empty lands, brings with its devastation also fertility: "The burning sun of those few weeks, with occasional rains at night, secured the corn."

Throughout the first book of *My Ántonia*, it is the world of nature rather than the human world which dominates, and even the human beings tend to identify themselves with the things of the land. One of Jim Burden's first vivid sensations in the new land is in his grandmother's garden: "I was something that lay under the sun and felt it, like the pumpkins, and I did not want to be anything more. I was entirely happy." During the pioneers' first year on the prairie the rotation of the decreed seasons imposes a primitive existence not far different from that of the plains' animals, and impresses on them a keenly felt truth: "In a new country a body feels friendly to the animals." If in the garden Jim imagined himself a pumpkin, there were other times when he and the rest felt a sympathetic resemblance to the gopher, in their intimate dependence on the land for sustenance and home. At the end of this first year's struggle with the land, Ántonia emerges with an essential and profound wisdom that only the cyclic seasons in their cruelty and their beneficence could bestow. She reveals to Jim, "Things . . . will be hard for us."

As Ántonia and Jim are shaped and "created" by the successive seasons, so their lives in turn are cycles of a larger order in time, and shape and create the nation. It is in the dramatization of Ántonia from the girlhood of the opening pages through her physical flowering in the middle books to, finally, her reproduction of the race in a flock of fine boys in the final pages of the book that her life is represented, like the year with its seasons, as a cycle complete in its stages of birth, growth, fruition and decline. Although Ántonia's life represents a greater cycle than that of the year, the pattern remains the same in both. The year, of course, is merely a term for the designation of a unit of time, and its resemblance to the life-cycle suggests that life, too, is a physical representation of time.

As the seasons of fall, winter, spring and summer impose a structure on the first book of Willa Cather's novel, the successive stages of Ántonia's life assist in imposing a structure on the total work. We may trace these stages through the various books into which the novel is subdivided. Some critics have called Ántonia an earth goddess. She is a re-creation of an archetypal pattern—woman as the embodiment of self-assured if not self-contained physical fertility which insures the endurance of the race. Ántonia never despairs, not even in the first book of the novel in which the hostility of the first prairie winter deprives her of her father; but throughout she works and lives with an innate dignity which springs from her intuitive knowledge of her appointed function in the continuation of the species. Even in the second book, called "The Hired Girls," Ántonia feels no sense of an enforced inferiority but rather a supreme reliance on the hidden resources bestowed upon her by the hard physical struggles of her past.

As Ántonia stands out sharply in the first book, in the second she merges with many "hired girls" in Black Hawk who are of her kind, and in the third, called "Lena Lingard," she does not even appear except as a remembered presence in the talks about the past between Lena and Jim Burden in Lincoln. In these conversations there is a foreshadowing of Ántonia's fate which is the subject of the fourth book, entitled "The Pioneer Woman's Story." If in Book I Ántonia represents the eternal endurance under supreme hardship of woman appointed propagator of the race, and in Book II she represents the overflowing liveliness and energetic abundance of physical woman come to the flower, in Books III and IV she symbolizes the calm and faithful endurance of woman eternally wronged. In Ántonia's fierce love for her fatherless child exists the full explanation of mankind's continuing to be. But Willa Cather insists on Ántonia's appearing in a double role, not only as woman wronged, but also as woman fulfilled in her destiny. In the last book of the novel, "Cuzak's Boys," Ántonia is glimpsed in her declining years surrounded by the "explosive life" of her many children. When Jim Burden sees her after the absence of all those years, he recognizes in her the persistence of that quality he had sensed when they roamed the prairie as boy and girl: "She was there, in the full vigour of her personality, battered but not diminished, looking at me, speaking to me in the husky, breathy voice I remembered so well."

In the closing books of *My Ántonia* ("The Pioneer Woman's Story" and "Cuzak's Boys"), Ántonia emerges as vividly as she did in the first. For an explanation of the fading of Ántonia in Books II and III ("The Hired Girls" and "Lena Lingard"), we must turn to a third principle of structure operating in the

DEPARTURES, DISLOCATIONS, DESCENTS

book, another cycle greater in scope than either a year or a life. For a foreshadowing of this cycle we may turn to Frederick Jackson Turner and his famous essay, "The Significance of the Frontier in American History." Turner asserted, in the late nineteenth century, that the distinguishing feature of America's development was the cyclic character of her movement westward, conquering over and over again a new wilderness. There was, Turner said, "A recurrence of the process of evolution in each western area reached in the process of expansion."[4]

My Ántonia exemplifies superbly Turner's concept of the recurring cultural evolution on the frontier. There is first of all the migration from the East, in the case of the Shimerdas from Czechoslovakia, in Jim Burden's case from Virginia, both lands of a high cultural level. In the West these comparatively sophisticated people are compelled literally to begin over again, on a primitive level, shedding their cultural attainment like an animal its skin, and, like animals, doing battle with the land and the elements for the meanest food and shelter.

The books of *My Ántonia* reflect the varying stages of this evolutionary process in cultural development. On this level of structure, not the seasons of the year, nor the phases of Ántonia's life, but the successive cultural plateaus of the nation operate as ordering elements in the novel. And it is on this level of significance and in the dramatization of this epic archetypal cycle of the country that justification for those sections of the book, so frequently condemned because they lose focus on Ántonia, may be found.

In the first book, "The Shimerdas," the newly arrived pioneers from the East discover nothing but their strength and the prairie's stubborn soil out of which to create for themselves a new world in their own image. In this primitive struggle with the prairie, on a level with the struggle of prehistoric man in the dawn of time, some lose their lives, some their spirit, and all lose that overlay of softening civilization which they brought from the East. There is not only the primitive struggle, but these pioneers become primitive men in the harshness of the struggle. Ántonia's father, sad for the old country, dies; and

[4] Frederick J. Turner, *The Frontier in American History* (New York: Henry Holt & Co., 1920), p. 2.

72

Ántonia takes a man's place behind the plow. On the prairie the elements, the sky and the land impose a communal democracy in all of the meager human institutions.

"The Hired Girls," the second book of *My Ántonia*, portrays a higher stage in the cultural evolution of the frontier: the small town comes to the wilderness. If Jim Burden discovers his own hidden courage and becomes a man in the snake-killing incident of Book I, in Book II he discovers the genuine complexity of adulthood, especially in a social context which the bare prairie does not afford. Jim is puzzled by the stratification of society in Black Hawk, a stratification that could not exist on the virgin prairie, and which does not tally with Jim's moral judgment: the "hired girls" are for Jim the most interesting, the most exciting and the liveliest of all possible companions, far superior to the dull conformists of the town. It is the strong lure of the hired girls, however, which precipitates Jim's first crucial decision: in spite of the strong spiritual and physical attraction of these girls, Jim turns to the study which will prepare him for college and which, in Black Hawk, culminates in the triumph of his high-school commencement oration. Already there has come to the frontier prairie that element whose absence caused Ántonia's father to despair. After Ántonia has heard Jim's speech, she tells him: "there was something in your speech that made me think so about my papa." In her instinctive way Ántonia dimly understands her father's sacrifice of his life and Jim's yearning for higher intellectual achievement, even though her own destiny, centered in the physical reproduction of the race, may be and is to be fulfilled on the innocent and unsophisticated prairie.

Jim's discoveries, both intellectual and emotional, of Book II, are continued and intensified in the next book, "Lena Lingard." Lincoln, Nebraska, is as far above Black Hawk culturally as Black Hawk is above the empty, untouched prairie, and though the university has the limitations imposed by the isolation of the plains, there is "an atmosphere of endeavour, of expectancy and bright hopefulness" which prevails. It is Jim's good fortune to develop a close association with Gaston Cleric, the intellectually alive and intense head of the Latin Department, who introduces Jim to the exciting world of ideas. Jim discovers that "when one first enters that world everything else fades for a time, and all that went before is as if it had not been." But the climax of Jim's awakening is a realization of the persistence of the past: "Yet I found curious survivals; some of the figures of my old life seemed to be waiting for me in the new." Jim's awareness of the crucial impingement of his prairie heritage on his involvement in a received culture seems an instinctive artistic confirmation of Turner's frontier thesis.

Culture does come to the Nebraska prairie, not only in the form of a world of ideas via Gaston Cleric, but also in the form of music and theater. The nature of the curious impact is revealed brilliantly when Jim describes his and Lena's reaction to the traveling "Camille": "A couple of jackrabbits, run in off the prairie, could not have been more innocent of what awaited them." Throughout Book III of the novel, there is a delightful rediscovery by the children of the pioneer genera-tion of a cultural world forsaken by their parents for the hard and isolated life of the prairie. But the pioneer values of fresh-ness and courage and integrity—and many more—survive and condition the responses.

Lincoln, Nebraska, though it offers much, offers a mere token of what waits in the rich and glittering East. Lured on by bright dreams of intellectual achievement, Jim Burden fol-lows Gaston Cleric to Harvard, which, in the book's develop-ing hierarchy, is to Lincoln as Lincoln is to Black Hawk and Black Hawk to the barren prairie. But with the dramatization of three stages of civilization as it comes to the wilderness, and with the suggestion of the future destiny by the "invocation" of "ancient" Harvard and by the suggestion of greater cultural riches farther East, Willa Cather shifts the focus from the dream of the nation and, indeed, of civilization, back to Ántonia of the prairies. The novel has, in a sense, come full circle when Jim, in the last book, finds himself in the midst of that very culture the nostalgic remembrance of which drove Ántonia's father to despair: "Once when I was abroad I went into Bohemia, and from Prague I sent Ántonia some photo-graphs of her native village." By this casual visit, the return to the point of origin, the cycle of cultural movement is symboli-cally completed. And when the sophisticated, world-traveled, perhaps even world-weary, Jim Burden returns to the prairie scenes of his boyhood and discovers Ántonia and her houseful of boys, he discovers at the same time the enduring quality of those values not dependent on cultural level, but accessible on the untutored prairies. Ántonia, "in the full vigour of her personality, battered but not diminished," not only endures but achieves an emotionally and physically fulfilled life. Her boys are her triumphant creative achievement.

My Ántonia closes with the dominant image of the circle, a significant reminder of the general movement of all the structural elements in the book. After his visit with Ántonia, Jim confesses, "I had the sense of coming home to myself, and of having found out what a little circle man's experience is." This vivid image reinforces the cyclic theme which pervades the book: the cycle of the seasons of the year, the cycle of the stages of human life, the cycle of the cultural phases of civilization. *My Ántonia* is, then, ultimately about time, about the inexorable movement of future into present, of present into past. Against the backdrop of this epic drama of the repetitive movement of time, man poignantly plays out his role. Ántonia, when she cries out to Jim, "I wish no winter ever come again," more nearly expresses the essence of the book's theme than does Jim when he asserts at the end, "whatever we had missed, we possessed together the precious, the incommunicable past." *Optima dies . . . prima fugit*, translated by Jim as "the best days are the first to flee," stands as the book's epigraph. This intensely felt awareness of the past *as past* is the emotional heart of the novel, and is evoked and sustained by the book's several levels of structure and their involvement with the revolving cycles of time.

5

Wharton and Cather:
The Quest for Culture

I. The Modern Scene

Modern America was born sometime around 1920, at the end of World War I. America for the first time got an inkling of what she was in for in the way of worldwide responsibility, a responsibility thrust upon her because of her emerging position as a world power. America was reluctant to take the position—she stayed out of the League of Nations—like a young adult temporarily reverting (in pique and in fear) to adolescence. But adulthood could not be avoided. The world insisted that America assume the position of maturity befitting her reserves of power.

This elementary history has interest for us only because, as students of literature, we are interested in literary periods. And that date, 1920, marks not only the birth of modern America but also the birth of contemporary literature: not only a literary era drew to a close, but a new and vigorous literary decade was launched. After 1920, it seemed impossible to write the kind of literature in America (and have it taken seriously) that was written throughout the nineteenth century and the early years of the twentieth.

Everybody knows the label we now give to the writers of the Twenties—even those not then conceived by the flappers and philosophers of the time: the lost generation. Gertrude Stein was the one who said it, and she said it to Ernest Hemingway who turned around and used it as the epigraph to his lost generation novel, *The Sun Also Rises*. And everybody knows what happened at the end of the golden decade, when the stock market crashed and the bread lines sobered up the jazz-age writers. Literature became deadly serious and terribly dull—except, of course, for some rare exceptions. The Great Depression (like the Jazz Age before it) lasted conveniently (conveniently, that is, for the literary historians) for exactly a decade: there is a unity of the depressed Thirties to match the unity of the wild Twenties. Then, of course, came the earthquake, the first tremors of which were heard on a quiet Sunday afternoon when everyone was listening to the symphony—the date was December 7. The violence grew and grew, reaching a climax in 1945 when a beautiful, terrible mushroom cloud arose over the American desert. Are the Forties the Age of the Atomic Bomb? Or the Age of Anxiety? Whatever age we call them, they were years not very productive of literature. In the holocaust, in the collapse of civilization, literature did not seem much to matter. There were books, of course, but most of the young poets and novelists found themselves in bootcamp or on the battlefield with a rifle in their hands. After the Forties came the Fifties and Sixties. And here we are. But where we are no one seems quite sure. The appearance of Sputnik could not inspire much reaction because the taste buds of our imaginations had been dulled. We are still spinning from the awesome possibilities of the worlds to be discovered in the atom; how were we expected to comprehend the worlds to be discovered in limitless space?

What has all this to do with Wharton and Cather? Before tackling that question head-on, let us quickly examine the literature of this Modern America we have been describing.

The Lost Generation of the Twenties produced such novelists as Ernest Hemingway, whose *The Sun Also Rises* became a kind of bible of behavior for the lostniks, a bible to which might be referred any question of the Code by which people who believed in nothing might live. Scott Fitzgerald became the symbolic jazz-age man, simultaneously living and recording the joy and agony of lostness of the Lost Generation. His finest book, *The Great Gatsby*, portrayed the life and death of a crazy mixed-up man who lost his love, himself, his country—and finally the world. In the background, as a chorus for this drama of the lost generation, were such novelists as Sinclair Lewis and Sherwood Anderson (both revolting from the mainstreet of Average Town, USA), and such dramatists as Maxwell Anderson and Eugene O'Neill, both breaking through the

77

bonds that had been stifling American drama ever since its dim origins in the eighteenth century. Toward the tail end of the lost decade, two powerful voices began to be heard, both with a slightly southern accent: Thomas Wolfe and William Faulkner. Wolfe and Faulkner, off the mainroads and out in the backwoods, were working different mines, shaping different styles: they did not identify with the Lost Generation so closely as the others—and thereby escaped its fate. Wolfe and Faulkner survived the '29 crash and continued to be vigorous voices in the decade ahead.

And the decade ahead proved to be a difficult decade for survival. The Depressed Generation had no time for the glitter and tinsel and liquor and flappers of the Twenties. People without jobs thought literature ought to be serious, not frivolous, somehow pertinent to real life, not irrelevant to the problems of existence. New literary Gods replaced the old. John Dos Passos came into his own with that strange, defective, weighty epic *U.S.A.* John Steinbeck became a national hero, even influenced legislation, somehow (nobody could say exactly how) prepared the way for a better world with his sympathetic, impassioned treatment of the Okies in their trek westward to California in search of the promised land (in *The Grapes of Wrath*). Erskine Caldwell seemed somehow to be facing the real facts of existence in dramatizing the appalling domestic and sex life of people barely literate, grubbing about in the dirt for their daily food and sensations—in *Tobacco Road* and *God's Little Acre*.

To those of us who grew to maturity in the Thirties, the depression seemed a permanent way of life, a perpetual fact of existence to which we had somehow to adjust. But then, late in the decade, we heard the cultivated, curiously weak voice of Prime Minister Chamberlain, the man with the umbrella, declaring war on Germany—all according to the rules of the game. And what a game it turned out to be! The Age of Anxiety turned at times into the Age of Agony! But we endured—and, astonishingly enough, the writers continued to write. New poets, like Karl Shapiro and Randall Jarrell, turned up in uniform to define the singular American sensibility in the boredom and sensation of war. New novelists also appeared, trained in the old schools, but bringing to light the new—but also ancient—experience of war. There is little excitement of

78

discovery in the novelists of the Age of Anxiety. There seem to be no brave new movements launched, no booming voices of prophecy raised. Somehow, this World War was more sobering than the First, and instead of firing the creative imagination sent it into a state of shock. Art was shattered into fragments—no man would attempt to embody the whole of experience. Irwin Shaw in *The Young Lions* tried to paint the war on a large canvas that included even the enemy, but, finally, the disparate materials would not fuse into great art. Norman Mailer tried to create the entire battlefield in a single mountain on a Pacific island—in *The Naked and the Dead*—but somehow the imagination seemed tired, perhaps too deeply engaged in the remembered experience. Robert Penn Warren, on the civilian front, explored in *All the King's Men* the psychology of demagoguery, but, except for the momentary excitement of McCarthyism, the issues did not really strike home as vital.

In spite of the Sputnik Fifties and the Space Race Sixties following close on the heels of the Atomic Forties, apathy rather than hysteria seems to prevail. We are no longer surprised or skeptical or shocked when we read an occasional reference to the awful Faustian knowledge that man has uncovered which makes it possible for him to blast both himself and his planet back into chaos, back into the primordial matter out of which God presumably found the materials for the beginning of it all. Perhaps the characteristic image of our time is the devil grinning down from the center of a neat, symmetrical mushroom cloud, or reclining casually on a rocket whizzing among the planets and stars, around the sun and the moon. Whatever the image, we have conjured it up mainly out of the newspapers, for the writers of our time have tended to shun it. None has cried the loud alarm, none has become our wild and screaming prophet of doom. Instead, we have all settled comfortably back into Suburbia, become adjusted Organization Men, been persuaded by the hidden persuaders and have set out seeking our own status. Literature seems stunted. The bold, sweeping imagination (like Whitman's or Melville's) no longer seems a possibility. When there is a thawing of the imagination, it seems to be for some precious, tightly restricted area of experience, an area small enough for the author to control completely and absolutely.

But the Fifties did witness the advent of one literary movement of peculiar vitality, a movement which might triumph by giving to history the decade's name: the Beat Generation. The most celebrated works to come out of this movement were Allen Ginsberg's book of poems, *Howl!* and Jack Kerouac's frenzied novel, *On the Road*. As these strange titles suggest, the Beat Generation seemed to be a movement of protest by a restless, rootless generation. Just what was being protested against was not quite clear, though there was much talk of suburban life, office routine, and gray flannel suits. Not clear, either, was how the protest justified conduct, frequently described in the literature, which bordered on juvenile delinquency—and might have been so labeled except for the advanced age of the participants. All of the talk of the collapse of morals suggested the same kind of talk of the same kind of behavior of the Lost Generation of thirty years before.

But if we were dancing in a merry circle, at least some new notes had been added to the piper's tune. Zen Buddhism was in the air, Walt Whitman had become respectable again among poets (T. S. Eliot had banished him from the canon in the 1920's), and long-haired, bright-eyed discussions went on about the *Bhagavad-Gita* and Kierkegaard. Perhaps one day we shall see that the Beat Generation was the old Lost Generation simply gone mystic, the cult of negation transfigured into the cult of beatification (Kerouac had insisted on the relation of *beat* and *beatify*). On one level the Beat Generation seemed to sink to sub-literary depths, to become a popular, mass movement that seemed real gone, jazz-created, mystic in a most mystifying and physical sense, not unrelated to the ritualistic rock-and-roll madness of the teen-agers and adolescents. On another level the Beat Generation rose to supraliterary heights, reaching out internationally to connect in oblique ways with the Angry Young Men of Great Britain, and the Existentialists of France.

II. The Age of Wharton and Cather

It is time now that I turn to Edith Wharton and Willa Cather. The picture I have painted has not been without purpose. It is against just such a background that discussion of our two "contemporary authors" must begin. We wince when we place

Wharton and Cather in the modern literary context, and it's the wince I wanted to evoke. Depending on our bias, we can say that we wince because Cather and Wharton suddenly seem old-fashioned; or we can say we wince because they remind us of solidity in a time of disintegration and decay. Whatever we say, we cannot escape the obvious incompatibility of the modern world and Wharton and Cather—though both lived long past 1920—Wharton died in 1937, Cather in 1947.

Even in novels which they wrote after 1920, Wharton and Cather have the pre–World War I flavor. If we judge them by their novels, we must conclude that they were too late for the nineteenth century and too early for the twentieth. They do not fit easily into any movement or period, and for this reason their reputations have suffered. Literary critics and historians have tended to relegate them to minor positions, Wharton dismissed as a second-rate Henry James and Cather as a tardy local colorist. It is too convenient to leap from the naturalistic movement in American fiction at the end of the nineteenth century to the rebellion of the lost generation of the 1920's. Those years in between are embarrassing: Stephen Crane and Frank Norris did not live on for very long into them, though Dreiser did, and both Mark Twain and Henry James were alive for a few of them—but there is, so the saying goes, not much there—nothing new, nothing fresh, nothing worth excitement.

It is this view that we must revise and for this reason we place Wharton and Cather together. We must call in question the conventional view: we must pry these two centuries apart and put back into the literary histories those lost years—and we might begin by testing a new name—The Age of Wharton and Cather, 1900–1920. The dates are a little untidy, but untidiness is the rule in defining any literary age. We shall neatly divide the reign, and let Wharton rule for the first half, Cather for the second.

Wharton and Cather thus belong together at the same time that they must remain separate. So far as is known, they never met and did not seem aware, in any vital sense, of each other's work. Indeed, in connecting them we yoke together two authors quite unlike—but there are subterranean connections. Old-fashioned as they are or seem, both yearn for an earlier time: both turn from the present in anguish and look longingly to the past; and both seem haunted by a sense of inevitable failure in the human pursuit of happiness. But if one cannot have happiness, he can at least discover for himself some sustaining values. Although the search for values is common to both, they traveled quite different roads in their quests and they arrived at different destinations in their discoveries. But the quests had behind them and in common the informing feminine and American sensibility. The femininity is perhaps too elusive to analyze, but the Americanism is visibly writ large.

It is this deeper sense in which Wharton and Cather belong together—the sense in which they symbolize the two conflicting elements in the American character. Wharton was the novelist of the East, satirist of high civilization, pursuer of Culture in the traditional sense: inevitably her gaze was fixed eastward, toward a half-real, half-mythic Europe. Cather, on the other hand, was the novelist of the West, critic of the mainstreet society replacing the pioneer prairie, pursuer of a Western spirit: inevitably her gaze was fixed westward, toward the receding frontier, also half-real, half-mythic. Out of just such an East-West conflict, or tug-of-war, has the American mind been formed and the American character shaped. Wharton and Cather belong together, therefore, in dramatizing the two sides of this conflict, in defining the two halves that somehow fuse and form the whole which becomes the Modern American.

For both Wharton and Cather, Europe seemed to provide some kind of key to the American experience. It was, of course, Europe as idea more than simply as a place to travel that was important. But both these women made various journeys to the Continent, and there can be no doubt that their travels were important to their themes and their work. Willa Cather made many trips abroad, particularly to France, and the direct results for her work are obvious in such books as *Death Comes for the Archbishop* and *Shadows on the Rock*. Edith Wharton traveled widely, and, in later life, settled down in France for many years. Important scenes in almost all her novels (including *The Age of Innocence* and *The Custom of the Country*) take place in Europe; and it is symbolically significant that her first novel, *Valley of Decision*, was laid wholly in eighteenth-century Italy. But more important than these somewhat casual connections is the presence of Europe in the work of both as culture symbol. The distance between Willa Cather's European immigrants and Edith Wharton's European nobility (or aristocracy) is not so great as at first might seem. The poor lost father in Cather's *My Antonia* who longs for his home in the old country and finally commits suicide on the Nebraska prairie is surely spiritual and symbolic kin to the poor lost French count in Wharton's *The Custom of the Country* who makes the mistake of becoming the third husband of the rapacious, vulgar, ruthlessly ambitious American society woman, Undine Spragg. Both men are deeply immersed in and committed to a tradition to which they cannot, dare not, become alien, at penalty of a sickness of the soul unto death.

III. The World of Edith Wharton

Before proceeding further with comparisons, it is necessary to peer more deeply into the individual worlds created by these two genuises.

Edith Wharton was a depressingly prolific writer, counting some forty-seven books published between 1878 and 1938. All of this outpouring is not fiction—there are verses, travel books, books on houses and gardens—but many of the volumes are, unfortunately, novels, novellas and short stories. I say "unfortunately" because many of the works are shockingly inferior writing. Such titles as *A Son at the Front, Twilight Sleep, Hudson River Bracketed* suggest an opportunistic seizing on the topic of the moment to cash in (though she was not poor) on the interests of the day. When we look into some of these books that gushed relentlessly from her pen, we are struck by the fatigue of the imagination, the awkwardness even in the turns of phrases, that characterize the writing. It is hard to remember, at such moments, that Edith Wharton's best work ranks with the best of our century.

Among that best work must be counted four novels: *The House of Mirth,* published in 1905; *Ethan Frome,* 1911; *The Custom of the Country,* 1913; and *The Age of Innocence,* 1920.

All of these novels are stories of the trapped sensibility, stories of individuals who married culturally incompatible mates or failed to marry the right person because of some curious, ambiguous weakness. Clearly this recurring theme derives from Edith Wharton's own marriage to a sportsman who was incapable of sharing her own restless intellectual interests.

But though the theme recurs, Edith Wharton is ingenious in working out variations to create the illusion of variety. In *The House of Mirth* the heroine Lily Bart is above yet at the same time deeply entangled in the empty and meaningless pursuit of pleasure of New York society, the turn-of-the-century leisure class that accepts no cultural responsibility; Lily goes down to defeat as she finds herself paralyzed, incapable of decision, as she is attracted alternately by the glitter and gold of high society life and the books and ideas of middle-class intellectual—almost bohemian—life, this last symbolized by the strongly attractive, curiously weak Lawrence Selden, a man of ideas who sees (if but murkily) through the vast pretenses of society. Lily could any number of times have had either life, but she dies with neither because always at the crucial moment of decision she backed off, incapable of an act of commitment.

Like Lily, Ethan Frome too is defeated. For this novel, Edith Wharton turned to the "low" society of the lonely, culturally starved life of the barren New England farmlands, a life she knew only as an outsider and observer. Ethan, his mind fired by the few books that have accidentally come his way, discovers the inadequacy of his life with his complaining, whining, hypochondriac wife Zeena, but his dream of escape with the sympathetic, warmly human Mattie Silver ends in an abortive suicide attempt that cripples Mattie's body and his own spirit beyond repair. Although the novel *Ethan Frome* is a kind of sport (in the biological sense) in Edith Wharton's work in that in it she abandons the New York society that she knows, still the obsessive theme of the trapped sensibility is present and dominant.

In *The Custom of the Country*, Edith Wharton takes under her sharp scrutiny not the customary sensitive, frustrated individual, but the rapacious, aggressive, attractive but essentially vulgar woman who cold-bloodedly plots her way to the top of the international social world. Undine Spragg, vaguely from the West, of the nouveau riche, financially but not socially secure, works her way ruthlessly through several marriages to her pinnacle of social and worldly success: the sensitive, bookish, poetic Ralph Marvell, the first husband we meet, is driven ultimately to suicide; the French count Raymond de Chelles, the second, after discovering Undine's unscrupulous and shallow nature, becomes a cynical, tight-lipped bystander busying himself with the limitless detail of his ancestral estates; even Elmer Moffatt, her last husband (but who was also, briefly, her first), whose own vulgarity is a match for Undine's, and whose immense, ill-gotten wealth has raised Undine to the social pinnacle, is uneasy at the end when he sees her already restlessly scanning the social horizons for new peaks.

In what is perhaps her best novel, *The Age of Innocence*, Edith Wharton shifts her focus back to a sympathetic hero, this time a man, male counterpart in a sense to Lily Bart, spiritual kin of Ethan Frome, and imaginative descendant of Undine's first husband, Ralph Marvell. Indeed, *The Age of Innocence* is *Ethan Frome* transferred from the barren New England soil to the sterile New York drawing room. Like Ethan, Newland Archer finds himself trapped in a marriage when his soul cries out for escape with the mysterious, intellectual Madame Olenska. But like Lily Bart's, his fate is of his own making. His weakness, his deep down desire to conform, paralyzes his will to rebel. He lives out his empty life with all its meaningless social ritual to wonder, at the end, the reason for his self-sacrifice, especially in the new age, the age of sophistication, in which all the old social ritual is being called into question, all the conventions observed in the breaking. The Age of Innocence with its old-fashioned values is gone forever. And we wonder as we close the book: Has Newland Archer been a fool to give up happiness or a gentleman to devote himself to duty? But our faculty for judgment, it seems, has been paralyzed by the ambivalence in Edith Wharton's own attitude.

The world of Edith Wharton is the tight little prescribed world of New York society. Although her obsessive theme is that of the trapped sensibility, a theme which makes inevitable a searching examination of such social questions as extramarital relations and divorce, yet her singular strength lies in another direction—in the creation of the social world in all its vanity, futility, intrigue, glitter, gluttony, and greed. It is a highly filled yet curiously vacant life which she describes, a life of endless activities of little significance. The lean spareness of

Ethan Frome clearly results from the absence in the New England countryside of that dense texture of social life which fired Edith Wharton's imagination to its greatest heights of satire. The fatness of the other books, especially *The House of Mirth* and *The Custom of the Country*, derives from the fine, full creations in them of an entire social world, with all of its infinite activity and all its character types—the divorcée, the poet, the stupid rich and the wise poor, the sexually restless and the financially aggressive, the brutal, the vulgar, and the delicate, the sensitive and the insensitive. Edith Wharton is always a severe critic, and at her best in her satire she is a master of humor, of sophisticated, quiet wit. For comparison one might well reach back to Jane Austen and the social world she satirized. The talents are not unsimilar. But on entering the world of Edith Wharton, we frequently sense the uncomfortable presence of sinister elements not clearly visible, elements alien to Jane Austen's pre-industrial world. And we are at times not sure of Edith Wharton's own awareness of their presence. And there is a sense of culture and tradition in Austen's world which is alien to Wharton's. It is precisely this alienation that is the object of so many of Edith Wharton's finest satiric thrusts.

IV. The World of Willa Cather

Willa Cather's prairies are half a continent away from Edith Wharton's New York, but the world they occupy is the same.

Unlike Edith Wharton, Willa Cather published a modest quantity of books during her life—the list reaches to only seventeen. In reading them next to Edith Wharton's, we begin to note a keener ear for language, a finer sense of style.

Selection with Cather is not so easy as with Wharton. We pass over, for better or worse, *The Song of the Lark* as too detailed, *My Mortal Enemy* as too slight, and even *Death Comes to the Archbishop* as too "got up" or manufactured. Those novels which seem to strike best the authentic note are: *O Pioneers!*, published in 1913; *My Ántonia*, 1918; *A Lost Lady*, 1923; and *The Professor's House*, 1925. Of these, *O Pioneers!* seems to mark the discovery of her talent, *My Ántonia* seems her masterpiece, *A Lost Lady* seems her most nearly perfect work, and *The Professor's House* her most complex and profound.

In a way, Willa Cather's constant theme is, like Wharton's, the trapped sensibility—but the issues never revolve around marriage and divorce, but rather around home and environment. If Wharton's unfortunate marriage became the chief substance transmuted into her novels, Cather's life on the Great American Prairie, especially in those early years after the childhood move from Virginia, became her primary imaginative resource. In Wharton, the means of livelihood and the availability of culture are taken for granted; in Cather they become matters for struggle—and for agony and triumph.

O Pioneers! is the history of such a struggle. Although there is a tale of a young man of weak nature wooing a young married woman, the two of them ultimately killed by the half-crazed husband, the real center of the story lies in the struggle of the heroine, Alexandra Bergson, immigrant daughter, to triumph over the challenge to her existence made by the hostile and unfertile prairies, and at the same time, the struggle to free herself from the heavy dead weight of mediocrity hung on her by her parasitic and somewhat stupid family. She wants not only to endure but also to rise to freedom. The one man of the family on whom the hopes had been pinned, and for whom an education had been provided, was the young lad caught up in the tragic love triangle. The remaining two brothers have neither the spirit nor resources to lead the struggle to survive nor the good nature to grant Alexandra her freedom for a small personal happiness. The brothers are dull conformists, selfish and weak, and want Alexandra to offer herself in sacrifice for them. In the end, her large, generous nature does win its freedom as she reaches out in defiance for the love her brothers would deny her.

The heroine in *My Ántonia* must, like Alexandra, begin by a struggle on the most primitive level for survival itself. First she must confront and somehow conquer the prairie, forcing its reluctant soil to yield its sparse fare. This fierce struggle forces the immigrant family to burrow for shelter in the sod like the prairie dogs, it plunges Ántonia's father into reveries about the old country and finally precipitates his suicide, it embitters her brother and bewilders her mother. Thrown back on her own resources, when she reaches young womanhood she moves into the small town to become a "hired girl." But even here the struggle is not over, for Ántonia along with the other hired girls becomes the victim of small town mores and small-minded prejudices: she is held beneath the level of middle-class respectability, outside the circle of accepted conformity. As many of the hired girls scatter over the world, Ántonia returns to the prairie. For a time she is a victim, a woman wronged by a scoundrel who fathers her child then runs into hiding. But Ántonia endures both the wrong and the new struggle with the soil—and finally she frees herself as Alexandra had done. She is last seen happily married and modestly prosperous in her home on the prairie, surrounded by her numerous fine sons, lively symbols of the final fulfillment of her obscure destiny.

In *A Lost Lady*, Willa Cather turns from the heroine whose story is a rise to a heroine whose sad tale is decline. In this book, too, she turns to a different level of culture, to another kind of pioneer. The lost lady of the book is married to one of the old, fast-disappearing builders of the west, a railroad man. Captain Forrester is old in years, retired, bypassed now in a small Nebraska town by the very railroad he helped to create. Mrs. Forrester is younger, still full of sophisticated charm and a warm love of gay life. But as they live on in the small-town isolation of their big house, Mrs. Forrester grows increasingly restess, increasingly aware of the waste of her remaining youth. Like Alexandra and Ántonia, she too is engaged in a struggle with a hostile or indifferent environment. But her actions turn out to be not heroic but somewhat shabby. As the Captain declines both physically and financially, Mrs. Forrester declines morally, first taking a coarse lover from her own class, and finally falling into a vulgar intimacy with the worst of the small-town, spiritually warped, imaginatively stunted, greedy and rapacious new order that has replaced the pioneer (a class close kin to Faulkner's Snopeses who despoil the war-weakened South).

Although *The Professor's House* may seem at first glance to hold little in common with Willa Cather's other novels, a deeper look reveals some close connections. Like Alexandra and Ántonia, Professor St. Peters is in conflict with the world in which he discovers himself. Like them, he possesses a superior spirit—superior in generosity, in feeling, in perception. The primary difference is that he has had the training to make him a historian—he is living in a period, after the primitive pioneer struggle, when such luxuries as education are possible.

On the superficial level, Professor St. Peters seems childishly attached to the old house in which he has lived out his career, the house in which both his children and his books have been born; he cannot bring himself to give up forever the attic room at the top of the house where in solitude he has lived the life of the mind. But as the society surrounding Professor St. Peters emerges in all its shabby pettiness, as we see the comfortable but essentially soulless new house which the professor's wife has built, as we see the showy, essentially vulgar mansion built by his daughter and her congenial but shallow husband—we then begin to sense the profounder feelings behind the professor's rebellion. And when we are carried back in time, through the tale of Tom Outland, the professor's student, now dead, and the only other character in the novel with a simple and superior spirit to match the professor's own, as we are carried back through his story to the houses of the ancient cliff dwellers of the American southwest, and witness their despoliation by the cheapness and the greed and the grossness of contemporary life, we come to realize that Professor St. Peters' desire to remain in the old house is basically his reluctance to move into the vulgar modern world. His conflict is essentially the same as Alexandra's and Ántonia's, but because of his highly developed and complex sensibility, it must of necessity be dramatized in more subtle terms. At the end, even though Professor St. Peters seems to have given in when he turns from his own past into the future planned for him by his wife and daughters, he still appears to have achieved that small measure of freedom won by Alexandra and Ántonia—but his freedom is visible only in his inner life, only in the spirit; his triumph has been a triumph of the aware mind.

The world of Willa Cather is the open, limitless world of the American frontier prairie. The real life of her novels exists not in her plots, no more than in Edith Wharton's, but in the world which she creates out of the barren and unlikely materials of the prairie. Her gift is not Wharton's, not the gift of humor, but rather of sentiment; her talent is not satiric but essentially poetic. Her greatest triumph in her art is her recurring use of genuine sentiment without lapse into a vitiating sentimentality. Willa Cather was as severe as Edith Wharton in her condemnation of society when in the deadweight of its mediocrity and dull conformity it stifled the gifted or imaginative spirit. Like Wharton, Cather deplored in society the vulgarity and shallowness of its culture; and like Wharton, she portrayed it as frequently preserving out of the past the mean and meaningless, the vacuous and fatuous ritualistic, while, at the same time, abandoning the genuine traditional values of moral substance. But unlike Wharton, Cather found some of her deepest values in the humblest of places, values of the human spirit which somehow transcended, rose above, the cultural mediocrity, values so subtle and so elusive they could be evoked only by the muted magic of poetry. For a parallel to the world of Willa Cather we can go back to no British writer. Startling as it may seem, we must instead go back to the American, James Fenimore Cooper. There is, of course, none of the poetry of Cather in Cooper, but there are some basic elements held in common. Cooper, too, wrote of the prairies; but more important than locale is the spirit. Before Cather, Cooper discovered certain fundamental values in the pioneer struggle, in the hard life of the frontier, and he deplored too the vulgarity of much of society. Although the world of suspense he created, filled with the endless chase of red man and white, white man and red, seems extremely remote from Cather's poetically shaped world, still he tried, as did she after him, to find the enduring values of both the old society and the new frontier where they came together in collision.

V. America, Europe, and Myth

Both Wharton and Cather were serious novelists in search of basic values. Wharton was an essentially negative novelist—she was at her best in satirizing the weaknesses and follies of society. Cather was essentially affirmative, at her best in portraying the struggle and spiritual triumph of a superior sensibility.

Wharton looked to the past, and particularly to the East, to Europe, for the values worth preserving. She seemed incapable of holding the West in anything but contempt in her imagination. Her characters who came out of the West were invariably vulgar in manners and frequently stunted in morals. The West to her was as far beneath New York culturally as New York was beneath Europe. And for Wharton, manners, culture and morals seemed inextricably interrelated. Cather, on the other hand, though she too looked to the past and to Europe, was able to perceive the moral value as not necessarily prescribed by the cultural: certain of the finest elements of character, she discovered, could flourish in the most culturally barren soil.

Indeed, in Cather, we find such characters as Alexandra and Ántonia transcending their realistic roles in the novels and assuming mythic dimensions. In their triumphant struggle with the soil, in their own magnanimity and generosity, they become earth goddesses, the affirming fertile female principle of life. Edith Wharton seems incapable of delineating either heroes or heroines of such proportions. Her "ideal" characters are men and women of culture who seem debilitated by some strange, spiritual weakness. Neither Lily Bart in *The House of Mirth* nor Madame Olenska in *The Age of Innocence* strike us with the force of some fundamental and enduring principle of life. Lawrence Selden in *The House of Mirth*, Ralph Marvell in *The Custom of the Country*, and Newland Archer in *The Age of Innocence* seem ultimately incapable, as Cather's characters are capable, of bending destiny to their will. Even Ethan Frome fails, and Undine Spragg's French count, perhaps the most cultivated and traditional of all Wharton's heroes, her truly ideal gentleman, is unable to dominate and direct his own life.

Central to the work of both Edith Wharton and Willa Cather is the basic American mythic drama, the conflict of East and West, the collision of Civilization and Frontier. In this myth Europe functions as symbol of the lost past, of a cultural Garden from which the American has been excluded by his eating of the Apple of the Innocent West. In its recurrence in American literature, the myth takes the form of the quest, a quest that heads significantly toward the East or the West, and which has as its goal the discovery of the old Garden or the creation of a new. And the myth is played out in real life as well as in art. Henry James and T. S. Eliot, for example, traveled East permanently, under the belief or the illusion that they could return to the Garden by their singular act of renunciation: theirs was salvation through faith. Cooper, Whitman, and Twain, on the other hand, made their commitment, at least imaginatively, to the West: they re-created the Garden in the western wilderness, achieving their salvation through good works. Wharton belongs to the first of these groups, Cather to the second. There is no need to judge one deficient, the other superior: each expresses a truth of the American experience; together they make our literature whole and complete.

II

BARBARIC YAWPS AND MYSTIC MURMURING

I too am not a bit tamed, I too am untranslatable,
I sound my barbaric yawp over the roofs of the
world.

WALT WHITMAN

6

Walt Whitman:
The Quest for Identity

The situation of Whitman and his critics, from the beginning in 1855 until now, may be summed up in two interlocking questions: Whitman asked, Who am I? His critics continue to ask, Who are you, Walt Whitman? It is not likely even yet that Whitman or his book will yield a definitive answer. But surely one of the reasons Whitman remains a central riddle of our literature is that he vigorously dramatized the questions that continue to haunt the American imagination—what does it mean, being an American? Who are we? Who am I?

The American search for identity must have begun deep in the consciousness of the first lonely settlers, awestruck by the immensity of the land that seemed to swallow them, isolated from the currents of the past that washed them to these shores. One of the first, halting attempts at answer came in 1782, when Crèvecoeur wrote: "Americans are the western pilgrims . . . they will finish the great circle. . . . The American is a new man, who acts upon new principles; he must therefore entertain new ideas, and form new opinions." Such brave assertions of such high destiny could spring only from the nagging uncertainties of self- and national-identity.

Throughout our literature, the question of identity has echoed insistently. James Fenimore Cooper ambivalently defined America (and himself) in the person of Natty Bumppo, a moral embodiment of the best of the old and the new, of civilization and the wilderness. Hawthorne probed his own and the national psyche in the puritan past of Salem and in the pagan present of Rome. Melville's central figure was Ishmael, cut off from home and father, a wayfaring orphan searching for a lost self. Emerson discovered the secret of identity deep within the hidden recesses of being—in the pure stream of a primitive and alien energy. Thoreau tested Emerson's theory by isolating and throwing himself rigorously back on the resources of that elusive spirit of the transcendent self. James sent his Americans across the sea to Europe where, in the shadows of the past, they took on moral configurations that appeared distinguishable and distinctive. Twain sent his Americans floating down the great mother river in search of freedom and exploration of self. In one of her brief lyrics, Emily Dickinson provided a whimsical commentary on this recurring theme:

> I'm nobody! Who are you?
> Are you nobody, too?

It is, of course, an oversimplification to attribute the endless search running through America's literature solely to the ancestral severance with the past. There are no doubt many complex causes, and an important one is the gradual loss of religious faith, which Darwin's mid-nineteenth century discoveries accelerated. To the question—What does it mean, to be an American?—was added the more puzzling dilemma: What does it mean, to be a man? Inextricably entangled are the questions, Who am I? What is man? What is his nature and destiny? These questions are not, obviously, peculiar to American literature, but they seem to flow naturally and directly out of the American experience of severance and isolation and loss.

Contemporary answers to these contemporary questions are varied, and tend to the subtle rather than the sweeping. In French existentialism, the British Angry Young Men, and the American Beatniks, the common denominator appears to be the search for identity, the longing for a soul—even of the self-created, do-it-yourself variety. In the existential doctrine of *substance preceding essence*, the discovery of self lies within the will of the individual: he literally creates himself, in an image of his own making. In another modern philosophy, Martin Buber's, the self is discovered only in relationships, the vital, living relationships of I-Thou: the individual creates himself in the connections he establishes with other men and the world.

The secret of Whitman's continuing relevance would appear

to be twofold. In American literature, he brings into sharp focus a central theme—the search for identity. In modern literature, he remains a remarkable example of an obsessive concern—the nature of the self. In the opening line of *Leaves of Grass* Whitman vigorously asserts his identity: "One's-self I sing, a simple separate person." And yet this individuality, this self, has significance only in the context of multiple social relationships, as the second line of *Leaves* hastens to assert: "Yet utter the word Democratic, the word En-Masse."

In a sense, the whole of *Leaves of Grass* is an answer to the question—What does it mean, being an American? In "A Backward Glance O'er Travel'd Roads," in the light of his fulfilled career, Whitman defined his purpose in the *Leaves* as something of a direct answer to the question. He had a "feeling or ambition to articulate . . . uncompromisingly" his "own physical, emotional, moral, intellectual, and aesthetic Personality, in the midst of, and tallying, the momentous spirit and facts of its immediate days, and of current America." He said, "I would sing, and leave out or put in, quite solely with reference to America and to-day." Although this statement implied an extremely personal content in the *Leaves*, it also suggested, paradoxically, its epic ambition. Repeatedly Whitman made clear that in its embodiment of democracy and science, in its intimate identification with the ideals of its time and place, *Leaves of Grass* was to fill the role of the American epic. His intention and ambition were made clear in the book's opening poem:

> Of Life immense in passion, pulse, and power,
> Cheerful, for freest action form'd under the laws divine,
> The Modern Man I sing.

As his epic hero, Whitman chose this Modern Man, one of the divine average, but, for all that, fit for the role of hero because of his supreme independence and individuality. Whitman said in "Inscriptions":

> For him I sing,
> I raise the present on the past,
> (As some perennial tree out of its roots, the present on the past,)
> With time and space I him dilate and fuse the immortal laws,
> To make himself by them the law unto himself.

Here was what it meant to be an American, a new man in a new society. The Modern Man, the American, was to find his identity not in a search of the past and in a voyage abroad—but here and now, in a present properly raised on the past, in a place filled by the new-found immensities of individuality.

The whole of the *Leaves* can be read as a sketching forth and a fleshing out of the epic hero, from his creation (or rebirth in a "new identity"), through his engagement in a crucial test of his maturity in America's Civil War, and concluding with his special insight into the meaning or fulfillment of death. The key poems in this progression are "Song of Myself," "Drum-Taps," and "Passage to India," each of which becomes a magnet of meaning, attracting to itself in its section of *Leaves* other poems and clusters which expand and elaborate its significance. In his use of the first person, Whitman appears as a lyric poet. But in reality he is dramatizing *himself* as the Modern Man of his epic. He is his own hero, not because he is in some sense special and superior, but precisely because he is not. He is representative. In a genuinely democratic society, everyman is his own epic hero:

> I celebrate myself, and sing myself,
> And what I assume you shall assume,
> For every atom belonging to me as good belongs to you.

But the secret of Whitman's contemporary appeal does not lie solely in his epic search for the American identity, in his attempt to dramatize what it means, being an American. Just as the modern American is likely to be puzzled not only by his American identity, but perhaps more overwhelmingly by his *human* identity, so Whitman in his deepest diving posed this profounder question:

> To be in any form, what is that?
> (Round and round we go, all of us, and ever come back thither)

The lines are from the most dazzling of Whitman's poems, "Song of Myself." If the whole *Leaves* tried to give expression to the American identity, "Song of Myself" attempted to plumb the depths of human identity—to solve the "puzzle of puzzles, . . . that we call Being." The evolution of the title of this longest of Whitman's poems suggests the manner in which Whitman groped his way to the innermost kernel of his subject—from American identity, to personal identity, to, finally, the phenomenon of human identity: 1856 title, "Poem of Walt Whitman, an American"; 1860, "Walt Whitman"; 1881, "Song of Myself."

We are just beginning to realize that "Song of Myself" is the greatest poem that America's nineteenth century produced, that it is, indeed, one of the great poems of the language of any century. It has the ring of a great primitive chant rising out of the dawn of history, but, at the same time, it has the tone of today in the reverberations of its language and its latent meanings. "Song of Myself" appears to us both eloquently ancient and curiously modern, precisely because it embraces the themes of the antique Bibles and of tomorrow's philosophy—the creation, the nature, the destiny of man.

Whitman realized that lurking beneath the question of what it meant to be an American lay the ever-mocking, ever-teasing question of what it meant to be a man. In leaning and loafing and inviting his soul, and observing a spear of summer grass, he determined to find out. And the first step was to divest himself of all the multitude of layers of civilization which stifled and obscured the genuine self within. He must abandon "creeds and schools," he must leave the "houses and rooms," and he must become "undisguised and naked"—all in order to "permit to speak at every hazard,/Nature without check with original energy." The substance of "Song of Myself" is this primal energy of unchecked nature—and such naked revelation always has its hazards.

"Song of Myself" is both a poem of discovery and a poem of creation, with a hero who is both passive and active. In his passive role, all the poet needs is the confidence of his own being and the profound knowledge waiting there for the taking:

> Sure as the most certain sure, plumb in the uprights, well
>   entretied, braced in the beams,
> Stout as a horse, affectionate, haughty, electrical,
> I and this mystery here we stand.

The very language vigorously asserts that the knowledge is not a secondhand book-knowledge but a firsthand man-knowledge, available to the ordinary individual in the depths of his human nature.

The mystery, the riddle, the puzzle—whatever it is called, it poses the question of being, the nature of self. The first half of "Song of Myself," through the strangely magnificent sections on touch (ending with Section 32), represents the poet as essentially passive, discovering within himself, through his awakened senses, the intimate relationship of body and soul—the key to the mystery of self. The second half of the poem reveals the poet as released from the bonds that held him, endowed by his new knowledge with a "supreme power." In the first half of "Song of Myself," the poet discovers the secrets of the self; in the second half, he proceeds to create the self in the image of his new awareness.

Throughout the first half of "Song of Myself," there is heavy emphasis on the senses—clearly the discoveries of the self must be made through them, not by suppressing them but by celebrating them. With the famous Section 5, in the sexual fusion of body and soul, the poet is launched on the journey within the realms of his own being. The vision of the "riddle and the untying of the riddle" beckons him on, deeper and deeper, in a series of discoveries alternating between identification of the self with all men in all human activities and identification of the insulated self individualized by its own creative senses. The outward identification reaches its climax in the long catalogue of human involvements of every kind, high and low, painful and ecstatic, of Section 15—". . . these tend inward to me, and I tend outward to them,/And such as it is to be of these more or less I am." But the mystery lies still deeper within—

> Who goes there? hankering, gross, mystical, nude;
> How is it I extract strength from the beef I eat?
>
> What is a man anyhow? what am I? what are you?

Gradually the poet penetrates the deepest recesses of self, and in profound response to his transfiguring senses exclaims—"Is this then a touch? quivering me to a new identity."

The new identity is the newly discovered self, the self transfigured by its encounter with the senses, the body made soul by the shock of touch. What the experience of the senses confirms is that the vital self is not the fragmented self, the body alone or the soul alone, but the body and soul fused into a single entity—a fusion achieved through the fully experienced senses. This new identity, then, is the body come spiritually alive, the physical self charged with the soul.

In short, in the realization of his new identity through the vitalized senses, the poet discovers that the self is of one's own creation, to be realized or not in accordance with one's will. With Section 33 the poet moves from passive to active stance, and begins to participate directly in the delineation of his own identity. He begins the creation of himself:

> My ties and ballasts leave me, my elbows rest in sea-gaps,
> I skirt sierras, my palms cover continents,
> I am afoot with my vision.

From this point on the poet is free to assume the identity of his choice, and he wanders about the earth and beyond, filling a variety of roles. Even "agonies are one" of his changes of garments, and he becomes for a time a mendicant; "I project my hat, sit shame-faced, and beg." But these roles are rejected finally for the identification with the ministering Christ fused with the "friendly and flowing savage." No longer embodying the "outlaw'd and suffering," the poet summons the "supreme power" of his revitalized being to share with all the outcasts of the world. In sharing the abundancy of his faith and spirituality with his fellow man, the poet shapes himself into his own deity—"Magnifying and applying come I/. . . Accepting the rough deific sketches to fill out better in myself, bestowing them freely on each man and woman I see." But each man must suffer his own freedom, must accept his own individuality, must shape his own destiny. The poet advises, "Shoulder your duds dear son, and I will mine, and let us hasten forth."

In his dramatic quest for identity in "Song of Myself," in his Thoreau-like drive of the self into a corner to reduce it to its lowest terms, Whitman made discoveries the complexity of which we are only now beginning to understand. To his transcendental contemporaries, Whitman seemed to be doing no more than what Emerson had done before him. In "The Over-Soul," Emerson said: "Man is a stream whose source is hidden. Our being is descending into us from we know not whence. . . . When I watch that flowing river, which, out of regions I see not, pours for a season its streams into me, I see that I am a pensioner; not a cause but a surprised spectator of this ethereal water; that I desire and look up and put myself in the attitude of reception, but from some alien energy the visions come." In "Song of Myself," Whitman placed himself from the beginning in this same passive state, permitting to "speak at every hazard,/Nature without check with original energy." His discoveries of the self seemed to be made in the alien energy of that same transcendent stream.

But unlike Emerson, Whitman discovered native sources for

that energy—sources that, though they shocked his own time, seem quite familiar to our own:

> Urge and urge and urge,
> Always the procreant urge of the world.

> Out of the dimness opposite equals advance, always substance and
>   increase, always sex,
> Always a knit of identity, always distinction, always a breed of life.

In opening himself to the flowing stream of Emerson's over-soul, Whitman appears to have delved deeply into the waters of the Freudian unconscious. Other poems in *Leaves,* particularly "The Sleepers," suggest that Whitman's modernity, at least in part, results, in his uninhibited explorations of the self, from his translation of the transcendental oversoul into the psychological unconscious.

But the central fact is that, in his journey into the depths of his own unconscious in quest of identity, Whitman found more than simply sex. Beyond the "procreant urge of the world" he found the substance of his own immortality, the essence of his own divinity. He said over and over again, in a variety of ways, "I know I have the best of time and space, and was never measured and never will be measured." If in his journey into the interior self Whitman found the soul more physical than did Emerson, earlier, he also found the body more spiritualized than did Freud, later. "Lack one lacks both, and the unseen is proved by the seen," he said.

In his quarrel with psychoanalysis, D. H. Lawrence wrote, "The Freudian unconscious is the cellar in which the mind keeps its own bastard spawn. The true unconscious is the well-head, the fountain of real motivity." It was this "pristine unconscious" of Lawrence that Whitman discovered in his explorations of the self—that still point of the interior, isolate self where body and soul merge and become one, a primal, *original* energy. It was surely this discovery that caused Lawrence to write, in what remains one of the most perceptive essays on Whitman, "Ahead of all poets, pioneering into the wilderness of unopened life, Whitman. Beyond him, none." In his quest for identity, Whitman made discoveries of the self that we have not yet come fully to understand. But he anticipated the delay when he said:

> Failing to fetch me at first keep encouraged,
> Missing me one place search another,
> I stop somewhere waiting for you.

7

Walt Whitman:
The Quest for Spirit

Whitman wrote in 1855, "The soul of the largest and wealthiest and proudest nation may well go half-way to meet that of its poets." In mid-twentieth century America, Whitman's words sound partly bluff, partly prophetic—the largeness and wealth and pride all are abundantly evident, but what about the soul? Whitman himself became its self-appointed comrade in the nineteenth century, nourishing it in sickness and health, but in the twentieth it has been cast out on its own, left naked and friendless to shiver in the cold—a gaunt, prematurely aged figure that most people, grown fat and warm with their plenty, solid and dull with their TV, have long forgotten.

Has this pitiful outcast, America's soul, gone halfway to meet America's poets? The question evokes a bizarre image: the starved, Ichabod-like figure grotesquely offering a furtive affection and meeting, not robust open arms, but the stern finger of T. S. Eliot pointing unwaveringly into the waste land, graveyard of America's dreams.

There are signs, however, that this thin hardy figure has survived his long exile and is turning up in some old haunts. He seems trying again to slip carefully out to that half-way mark Whitman set for him over a hundred years ago. And his appointed rendezvous seems to be with the Good Gray Poet himself.

There have always been voices raised in Whitman's defense. Even at that low ebb of his reputation in the early Twenties when Eliot and Ezra Pound banished Whitman and took over the direction of poetry and criticism for several decades, Hart

Crane cried out in the wilderness for America's meistersinger, and D. H. Lawrence restlessly searched the hard face of the world for Whitman's lost spirit. Now, some thirty years later, when the deity-prophet roles of Pound-Eliot seem tarnished, suspect, even a bit phony, Whitman's voices are not so easily drowned in the din of desert-gabble. Notable as contemporary explorers of *Leaves of Grass* are poets Randall Jarrell and Karl Shapiro. Dylan Thomas, before his early departure, quietly noted his affinity and affection.

But even below these heights there are signs. In such mundane things as college anthologies, Whitman's section has grown thicker and thicker, and the high school books have finally started including selections beyond the tired public chant, "O Captain, My Captain." Editions of *Leaves of Grass* proliferate, the fancy, illustrated, handlaid-paper editions side by side with the cheap paperbacks.

Indeed, there has been a revolution in Whitman's reputation and he has emerged in a new role, one that might create for him his unique and permanent niche in American and world literature. In the nineteenth century, after the charge of indecency, Whitman turned up as the Good Gray Poet, and his hot little prophets even tried to fit his head for a halo. This role never really caught on, and after his death, when his reputation passed on to unsympathetic and even hostile hands, he became Whitman the phony chauvinist, an indiscriminate Enthusiast who tumbled about wildly in the messy bin of poetic materials without ever emerging with a poem properly proper.

Now, in our own time, in an age of unbelievable complacency and prosperity in America and an age of incredible fear and hunger in the world, Whitman has become the Mystic Vagabond. That furtive, wizened figure—America's soul—has no doubt come across this wild, mad mystic during his waste-land banishment and has brought him back, their arms around each other's neck, chanting together their songs of democracy and religion.

Even in his barbaric yawp, Whitman always insisted on the transcendence of his religious themes, but the waste-land poets of the Twenties never read beyond his inventories. Now that the poetic religious revival that Eliot started has escaped its intellectual prison and has plummeted downward to the heart and even to the belly, flirting with the soul in the plunge, the resurrection of Whitman seems not only natural but inescapable.

With the recent fascination for the Oriental religions, symptomatically manifested in all the Beatniks—including Kerouac's *On the Road* and Ginsberg's *Howl!*—and emerging centrally in the work of such a first-rate writer as J. D. Salinger, Whitman's "Passage to India" seems on the verge of final discovery. For the first time in years, Richard M. Bucke's treatment of Whitman in *Cosmic Consciousness* seems symbolically relevant.

Many discussions of mysticism have been derailed before they begin, simply because no agreement could be reached on a definition of such a vague and disputable term. Without becoming tied up in knots distinguishing among religious, psychological, or philosophical concepts, I propose that we define mysticism, along with William James in *The Varieties of Religious Experience*, as a state of consciousness characterized by the *noetic* (states of transcendent, non-intellectual insight, revelation) and the *ineffable* (the "knowledge" cannot be imparted; to be known it must be experienced). This minimum definition should be an acceptable area of truce for the skeptical, who view the mystical experience as purely psychological phenomenon, and the orthodox, who are committed to an official definition.

With this definition we should be able to make a brief exploration of Whitman's poetry, discovering where signs of mysticism appear, and then, after a glance at critical commentary on Whitman's mysticism, attempt to describe it more fully by distinguishing it from other kinds of mystical experience. For the sake of clarity and emphasis, we shall pass over many minor instances of mystical moments (such as those in "Prayer of Columbus"), and even the major example of "Song of Myself" (which has been repeatedly analyzed for its mysticism), and concentrate on four key poems, each a masterpiece of its kind, which in their chronological arrangement admirably demonstrate Whitman's development over his most productive and creative period of fifteen years, from about 1855 to 1870.

"Crossing Brooklyn Ferry" (1856) is a "public" philosophical poem dramatizing and celebrating the part played by the "dumb, beautiful ministers" (all the diverse inventory of the universe) in bestowing spiritual insight into the unity of all mankind. "Out of the Cradle Endlessly Rocking" (1860) is a "private" love poem which describes the symbolic love experience that granted spiritual insight into the meaning of death—and the origin of the poetic impulse. "When Lilacs Last in the Dooryard Bloom'd" (1865) is an elegy which dramatizes the grief at a national loss that, through its profundity, results in "knowledge of death" and spiritual insight into eternity. "Passage to India" (1871) is a religious chant on the achievement of man in circling the globe, and concludes in an ecstatic apprehension of divine presence that culminates in spiritual insight into the nature of man's fate. All of these poems turn in their crucial passages on some kind of intuitive insight that is both profoundly revealing and ultimately ineffable. All of them are, by whatever definition, deeply mystical in nature.

Of all four poems, "Crossing Brooklyn Ferry" seems the most deeply involved in the materials and content of the world. Indeed, it is the physical body of the world, the world as perceived through all the senses, that leads to the poem's spiritual assertion. The dramatic structure of the poem is essentially mystical—the successive stages constitute a progression toward ultimate mystical penetration of the barriers to union, as indicated by the carefully spaced and timed outcries—"It avails not, time nor place—distance avails not" (Sec. 3), "Whatever it is, it avails not—distance avails not and place avails not" (Sec. 5), "Closer yet I approach you" (Sec. 7), and finally: "We understand then do we not?/What I promis'd without mentioning it, have you not accepted?" (Sec. 8). All of these assertions confirm two movements in the poem, one on the surface, the other subterranean, the latter more vital than but only hinted at by the former. Just what is understood or accepted is what the "study could not teach—what the preaching could not accomplish"—it is intuitive awareness of unity that fuses Whitman into the reader, that resolves all things into one. It is a *mystical* knowledge, not intellectual but spiritual in origin.

In "Crossing Brooklyn Ferry," Whitman focused on an unexceptional event, the common experience of multitudes in making their daily rounds, to dramatize a kind of mysticism of the masses; in "Out of the Cradle Endlessly Rocking," the central event is secluded and private, a part of the poet's distant past. We might speculate that Whitman (following the process of what T. S. Eliot called the objective correlative) transfigured his personal emotions (a disappointed love affair?) into art by inventing (or fusing out of many events) a set of symbols that correlate with (but do not necessarily—even symbolically—re-create) original experience. The poet's emotional distance is achieved not only by placing the event in his boyhood (he is singing a reminiscence), but also by becoming an observer of the tragic love of the mocking-birds. But the narrative of the poem is not related for its own sake: the meaning of the poem lies in the mystical knowledge bestowed by the experience enabling (or compelling) the boy to become a poet. As elsewhere in Whitman, this knowledge is never fully revealed, only hinted at. In the latter part of the poem, after "tallying" the he-bird's carol of unsatisfied love, the boy passionately invokes the night for a "clew"; and in answer to his spirit's anguished cry, the sea sounds repeatedly the single word "death," pouring its mystic meaning into the boy's ecstatic soul ("Creeping thence steadily up to my ears and laving me softly all over/Death, death, death, death, death"). Out of this mystical experience, out of insight into the mystic link of love and death, comes the boy's assurance of his role and theme as a poet.

Of Whitman's four major poems, "When Lilacs Last in the Dooryard Bloom'd" and "Out of the Cradle" seem more closely related than the others. Both involve the nature of love and the grief of death, and both conclude with mystic affirmation. But in the elegy the love is less personal, more exalted, as symbolized by the dooryard lilacs of the title. The western star suggests Lincoln, and the black cloud obscuring it represents his assassination. And it is the bird, the hermit-thrush, with its secluded and ecstatic eulogy of death as the "dark mother" and "deliveress," that finally brings about a reconciliation of the grief. The poet's visit with the hermit-thrush in the swamp cedars (and his soul's "tally" of the bird's song) is a symbolic dramatization of the mystical experience. While he listens, the "pure deliberate notes" of the bird pour into him (much as did the sea's voice in "Out of the Cradle"), and in his ecstatic, trance-like state, he sees beyond human ken: "While my sight that was bound in my eyes unclosed,/As to long panoramas of visions." The "visions" begin with the grim confusion and chaos of the battlefield, with its "debris of all the slain soldiers," but end with intuitive realization that it is the dead who are at rest, the living who suffer. The bird's spiritually "tallied" song together with the poet's vision represent an ultimate mystical affirmation much like that inspired by the bird's song and the sea's voice in "Out of the Cradle": in both poems, the dramatic speaker (or the poet) undergoes an experience that appears the very essence of the mystical.

Of all Whitman's poems, "Passage to India" seems the most ecstatic, perhaps in part because of the recurring fervent and intimate address to the soul ("Passage O soul to India!"). Although it seems closer in structure to "Crossing Brooklyn Ferry," it differs markedly in its attitude toward the material world. Whereas "Crossing Brooklyn Ferry" celebrated the physical contents of the world as the "ministers" that furnished their part to the soul, "Passage to India" calls for a spiritual achievement to match the engineering feats of the Suez Canal, the transatlantic cable, and the transcontinental railroad—feats which together have rounded the globe. In the first poem Whitman's love affair is with the world's body, in the second with the world's soul. But both affairs are Platonic—or mystical. In "Crossing Brooklyn Ferry," the poet achieves a spiritual fusion with the reader and all mankind; in "Passage to India" he merges with his own soul—and with God. The spiritual India for which the poet seeks passage is remote in both space and time; only by transcending both, as he does metaphorically in the early sections of the poem with their eager encompassment of the "vast Rondure, swimming in space" and "all history," running its course "down the slopes" of time—only by embracing them as One in his expanding vision is he granted (in the latter part of the poem) his mystic merge beyond their barriers. As he soars in his mystic vision into the "regions infinite," where he hears the "ripples" and is "laved . . . all over" (much as the boy-poet by the seaside in "Out of the Cradle"), he cries out in spiritual ecstasy: "Bathe me O God in thee, mounting to thee,/I and my soul to range in range of thee." This seems to be the moment of mystic Union, for there follows the frantic search for language to express the ineffable—"Thou transcendent,/Nameless, the fibre and the breath," "Light of the light, shedding forth universes," "Thou moral, spiritual fountain," "thou reservoir." More than Whitman's

other poems, "Passage to India" represents imaginative achievement of the mystic goal, Union with the One—or, as Whitman
puts it in one striking metaphor—"the Elder Brother found,/
The Younger melts in fondness in his arms."

Whitman's four key poems, his "Ferry" and "Cradle," his
"Lilacs" and "India," are not only his masterpieces but also his
most mystical poems (aside from the unique "Song of Myself"). It is perhaps easiest to trace the mysticism to Emersonian transcendentalism, and to envision Whitman as merely
fulfilling Emerson's doctrine of self-trust, the doctrine which
asserts that every man should commune with the divinity (or
the animating over-soul) within himself. And there can be no
doubt that in the mystical insights of his poems Whitman
resembles the ideal American scholar, in describing which
Emerson declared: "In self-trust all the virtues are compre-
hended. Free should the scholar be,—free and brave." (In his
famed 1855 letter to Whitman, Emerson used precisely these
words: "I give you joy of your free and brave thought.")
Emerson recognized what he had been calling for, but he also
knew that Whitman's poetry was no mere parroting of transcendental doctrine; he said, "I find it the most extraordinary
piece of wit and wisdom that America has yet contributed."
Thoreau, too, found more than mere imitation transcendentalism in Whitman; he found him so "wonderfully like the Orien-
tals" that he asked Whitman if he had read them, to which
Whitman replied, "No: tell me about them" (letter to H. G.
O. Blake, 1856). But in any event, to label Whitman's mysticism as Emersonian transcendentalism is but to duck the intricate question of the mystical elements in the New England
philosophy.

From the very beginning Whitman's critics attempted to
define the intangible mystical element in *Leaves of Grass*. In
"The Good Gray Poet" (1866), W. D. O'Connor detected a
"sacerdotal and prophetic character which makes it a sort of
American Bible." In *Notes on Walt Whitman as Poet and
Person* (1867, revised 1871), John Burroughs spoke of the
"long train of revelations" which made *Leaves* "like the bibles
of nations." But it was Richard M. Bucke, a Canadian psychiatrist, who first tried to describe with some precision the essential distinctiveness of Whitman's mysticism. Bucke's book,
Cosmic Consciousness (1901), expounded a theory of three

levels of consciousness, Simple, Self, and Cosmic, the first an attribute of animals, the second of man, and the third of the rare human who is prophet, seer, mystic—including Gautama the Buddha, Jesus the Christ, and (among others) Walt Whitman. Bucke's book was a signal if unscholarly work which brought together for comparison examples of transcendent spiritual insight of every type from every variety of faith and philosophy. William James supplied the scholarship in *Varieties of Religious Experience* (1902), not only quoting Bucke approvingly but citing Whitman as an example of the "sporadic type of mystical experience." Both Bucke and James seemed to accept the notion of some specific spiritual experience in Whitman's life underlying the mystical elements of his poetry.

More recently there have been two attempts to define the essence of Whitman's mysticism. In *A Critical Guide to Leaves of Grass* (1957), I attempted to demonstrate the relevance of the Mystic Way (as defined by Evelyn Underhill in a study of Christian mystics, in *Mysticism* [1911]) to Whitman's poetry by showing his dramatization of the Awakening of self, the Purification of self (Whitman inverts this traditional step), the Illumination, the Dark Night of the Soul, and, finally, Union. If we were to consider these terms in relation to the poems discussed here, we probably would find Awakening most clearly connected with "Crossing Brooklyn Ferry," Illumination most relevant to "Out of the Cradle Endlessly Rocking" and to "When Lilacs Last in the Dooryard Bloom'd," and Union most applicable to "Passage to India." But Malcolm Cowley, in *Walt Whitman's Leaves of Grass: The First (1855) Edition* (1959), has contended that Whitman's mysticism is more oriental than Christian, that it includes such non-Christian concepts as metempsychosis and karma, and that it resembles more closely the *Bhagavad-Gita* than it does Christian documents. But Cowley contends that Whitman's sources are not literary; he believes, as did Bucke and James, that Whitman actually had a mystical experience, sometime between 1850 and 1855, from which he derived the ecstatically spiritual quality of his verse.

Whatever the origin of the mysticism in Whitman, it seems now clear that his most dynamic connections run more deeply than merely to Emersonian transcendentalism or even to

Wordsworthian romanticism. He goes back in a vital way to a prophetic poet like Blake, whom he apparently did not read, or looks forward to a prophetic philosopher like Nietzsche, whom he could not have read. And although Whitman has been called many poets—poet of democracy, poet of sex, poet of science—it might be that he will have had the last word in his frequent assertion that his "religious" themes dominated *Leaves of Grass*. Certainly in his great and memorable poems, the mystical current is strong, and other themes seem to be carried along by its sheer power and vitality. Perhaps the critical task that lies ahead is not so much the identification of Whitman's mysticism as Eastern or Western, but rather the reconciliation of his mysticism with his strong materialism, his assertion of self, his restless vagabondage, and his celebrated sexuality. In the last analysis, Whitman's temperament seems eminently unsuited to the selflessness of the Christian mystic and to the passivity of the Oriental. He is far too much bound up in his own consciousness and self-hood and far too fully committed to wandering the open road. It is possible that Whitman, out of multiple obscure sources and out of his own soul, created a unique mysticism designed for America, a "democratic" mysticism available to every man on equal terms, embracing both the body and the soul, science and myth, life and death, the active and passive, material and spiritual. But whatever the ultimate nature of his mysticism, it must be granted a central role in the meaning of his greatest poetry in *Leaves of Grass*.

8

Whitman and Eliot:
The Poetry of Mysticism

A test of the breadth and durability of one's poetic taste might well be based on the ability to experience and appreciate two vastly diverse poems—Walt Whitman's "Song of Myself" and T. S. Eliot's "Four Quartets." Despite the gulf in mood, feeling, poetic sensibility, temperament, and general attitude that constitutes a permanent barrier between these two poems, there exists a remarkable number of similarities of idea and technique which renders a comparative study of value: in understanding the likenesses we can better know the differences. And when we can place these two poems, separated in time by about one hundred years, in proper perspective, we have immensely deepened our understanding of the complex nature of contemporary poetry. Moreover, a recent work has made an exploratory study of the relationship of Whitman and Eliot and has concluded, persuasively, that the influence, though perhaps largely unconscious on Eliot's part, was extensive.[1]

I. Two "Opposed" Poets

In spite of the reputation as poet of the modern which Whitman after hard struggle won, both Eliot and his mentor Ezra

[1] S. Musgrove, *T. S. Eliot and Walt Whitman* (Wellington: New Zealand Univ. Press, 1952).

Pound have expressed their deeply rooted distaste of the elder American poet and have set busily about producing a poetic revolution of their own in which Whitman amazingly emerges among the routed "old guard" (much as W. D. Howells, a great prophet of realism, was finally discarded by the literary rebels of the Twenties as hopelessly dedicated to realism's deadly enemy—the genteel tradition). Eliot, in his few scattered statements about Whitman, has confessed that he "had to conquer an aversion to his form, as well as to much of his matter," in order to be able to read him. In a brief review Eliot discusses Whitman by insisting on his similarities to Tennyson: "Whitman succeeds in making America as it was, just as Tennyson made England as it was, into something grand and significant"; and, Eliot asserts, Whitman's " 'frankness' about sex . . . did not spring from any particular honesty or clearness of vision," and concludes, "There is, fundamentally, no difference between the Whitman frankness and the Tennyson delicacy."[2] One might conclude from Eliot's remarks that he had not read *Democratic Vistas*, which envisions nineteenth-century America as anything but "grand and significant," and that his concept of Whitman's treatment of sex is limited to a hasty, perhaps squeamish, reading of "Children of Adam," the least remarkable of Whitman's handling of the sex motif.

No two poetic careers seem more widely divergent than Whitman's and Eliot's. Yet beneath the superficial differences lie some astonishing parallels. Probably no two poets appear, from their first published work, as greater rebels against established religion (cf. "The Hippopotamus" and the 1855 Preface to *Leaves*), and probably no two poets have asserted with greater vigor in their maturer years their intensely felt "religious" sensibility (manifested in Eliot by his Anglo-Catholicism and in Whitman by his obsession with "Religion" as the informing and unifying theme of *Leaves of Grass*). Although their assumptions and attitudes vary considerably, both Whitman and Eliot have a common obsessive compulsion for "defining" the modern world, and, particularly, for assessing the contemporary period in relation to the past. It was

[2] For a full exploration of Eliot's comments on Whitman, see Musgrove.

Whitman's eccentricity to identify the modern world almost exclusively with an optimistic American democracy, as it was Eliot's to discover the contemporary scene a vast and arid land of waste. But as Whitman admitted (in *Democratic Vistas*) some cause for despair, so Eliot found (in his later affirmative "religious" pieces) some cause for hope. Whereas both Whitman and Eliot felt it incumbent on the poet to possess a keen awareness of his specific relation to the past, they diverged in their definitions of what that relationship should be. Although Whitman asserted in the opening lines of his 1855 manifesto that "America does not repel the past," he made it clear in that preface and later that the ideal poet (the "poet of the kosmos") was a poet of the modern who must "assume" the two great modern "developments"—science and democracy. Eliot decried the rootless present and asserted that the individual talent must discover a tradition or perish. Whitman's trips West from New York and Eliot's travels East from St. Louis are symbolic: though both poets restlessly journeyed in search of a valid poetic subject matter, a new "truth" which would not become half-false on the utterance, their spirits came finally to rest in places separated by oceans and continents. Whitman's spirit alighted in the far West, amidst the raw beauty and terrifying grandeur of the New World Rockies; Eliot's spirit found a sympathetic haven amidst the neatly ordered hierarchy and the elegant, "refined" beauty of the highly "cultured" old world civilization.

But even the half-world and the whole century that separated these two poets did not prevent the two from brooding on the nature of self and God, life and death, and setting forth the results of their contemplation and insight in two of the finest poems in the language—"Song of Myself" and "Four Quartets." Although Whitman's great poem came at the opening of his "serious" poetic career, he continued with care and precision to prune, change, shift, group, until finally the infirmities of old age forced him to abandon to the world a "last" version. "Song of Myself" represents as much as does "Four Quartets" the "philosophy" of a matured and sensitive mind. Both are the poems of the inspired judgments of men who have looked long and hard at life, at death, and at that complex creature intimately involved in both—man.

114

II. Two "Mystical" Poems

The reader who encounters "Song of Myself" and "Four Quartets" for the first time might be struck by what appears to be in both an indiscriminate and disorderly mixture of narrative episodes, songs, chanted prophecies side by side with intimate confessions, soaring ecstasy intermixed with supreme dejection—the whole constituting not a coherent experience but a kind of verbal dance, primitive, magic, drawing the reader within the circle but failing to disclose the full mystery. Whitman's title suggests a celebration of the individual, one's identity, a glorious paean dedicated to body and soul which constitute the "self." Eliot's main title is suggestive of the harmony and rhythm of music, and his subtitles ("Burnt Norton," "East Coker," "The Dry Salvages," and "Little Gidding"), all place names, suggest the not-self, that which exists outside the self, the world of *place* in *time* rather than the world of *self*. As the titles imply, "Song of Myself" is inwardly oriented, directed toward *being, existing*, both physically and spiritually, while "Four Quartets" is projected outward, engaged with non-being, focused on the other-than-self.

Attempts at examining these poems in a "subject matter" structural analysis are doomed to failure. Neither poem, as has been frequently supposed, is a "philosophical" statement, presenting an orderly and systematic view of the world, or concept of the universe, or attitude toward existence. Both poems are essentially dramatic and derive their form not from an orderly arrangement of subject matter but from revelation of an action. There is a narrative thread which informs and makes meaningful the "lyricism" and the "philosophy" of the poems, and which has a beginning, middle, and end, beginning at one place, developing in a specific direction, and finally arriving at a destination. It is in the nature of this "plot" that "Song of Myself" and "Four Quartets" exhibit a multitude of striking similarities.

Critics of both Whitman and Eliot have usually resorted to metaphor when confronted with the problem of structure, and the figure most frequently relied upon is *music*. The poets themselves have called attention to the analogy of the structure

115

of their poems and music. Whitman once jotted in his note-book, "My poems when complete should be a *unity*, in the same sense . . . a perfect musical composition is."[3] T. S. Eliot has said "the music of verse is not a line by line matter, but a question of the whole poem. . . . It is a music of imagery as well as sound." And he has asserted that he believes that "the properties in which music concerns the poet most nearly, are the sense of rhythm and the sense of structure."[4] Indeed one need but look at the titles of the two poems under examination to discover the poets' own consciousness of the music analogy; Whitman's poem is a *song* of the self, while Eliot's poem derives its title from the musical form of the quartet. If Whitman's title connotes a musical performance of celebration with the whole world as audience, Eliot's suggests a semi-private performance with the select audience of chamber music.

Much criticism and scholarship have already been devoted to discovering the intimate relationship of music—particularly opera—and *Leaves of Grass*.[5] And an understanding of Whitman's poetic use of such techniques as the aria and recitative helps immeasurably in understanding the meaning and structure of the poems in *Leaves of Grass*. Similarly, a number of musical analyses have illuminated Eliot's work. Insight into the significance and order of "Four Quartets" is increased by a knowledge of the applicability to its structure of the "movements" of the "sonata form."[6]

But when we talk of poetic structure in musical terms, we must remember that we are speaking in metaphor, that we are drawing an analogy which ultimately must be abandoned. It is not to deny the validity or usefulness of the music-analogy to assert that a "poetic" plot exists in "Song of Myself" and "Four Quartets." Both poems are dramatic representations of a mystical experience, with the poets themselves cast in the main roles.

---

[3] *The Complete Writings of Walt Whitman* (New York: G. P. Putnam's Sons, 1902), IX, 3.

[4] T. S. Eliot, *The Music of Poetry* (Glasgow: Jackson, Son & Co., 1942), pp. 25–28.

[5] See Robert D. Faner, *Walt Whitman and Opera* (Philadelphia: Univ. of Pennsylvania Press, 1951).

[6] See, for example, Helen L. Gardner, "Four Quartets: A Commentary," *T. S. Eliot: A Study of His Writings by Several Hands*, ed. by B. Rajan (New York: Funk & Wagnalls Co., 1948), pp. 57–77.

The parts of the poems correspond to the progressive states of the experience, which are differentiated by an increasing emotional intensity as well as a deepening penetration of the barriers of time and space. The climax is reached, as with all mystics, in an apparent escape out of time and space into some kind of union with the Absolute which grants spiritual strength and cosmic knowledge. Neither "Song of Myself" nor "Four Quartets" offers proof that Whitman or Eliot actually had mystical experiences or *are* mystics, but the poems do demonstrate that it is the nature of the genius of both poets to be able to discover and use dramatically in their work, either by intuition (as with Whitman) or through assimilation (as with Eliot), the quality of feeling implicit in the various complex phases of the mystical experience.

III. Whitman's Dramatized Mysticism

Inasmuch as I have in a previous essay analyzed at length "Song of Myself" as a dramatized mystical experience, I shall confine my observations here to a brief summary of my findings.[7]

The progressive stages of the mystical experience, as revealed and examined by Evelyn Underhill's valuable study of the Christian mystics in *Mysticism*, informs "Song of Myself" with an intelligible structure. Indeed it is possible to discover in the poem the precise points at which one stage of the experience concludes and a new stage begins: Sections 1–5, entry into mystical state; 6–16, awakening of self; 17–32, purification of self; 33–37, illumination and dark night of the soul; 38–49, union (supreme spiritual power and perception); 50–52, emergence from mystical state. The first five and the last three sections of the poem represent the popular concept of the mystic's behavior in portraying the poet's entry into and deliverance from the mystic trance; the remainder of the poem dramatically portrays the poet as traveling step by step the Mystic Way until he has achieved the goal of all mystics— Union.

In the opening sections of "Songs of Myself," the poet prepares himself for the mystical journey by loafing, contemplat-

---

[7] "'Song of Myself' as Inverted Mystical Experience," *A Critical Guide to Leaves of Grass* (Chicago: Univ. of Chicago Press, 1957).

ing a spear of summer grass, and inviting his soul. In section 5 the soul and body consummate a union which precipitates transcendent insight—"I know that the hand of God is the promise of my own/And I know that the spirit of God is the brother of my own."

After this initial symbolic trance, the mystic journey is launched. The first stage is the "awakening of self" (sections 6–16), in which the poet discovers a multitude of relationships of the self with all else outside the self—to nature (the grass), to other men and women, to God. In these sections of the poem appear some of the longest (and finest) catalogues in which the poet "discovers" the complex multiplicity of the universe: he seems to be "awakening" to an obscure consciousness of some subtle significance lurking within the world's inventory.

In sections 17–32, the focus of "Song of Myself" shifts from the "awakening" to "purification," as the poet ceases marveling at the multiplicity of things and begins to insist on their "equality." It is by means of this theme of equality, particularly the recurring concept of the equality of body and soul, that the poet achieves purification of self. It is in this stage of the mystical journey that the fundamental difference between the traditional mystic's experience and the poet's drama emerges. Whereas the traditional mystic purged and mortified his senses in order to purify himself, Whitman transfigures and celebrates the senses, purging not the senses but the notion of the senses as evil, as the means to achieve purification.

The next two phases (sections 33–37) of the mystical experience occur almost at the same time. The poet's illumination is swift as he cries out at the beginning of section 33: "Space and time! now I see it is true, what I guess'd at." "Afoot" with his vision at last, the poet seems to apprehend Divine Reality directly as the bonds of time and space fall away and he soars through eternity and infinity. But just as swiftly as illumination was granted, the "dark night of the soul" descends upon the poet. As he at first appears to feel the Divine Presence, so suddenly he seems to feel a withdrawal of Divinity. This sense of degradation and agony reaches a climax at the end of section 37, as the poet identifies himself with common beggars: "Askers embody themselves in me and I am embodied in them,/I project my hat, sit shame-faced, and beg."

The desired goal of union is achieved and the emotions the poet feels are dramatized in sections 38–49. At the opening of section 38, the poet disclaims the attitudes assumed in the foregoing "dark night" sections: "Enough! enough! enough!/ Somehow I have been stunn'd. Stand back!" He has discovered his "usual mistake," ceases his identification with the degraded, miserable, and outcast, and begins instead an identification with Christ as he feels pulsing within him the supreme spiritual power of the Divine. The faith and love granted by his mystic union are abundant enough to share generously with others. And he makes an attempt (in sections 44–49) to convey some impression of the "supreme perception" which the mystical journey has brought: "What is known I strip away,/I launch all men and women forward with me into the Unknown."

The final sections of "Song of Myself" (50–53) portray the poet as emerging from his mystic trance, physically exhausted by the spiritual journey: "Wrench'd and sweaty—calm and cool then my body becomes, I sleep—I sleep long." And as the poet looks back over the experience, he searches for the "word unsaid" ("not in any dictionary, utterance, symbol") which will convey some sense of the significance of his ultimate spiritual discovery: "It is not chaos or death—it is form, union, plan—it is eternal life—it is Happiness." With this attempt to express the inexpressible, the poet turns to bid his farewell to the reader, identifying himself as he goes with the swooping hawk and its "barbaric yawp."

IV. Eliot's Dramatized Mysticism

What contemplation of the spear of summer grass does for Whitman in "Song of Myself," meditation of the rose seems to do for Eliot in "Four Quartets." Whereas Whitman felt a compulsion to abandon "creeds and schools" and to "go to the bank by the wood and become undisguised and naked" and let "speak at every hazard/Nature without check with original energy," Eliot is beckoned by the thrush into the formal garden filled with shrubs and roses, bordered by an "empty alley," and containing a "drained pool." And one feels instinctively from the beginning that Eliot in his mystic "frenzy" does not abandon "creeds and schools" but seeks and discovers their ultimate significance. The mystical experience of "Four

Quartets" begins in "Burnt Norton" with the speculation on time ("Time present and time past/Are both perhaps present in time future"), and the almost immediately following incident in the garden ("the pool was filled with water out of sunlight") which momentarily grants the poet a vision outside time. From this opening insight the poet progresses on the mystic journey (not the vertical line but the spiral would best image the nature of the route), seeking always (as he says in "East Coker"), "another intensity," "a further union," or a "deeper communion." The main body of "Four Quartets" is meditative, an account of the poet's gradual and difficult achievement of these goals. In the last of the "Four Quartets," "Little Gidding," the climax is reached in section II, in which the poet, first noting the "death" of air, earth, water, and fire, finally bursts the bonds of time and space and encounters the "first-met stranger" in a "meeting nowhere, not before the after." This event, the poet's "mystic union," grants an intuitive faith and an insight symbolically represented in the joining of the poem's two major symbols in the last line of "Four Quartets"—"And the fire and the rose are one."

Elements of the traditional mystical experience may be discovered in each of the "Four Quartets," and perhaps it is useful to note specific parallels. "Burnt Norton" is the poet's "awakening of self," not only in the intense but brief insight experienced in the opening section, but also in the realization throughout of the nature of "the way." The dominant image for *there* (the mystic's goal, union) is "the still point of the turning world" (a figure ingeniously suggesting escape from both time and space—and also introducing a word—*still*—charged with a number of meanings the poet can exploit poetically, much as Whitman exploited *leaves*), while the *here* (the world we live in) is grossly saturated in time and place, a waste land "empty of meaning" where "men and bits of paper" are "whirled by the cold wind." The way from *here* to *there*, the poet realizes in his "awakening," is the way of "perpetual solitude," "deprivation/And destitution of all property" and "desiccation of the world of sense."

If the cottage garden of Burnt Norton offers the solitude and the world of nature appropriate for the poet's *awakening* to the potentiality of the spiritual attainment of self, East Coker, a Somersetshire village, suggests the nature of the next stage of the mystical experience—purification as voyage. In "East Coker" there seems to be a traveling back in time as well as a journeying forth in space. The refrain which opens "East Coker," "In my beginning is my end," is altered at the close, "In my end is my beginning," a reversal suggesting the extent of the change which transpires in the progress of the poem. At first the poet realizes that a spiritual beginning necessitates the end of the physical or the life of the senses; at the close, the poet seems to have attained, at least partially, the end of the material distractions of physical life and to be anticipating the beginning of that phase of the mystical experience most desired. After the vivid opening description of the ancient fertility rites, the poet states "I am here/Or there, or elsewhere," an assertion of omnipresence which in itself suggests the poet's intense consciousness and reexamination of his intimate engagement in the cyclic "business" of living. The poet comes to a gradual realization that "the way" is through "a dark wood, in a bramble," and that there "is no secure foothold"; and he discovers that the "only wisdom we can hope to acquire/Is the wisdom of humility." In section III of "East Coker" the poet seems plunged into the terrifying and agonizing act of mystic purification, in a vision of darkness engulfing all, including the poet and his goal: as this "darkness of God" descends, the poet must abandon materialistic hope, faith, and love in order to attain all again on a spiritual level. As "East Coker" ends, the poet, in the "middle way," can assess his meager accomplishments and re-dedicate himself to the attainment of "another intensity" and a "further union," but always with the realization that "the way" is through "the dark cold and the empty desolation."

If "East Coker" seems a symbolic setting forth, "The Dry Salvages" (off Cape Ann, Massachusetts) appears a symbolic arrival. If the voyage is *purification* then the destination is *illumination*. The poet's insight at the opening of "The Dry Salvages" into the significance of the "strong brown" river-God, his realization that the "river is within us, the sea is all about us," and his vision of a time "older than the time of chronometers," an hour when "time stops and time is never ending," constitute his illumination. This emotional verification of eternity, a consciousness of existing outside time, is accompanied, however, by questioning and doubt, by an awareness of

121

the possibility of the withdrawal of the divine presence. At the opening of section II of "The Dry Salvages," the poet cries out, "where is there an end of it, the soundless wailing,/The silent withering of autumn flowers," followed, finally, by the answer, "There is no end of it, the voiceless wailing." The vision of abiding agony, the awareness that the "primitive terror" is "likewise permanent/With such permanence as time has," this "somber season" and "sudden fury"—constitute the poet's dark night of the soul. The "sudden illumination" and the agony of the dark night seem to descend on the poet almost simultaneously—as they have done on many of the traditional Christian mystics. In the latter part of "The Dry Salvages," the poet, having come a distance on his own spiritual voyage, turns to the fate of others as he advises, "Fare forward [not fare-well], travelers"; conscious that "death is every moment . . . do not think of the fruit of action." The "occupation for the saint" (and the goal of the mystic) is "to apprehend/The point of intersection of the timeless/With time," an accomplishment requiring "a lifetime's death in love,/Ardour and selflessness and self-surrender." This apprehension is, certainly, union, as far beyond illumination as illumination is beyond the awakening of self. "For most of us," asserts the poet in his keen awareness of the difficulties of "the way," there is only the "unattended/Moment, the moment in and out of time,/The distraction fit, lost in a shaft of sunlight." The poet's dark night, following his illumination, has sobered him with uncertainty; for "most of us," he says, "the impossible union/Of spheres of existence"—"the aim"—is "never here to be realized." Our attempt to achieve such union (whether the individual with the absolute or the temporal sphere with the timeless—the goals are the same) in itself constitutes a triumph.

"Little Gidding" returns the poet from the distant shore and from out of the past—to "now and England," to "end" where he "began." Whereas throughout the previous portions of "Four Quartets" the poet speculates on "the way" and envisions what might lie at the journey's end, in "Little Gidding" he speaks with the assurance of knowledge gained through experience of "this way"—the way he has come and the end he has reached. "Little Gidding" opens with a series of images connoting intense illumination and even union—"midwinter spring," "a glare that is blindness," the "spring time . . . not in

time's covenant." If this spring, "not in the scheme of generation," constitutes such an intense "glow," speculates the poet,
what will be the nature of the summer—"the unimagina-
ble/Zero summer"—perhaps the full fruition of that union
precipitated by death. It becomes quite clear in the progress of
section I of "Little Gidding" that the poet has travelled "this
way" and has reached that "impossible union" of two spheres
of existence, as he concludes:

> Here, the intersection of the timeless moment
> Is England and nowhere. Never and always.

The poet has indeed apprehended "the point of intersection of
the timeless/With time," as he has accomplished what he himself has designated the "occupation for the saint."

In section II of "Little Gidding," a series of three stanzas
represents the "death" or disintegration of the elements of the
material world—air, earth, water and fire, as the poet makes
preparation for the climactic act of his union—a mystical "encounter" outside time and space that is to bestow prophetic
knowledge. It is perhaps inevitable that a poet of Eliot's temperament, instead of endowing the meeting-ground with the
vague attributes of heaven, would describe the setting as a
lonely suburban scene, with asphalt streets, dead leaves, and
smoke. The "dead master," whom the poet encounters and with
whom he trods "the pavement in a dead patrol," is, surely, the
poet's self, an identification hinted at in such phrases as—"so I
assumed a double part," "knowing myself yet being someone
other." This encounter with self occurs without the limits of
time—"at this intersection time/Of meeting nowhere, no before and after"—and represents the highest insight the individual can achieve.

The poet's physical self is informed by his spiritual self of his
future fate, of the three "gifts reserved for age"—of "the cold
friction of expiring sense," of the "impotence of rage/At
human folly," and of "the sham of motives late revealed." But
this prophecy is qualified by advice. The spirit will move
"from wrong to wrong . . . unless restored by that refining
fire/Where you must move in measure, like a dancer." The
suggestion implicit in this knowledge granted by the union
achieved in the mystical experience is that all life, if it is to
achieve spiritual fulfillment after death, must be devoted to the

123

process of purification, the essence of which is the "expanding/ Of love beyond desire."

In section III of "Little Gidding," the poet exclaims

> See, now they vanish,
> The faces and places, with the self which, as it could, loved them,
> To become renewed, transfigured, in another pattern.

Motivating this exclamation is the realization of the achievement of the purified state, in which love is expanded beyond desire. This transfigured self knows intuitively, out of the glimpse of the cosmos granted in union, that "all manner of thing shall be well," and that, paradoxically, "the end is where we start from." History—that "true" history which lies "Behind the assurance/Of recorded history" and which is the succession of illuminated moments grasped outside time—is "now and England," this "time" and "place." The moments of insight are not a permanent part of a "past," but constitute an "eternity" into which the purified self may briefly glimpse, any time, any place. The essence of the knowledge derived from the mystical experience "will be to arrive where we started/And know the place for the first time"—in a spiritual rather than a material context. The poet who began with "I" concludes with "we": there is the tacit assumption that each man may—or must—travel for himself "the way" and create out of his transfigured self the opportunity of "discovery" which in reality is an essential knowledge of the known.

V. Happiness and Humility

If there are major similarities in the experiences dramatized in "Four Quartets" and "Song of Myself," there is one basic distinction which markedly differentiates the emotional impact of the two poems. This element gathers to a focus in a single word in both poems. In "Song of Myself," in the final sections of the poem in which the poet seems to be emerging from the mystic trance, he gropes about for a word, however inadequate, which will hint at the supreme truth intuitively grasped in his experience: "It is not chaos or death—it is form, union, plan—it is eternal life—it is Happiness." In "Four Quartets," the poet (in "East Coker") discovers the inadequacy of the "wisdom of age" and concludes: "The only wisdom we can hope to acquire/Is the wisdom of humility: humility is endless."

These two key words—happiness and humility—relate directly to the stage of the mystical experience known as *purification*. Whitman's concept is an inversion of the traditional pattern of mortification of the senses: instead of annihilating the body and physical sensation, Whitman celebrates them, and purges them of their associations with evil, by identifying them with the great rhythmical, creative forces in nature and in the universe—in such passages as that beginning "Smile O voluptuous cool-breath'd earth!/Earth of the slumbering and liquid trees!"

In contrast, the poet in "Four Quartets" is burdened with an obsessive sense of sin, and the dominant image of purgation is *fire:* to be purified, one must be "restored by that refining fire" where one moves "in measure, like a dancer." But the poet of "Four Quartets" would not disown *happiness:* he would redefine it. In "Song of Myself" the word seems synonymous with "fulfillment." Eliot seems to glance directly at Whitman with scorn when he asserts—

> The moments of happiness—not the sense of well-being,
> Fruition, fulfilment, security or affection,
> Or even a very good dinner, but the sudden illumination—

If *happiness* may be associated with *illumination*, then for Eliot humility becomes happiness, for it is through humility that insight is achieved.

VI. Voices Personal and Public

Once this fundamental divergence in the two poets is recognized and isolated, many startling likenesses beyond that of the dramatized mystical experience emerge. One of the most striking elements common to both "Song of Myself" and "Four Quartets" is the large amount of specifically personal reference. The lifetime editions of Whitman's poem were always faced by the "vagabond poet" photograph which Whitman insisted was an integral part of the poem. Supplementing the photograph were the biographical lines in the opening section of "Song of Myself"—

> Born here of parents born here from parents the same, and their
> parents the same,

> I, now thirty-seven years old in perfect health begin,
> Hoping to cease not till death.

And in a later section appears the direct identification, "Walt Whitman, a kosmos, of Manhattan the son."

In the progress of "Four Quartets," Eliot also makes similar personal revelations. He confesses in "East Coker"

> So here I am, in the middle way, having had twenty years—
> Twenty years largely wasted, the years of *L'entre deux guerres*—
> Trying to learn to use words. . . .

Neither Whitman nor Eliot reveals biographical data through naïvete or ineptitude: both are more fully aware of their purposes in such personal "outbursts" than is commonly supposed. "Song of Myself" and "Four Quartets," as dramatizations of mystical experiences, necessarily have as their protagonists the poets themselves, and a high degree of verisimilitude is achieved by the injection of enough of the actual self to suggest *total* sincerity (the device offers advantages similar to those of first-person narration in fiction).

Similar to this inclusion of personal elements is the startling comment on the problems of writing or on the art of poetry. It is as though the poet examines and comments on the problems of his craft in the work of art itself. Whitman once said, "No one will get at my verses who insists upon viewing them as a literary performance, or attempt at such performance, or as striving mainly toward art or aesthetism."[8] Throughout *Leaves of Grass* Whitman creates the image of himself as poet of the New World and in "Song of Myself" he asserts, "I am the poet of the Body and I am the poet of the Soul." Like Whitman, Eliot in each of the "Four Quartets" calls attention to his role as poet and comments upon his success or failure. He says of one series of images, "That was a way of putting it—not very satisfactory:/A periphrastic study in a worn-out poetical fashion," and he finally exclaims, "The poetry does not matter." Both Whitman and Eliot were capable of assuming the role of dedicated prophet obsessed with a consuming message which is all but inexpressible and which transcends the significance of "mere" art; it is important in the evaluation of their poetry to realize that they understood that

[8] *The Complete Writings of Walt Whitman*, III, 65.

they were striking a pose and that they did so for dramatic purposes: the prominent display of a scorn for the "pettiness" or "inadequacy" of art is, by the very irony of its appearance in a poem, charged with a "concealed" artfulness.

Revelation of what appears to be the art behind the art in both Whitman and Eliot suggest an intimate relationship with the reader: nothing is to be concealed, nothing is to stand in the way of a direct infusion of meaning. Could Eliot be more honestly simple than when he says:

> You say I am repeating
> Something I have said before. I shall say it again.
> Shall I say it again?

This disarmingly fresh or naïve tone seems an echo of Whitman's own famous confession:

> Do I contradict myself?
> Very well then I contradict myself,
> (I am large, I contain multitudes.)

In the remarks by both poets there is the same note of supreme confidence underlying the acknowledgment of the truth of what some "critic" might mistakenly assume to be a serious charge. In each instance the effect is that of the poet who has nothing "to hide," who is able to convert even his weaknesses into strengths. Certainly one can assume that behind the superficial "artlessness" lies an intense concern for the "artistic" effect.

If there is an "intimate" tone approaching personal confession in both "Song of Myself" and "Four Quartets," there is also the unmistakable tone of prophecy with its contrasting public or even cosmic quality. Such a tone is omnipresent in "Song of Myself"—

> I fly those flights of a fluid and swallowing soul,
> My course runs below the soundings of plummets.

And the chant of the prophet bursts forth frequently in "Four Quartets"—

> . . . there is a time for building
> And a time for living and for generation
> And a time for the wind to break the loosened pane. . . .

Such a tone is present in the authoritative command both poets have over their souls. Whitman exclaims: "I believe in you my soul, the other I am must not abase itself to you,/And you must not be abased to the other." Eliot says, perhaps more politely but no less firmly, "I said to my soul, be still,/And let the dark come upon you/Which shall be the darkness of God." In both "Song of Myself" and "Four Quartets," the voice of the seer who chants his chant of the mystic vision is never far beneath the surface.

VII. Concepts and Attitudes

One might expect Whitman and Eliot to differ immensely in their concept of time and place, especially in view of Eliot's stress throughout his career on tradition, in contrast with Whitman's embracement of the modern; and also in view of Eliot's journey, both physical and spiritual, to Old World Europe, in contrast with Whitman's insistent celebration of America as a culmination of the "scheme." It is perhaps surprising, therefore, to discover in "Four Quartets" as well as in "Song of Myself," a "mystic" affirmation of the transcendent significance for the individual of the *here* and *now*. When Whitman exclaims, "I am an acme of things accomplish'd, and I an encloser of things to be," he is not being merely egotistical but is simply asserting his own supreme sense of existence in "this place" at "this time," and his own keen consciousness of playing a crucial part in the evolution of Time's spiral. Implicit in the line (as elsewhere in "Song of Myself") is the suggestion that the *now* and *here* are the most important facts, spiritual as well as physical, for the individual. Indeed it is this vision of time and place that informs the whole of *Leaves of Grass*, and not some limited, chauvinistic view as is sometimes supposed. Eliot expresses a concept almost identical with Whitman's when he says, "Here, the intersection of the timeless moment/ Is England and nowhere," or again—

> So, while the light fails
> On a winter's afternoon, in a secluded chapel
> History is now and England.

In both Whitman and Eliot, the motive for elevation of the *here* and *now* is not a super-patriotism but rather a realization of the mystic, and paradoxical, truth: "Only through time time is conquered." It is only through a comprehensive engagement with his own time and place that the individual may achieve the supreme knowledge that lies outside both.

In the mystic view of Whitman and Eliot, the aspect of life which predominates is its cyclic quality. Near the opening of "Song of Myself," Whitman evokes a compelling sense of the "Sexual life force"—"urge and urge and urge,/Always the procreant urge of the world." And throughout the poem recurs the vision of life as birth, fruition, and death: "The little one sleeps in the cradle. . . . The youngster and the red-faced girl turn aside up the bushy hill. . . . The suicide sprawls on the bloody floor of the bedroom." In the scene in the "open field" in the first section of "East Coker," Eliot recreates a similar vision of the dance of life in a dramatization of a country "fertility rite." The dancing of the rustics beats the rhythm of—

> The time of the seasons and the constellations
> The time of milking and the time of harvest
> The time of the coupling of man and woman
> And that of beasts. Feet rising and falling.
> Eating and drinking. Dung and death.

In both poets the "cyclic" vision is achieved by the development of the self as a great, universal being transcending the barriers of time and place. As Whitman exclaims amidst his long catalogues of the overwhelming diversities of life, "I am there, I help," or "In me the caresser of life wherever moving," so Eliot asserts, "I am here/Or there, or elsewhere." And if Whitman envisions the grass as transpiring from "the hearts of young men," or tells his reader that if they want him again they must look under their boot-soles, Eliot presents much the same concept of a cyclic immortality of the physical in his vision of "Those long since under earth/Nourishing the corn."

Closely related to the vision of Time's spiral is the view of the paradoxical conjunction of opposites. Whitman's stage of purification in the mystical experience is in reality one extended paradox in which all is embraced, nothing excluded. The defeated are elevated with the triumphant, the evil with the good, the sick with the healthy, because, says the poet of his gift—"This is the meal equally set, this the meat for natural hunger." And the climax of the poet's joining of the disparate is achieved in his celebration of the body alongside the soul: "Voices indecent by me clarified and transfigured." Although Eliot by no means holds Whitman's view of the physical, the contemporary poet does see a world filled with paradoxical union and he exploits that world, as did Whitman, for its full poetic effect of surprise and sometimes shock. Such union is vividly incorporated in the imagery in—"Garlic and sapphires in the mud/Clot the bedded axle-tree." If Whitman imagines himself an entire band, and cries out, "I play not marches for accepted victors only, I play marches for conquer'd and slain persons," Eliot asserts,

> These men,[9] and those who opposed them
> And those whom they opposed
> Accept the constitution of silence
> And are folded in a single party.

The paradoxical joining of both quiet and movement is implicit in the refrain of "Burnt Norton": "At the still point of the turning world." The poet can only hint at the nature of this "still point" by suggesting the coupling of opposites to form a new, third element unknown to man's mind:

> Neither flesh nor fleshless;
> Neither from nor towards; at the still point, there the dance is,
> But neither arrest nor movement.

Eliot's assertion that it is only "through time" that "time is conquered" seems closer than the poet realized to a recurring concept in *Leaves of Grass*—that it is only through the physical that the spiritual is achieved. At last there is the same paradoxical reconciliation at the root of both ideas. The refrain introduced in "East Coker"—"In my beginning is my end"—is a poetic exploitation of the same kind of reconciliation. Eliot seems sometimes bent on mystifying the reader by his sudden juxtaposition of opposites, as in "and the way up is the way down, the way forward is the way back." In passages such as these in "Four Quartets" as well as in "Song of Myself," one detects the tone of primitive man chanting his chant or intoning his incantation as the ritualistic dance of life is performed around the sacred fire. As Eliot finds, at the end of his poem, that the result of all one's effort is "to arrive where we started," so Whitman asserts, "I find one side a balance and the antipodal side a balance,/Soft doctrine as steady help as stable doctrine."

VIII. Methods and Techniques

One of the best known features of Whitman's poetry is the catalogue, a device that has been both damned and praised. But

[9] The founders of Christianity.

the poetic variety and intensity such a device makes possible
have never been sufficiently examined or demonstrated. Such
catalogues are in one sense a forerunner of contemporary
poetic passages in which syntax has been abandoned for a
subterranean connotative coherence. In section 33 of "Song of
Myself," the poet, suddenly "afoot" with his vision, launches
the longest of his catalogues to demonstrate the comprehen-
siveness of his insight and expansiveness; only a brief portion
may be quoted—

Where burial coaches enter the arch'd gates of a cemetery,
Where winter wolves bark amid wastes of snow and icicled trees,
Where the yellow-crown'd heron comes to the edge of the marsh at
    night and feeds upon small crabs,
Where the splash of swimmers and divers cools the warm noon
Where the katy-did works her chromatic reed on the walnut-tree
    over the well. . . .

In this entire catalogue the poet seems to imagine himself as
some kind of life principle—at times the motive-force of the
universe—infusing all existence everywhere. If Whitman's catalogues generally are concerned with the diversity of life, it is
perhaps appropriate that the most notable catalogue in "Four
Quartets" relates to death:

O dark dark dark. They all go into the dark,
The vacant interstellar spaces, the vacant into the vacant,
The captains, merchant bankers, eminent men of letters,
The generous patrons of art, the statesmen and the rulers,
Distinguished civil servants, chairmen of many committees,
Industrial lords and petty contractors, all go into the dark,
And dark the Sun and Moon, and the Almanach de Gotha
And the Stock Exchange Gazette, the Directory of Directors,
And cold the sense and lost the motive of action.

The primary concept expressed in this passage is the rather
commonplace idea of death as the great leveler, the great
equalitarian. But the extensive "listing" of those who "go into
the dark," and particularly the sudden movement from "petty
contractors" to the "Stock Exchange Gazette," are Whit-
man-like in technique if not in tone. In both passages,
there is in the mere "piling" of detail on detail the suggestion
of emotional "frenzy" and there is in the juxtaposition of
the unusual the poetic reliance on a complex interaction of
connotative meaning.

Similar to the catalogue, but different in composition and
function, are the notable passages in Whitman's poems which

are not just "lists" but meticulous arrangements of dominant and secondary images. The first some twenty-two lines of "Out of the Cradle Endlessly Rocking," and the last sections of "Crossing Brooklyn Ferry" and "When Lilacs Last in the Dooryard Bloom'd" are "symphonic" recapitulations of the primary images of the poems. In the last section of "Little Gidding," Eliot fuses a number of his images in the "farewell" lines of his poem:

> When the last of earth left to discover
> Is that which was the beginning;
> At the source of the longest river
> The voice of the hidden waterfall
> And the children in the apple-tree
> Not known, because not looked for
> But heard, half-heard, in the stillness
> Between two waves of the sea.
> Quick now, here, now, always—

The reader will quickly recognize images and phrases garnered from earlier passages of "Four Quartets," some even from the opening lines of "Burnt Norton." And in the very last lines of his poem, Eliot does indeed fuse his major images in the "crowned knot of fire" as the "fire and the rose" become "one." Such recapitulation of the imagery in Whitman and Eliot suggests the importance of the dramatic roles individual images assume in their poetry, and implies, further, that a comprehensive analysis of the "movement" or "action" of the images will bring to light significant elements of form.

In view of the close relationship of the experiences represented in "Song of Myself" and "Four Quartets," it is perhaps not surprising that there is a good deal of imagery common to both. Throughout *Leaves of Grass* the dominant image is the sea, together with a cluster of water images—lakes, rivers, rivulets. In "Song of Myself" as elsewhere, the sea symbolizes the world of "eidólons," the world of spirituality: "Sea of the brine of life and of unshovell'd yet always-ready graves." The whole of "The Dry Salvages" in "Four Quartets" is dominated by water-imagery, particularly in the form of the river and the sea:

> The river is within us, the sea is all about us;
> The sea is the land's edge also, the granite
> Into which it reaches, the beaches where it tosses
> Its hints of earlier and other creation.

Throughout "The Dry Salvages," the sea, with its "many gods and many voices," seems to function much as it functions in "Song of Myself." And the fusion of sea-voices—the howl, the yelp, the whine, the "menace and caress of wave," the "wailing warning," the "tolling bell," and more—closely resembles Whitman's catalogue-fusions, particularly in the passage in "Song of Myself" in which the poet, after stating, "Now I will do nothing but listen," is inundated by a multiplicity of sounds so various as to appear to encompass all life—"Sounds of the city and sounds out of the city, sounds of the day and night."

In both "Song of Myself" and "Four Quartets," the mystical experience emerges metaphorically as a journey or trip. Whitman's movement, gradually increased in pace, not only throughout the world but also out into the universe, is paralleled by Eliot's eternal search for "the way" which paradoxically leads back to the starting point. Near the end of "Song of Myself," the travel imagery becomes dominant as the poet asserts "I tramp a perpetual journey," and advises his listeners that they must travel their own road:

> I have no chair, no church, no philosophy,
> I lead no man to a dinner-table, library, exchange,
> But each man and each woman of you I lead upon a knoll

The poet recognizes that those who would merely "follow" him in his footsteps would be violating one of the primary elements of his credo—self-reliance. "Not I, not any one else can travel that road for you,/You must travel it for yourself," the poet advises; and he suggests that he and his listeners both be about the business of the journey: "Shoulder your duds dear son, and I will mine, and let us hasten forth." Implicit throughout the poet's advice is the suggestion that the experience of the journey itself will grant insight, will in some measure renew the self-hood of the individual. "You must habit yourself to the dazzle of the light," he asserts: "Long have you timidly waded holding a plank by the shore,/Now I will you to be a bold swimmer." In "Four Quartets," too, the poet suggests that each man must travel "the way" of his own volition. He asserts paradoxically, "We must be still and still moving/Into another intensity." And, after the manner of Whitman, he passes forth advice about the journey validated by his own experience of the route: "Fare forward, travellers!

not escaping from the past/Into different lives, or into any future." As in "Song of Myself," the road is long, the hazards of the journey many, and the destination uncertain. But the experience of travel itself will transfigure the individual: "Fare forward, you who think you are voyaging;/You are not those who saw the harbour receding, or those who will disembark." In dramatizing the progressive stages of the mystical experience and in converting the experience into meaningful terms for the reader, both Whitman and Eliot find the metaphor of the journey indispensable.

IX. A Kelson of the Creation Is Love

Both Whitman and Eliot achieve through mystical experience insight into the significance of such complex concepts as Time, Space, Life, Death, and God, but perhaps their most *illuminating* discovery relates to the role of love in the universe. A recurring theme in *Leaves of Grass*, dominant in the "Calamus" section and central in such poems as "Out of the Cradle Endlessly Rocking" and "When Lilacs Last in the Dooryard Bloom'd," is the fulfillment of spiritual love after death. Such a love is, of course, an emotion transcending time and place and expanded far beyond the physical. In "Song of Myself," the power of such love is granted the poet in his achievement of union, and he goes about the earth aiding and comforting:

> I dilate you with tremendous breath, I buoy you up,
> Every room of the house do I fill with an arm'd force,
> Lovers of me, bafflers of graves.

This kind of love does indeed "baffle" the grave, for it is an emotion of the spirit, not the body, related to eternity and not the hour. Among the most significant discoveries the poet makes is that "a kelson of the creation is love." So, too, in "Four Quartets," a central discovery made by the poet is the significance of the love that transcends time and space:

> Love is itself unmoving,
> Only the cause and end of movement,
> Timeless, and undesiring

Located at that "still point of the turning world," love is identified with spirituality itself. "Love is most nearly itself/ When here and now cease to matter." This love "beyond desire" becomes, near the end of "Four Quartets," the motive-force behind the allurement on "the way":

> Who then devised the torment? Love.
> Love is the unfamiliar Name
> Behind the hands that wave
> The intolerable shirt of flame
> Which human power cannot remove.

Eliot's vision of love as the "unfamiliar Name" that "devised the torment" of "the way" is, although superficially different from, ultimately identical with Whitman's view of love as "a kelson of the creation": in both poets it is love that pervades, informs, and gives meaning to the world and universe, and it is spiritual love that is fufilled in the supreme achievement of mystic insight or in the "total" release of death.

Although Whitman and Eliot are in disagreement in some of their basic attitudes and concepts, their work exhibits an astonishingly large number of areas of similarity in idea and technique. The fundamental relationship of "Song of Myself" and "Four Quartets" is the use in both of the mystical experience as a dramatic frame. It is of transcendent importance to understand that neither poet is recording factual experience but that both are creating out of their emotional and intuitive insight a vivid drama profoundly convincing as "imaginative" truth.

In spite of the poetic form of Whitman and Eliot, readers have persisted in judging them not as poets but as philosophers. The orthodox and the iconoclast, as guardians of special points of view, have aligned themselves with one poet or the other because of the dubious pleasure they derive from discovering written assurances of their own certain certainties. Some have been at first attracted but, on the emergence of an unexpected or disturbing attitude, have later been repulsed. The poets' best friends have been their worst enemies; there is an amazing parallel between Whitman's "hot little prophets" and the dedicated interpreters and worshippers that now surround Eliot. As there were many who were sadly dismayed when it became clear that Whitman relished playing a role, whether of the vagabond poet or of the carpenter-Christ, so one might predict a similar disillusion in Eliot when his life has been scrutinized as closely as Whitman's and when it is discovered that his poetry is not autobiography.

It seems that each generation must learn through bitter experience that the poetic pose, because it is a pose, is not therefore fraudulent: it is of the nature of poetry to create out of the emotions and out of the imagination as much as out of factual experience. The reader who aspires to unbiased and disinterested judgment may well test his critical faculty by exploring the poetic merits of both "Song of Myself" and "Four Quartets" read not as philosophy but as poetic dramatizations.

9

Emily Dickinson's
Bright Orthography

In 1956 the American Literature Group of the Modern Language Association solemnly established the official canon of Great American Authors with the publication of a bibliographical volume which seemed a dignified and permanent entombment of their genius. Their number, Eight, appeared symmetrical and conclusive, and the roster of their names seemed academically definitive: Poe, Emerson, Thoreau, Hawthorne, Melville, Whitman, Twain, James. There was widespread congratulation that at last such writers as Cooper and Howells, Lowell and Longfellow were put in their respectable, second-rate places.

The Amherst gnome who wrote "How dreary—to be—Somebody!/How public—like a Frog" would have found in the pronouncement excellent material for a short but piercing poem on the furtiveness of fame. Indeed, someone with Emily Dickinson's keen wit seems to have planned her reputation in the twentieth century to compensate for her obscurity in the nineteenth—all as a series of jokes on professors of poetry. There is a small but persistent knock at the back door of the Academy which the scholars can continue to ignore only at risk of their own reputations, not the knocker's. And the petite Nobody ready to enter might turn out to be more quietly cataclysmic than the imposing Somebodies already on the roster of Eight.

Emily's knocking began with an impressive whack in 1955, with the publication of T. H. Johnson's three-volume schol-

137

arly edition of the *Poems*, the first complete and accurate edition ever to appear, correcting errors of previous editors, lining up all the extant versions of each poem, and, by meticulous detective work, establishing a chronology of the poems. This monumental work was followed in 1958 by a three volume edition of the *Letters* (T. H. Johnson, editor), an event more important for Emily than for most poets because her letters captured as much of the evanescent stuff of her genius as her poetry. The knocking has continued unabated, rising to something of a clamorous staccato in 1960, punctuated by three magnificent super-blows: Jay Leyda's two-volume biography-in-sources, *The Years and Hours of Emily Dickinson*, Charles R. Anderson's critical study, *Emily Dickinson's Poetry: Stairway of Surprise*, and T. H. Johnson's one-volume edition of the *Complete Poems* (which achieves its brevity by dropping the scholarly apparatus of the three-volume edition).[1]

These publishing events are a feast for Emily compared to the meager crumbs which were the sole nourishment of her reputation in the past. When she died in 1886, she had published, in most cases reluctantly, some seven poems—out of a total of some 1775 she had written. When her sister Lavinia gathered together the poems—on scraps of paper, in letters, in the neat manuscript booklets—and took them to her friend Mabel Loomis Todd, there began one of the strangest stories in the annals of publishing. The poems began to appear, with editorial revision, in the 1890's, and new poems were still appearing in piecemeal publication as late as 1945 (*Bolts of Melody*). All critical and scholarly work on Emily's poetry was frustrated by the simple fact that no one could be sure to what extent the poems as published had been tampered with by her editors. Many a critical insight built on a word or phrase blushed with embarrassment on the discovery that the language was not Emily's but Mabel Loomis Todd's or Thomas Wentworth Higginson's. Such a situation is enough to cause critics to stammer and scholars to stand mute, paralyzed by

[1] Jay Leyda, ed., *The Years and Hours of Emily Dickinson* (New Haven: Yale Univ. Press, 1960); Charles R. Anderson, *Emily Dickinson's Poetry: The Stairway of Surprise* (New York: Holt, Rinehart & Winston, 1960); Thomas H. Johnson, ed., *Complete Poems of Emily Dickinson* (Boston: Little, Brown, & Co., 1960).

fear of hailing a synthetic genius. Never before has biblio-graphical chaos created so much critical uncertainty or schol-arly irresolution.

But the recent events have dispelled the chaos and instituted the certain certainties so vital to the scholar's work. It is no longer possible to dismiss Emily as the quaint recluse of Am-herst, the little tippler genially leaning against the sun, the fantasy bride whose life had stood "a loaded gun" until her imaginary hunter carried her away, the melancholy seer who heard a fly buzz when she died and who rode in a carriage with her lover Death off to a Swelling of the Ground—in short, as a minor talent with an occasional charming, but tortured, turn of phrase. She must be invited to the feast with her peers, and if the places set are not enough, then one of the Immortal Eight must politely withdraw—and Edgar Allan Poe would be just the southern gentleman to excuse himself for a lady. But the French would object, and in an age of International Relations, we must respect their feelings. We'll lay another place and raise the Eight to Nine, a mystic number that once counted the old world muses, surely appropriate to measure the geniuses of the new.

In short, it is time to recognize Emily Dickinson as being, with Walt Whitman, one of the two original poetic geniuses of America's nineteenth century. And it is surely only a matter of time before the psychological critics point out that Walt with his barbaric yawp and public parade of self represents the aggressive male ego while Emily, with her quiet voice and private shyness of spirit, represents the passive female. The critic who demands that we choose between them should consider first our keeping both. Separate they are frag-ments—however large, still incomplete; together, as one embraces and the other shrinks, they complete each other like the union of magnetic opposites. The fruit of their union is the modern idiom of twentieth-century poetry.

The most recent works on Emily are calculated to restore her to her rightful place in the American literary tradition. But these works do not bring affairs to an end so much as to a new beginning. What they settle is less than what they arouse.

Jay Leyda's *Years and Hours* is a massive compilation of the documents, large and small, important and trivial, that relate to Emily's life. The thought of so huge a work imposed on so frail a figure causes an involuntary shudder, but the results are surprisingly uncrushing. In spite of their density, these documents do not seem to have the weight of all their words; they remain on the edge of Emily's life, beyond the perimeter, where they seldom traffic with her spirit. There are, of course, her own letters, but these bear out rather than weigh in—they seem to offer release and to give buoyancy. In his Introduction, Leyda states as his single aim "to get at the truth of Emily Dickinson." And then, a few pages on, he confesses his failure: "most of our biggest questions about her must remain unanswered." The frankness is refreshing. In all the pages of these two huge volumes, the big questions do indeed elude the reader, and even some of the small shrink and disappear in the multitude of unassimilated details. The greatest service of these volumes is to demonstrate graphically that Emily's life, like the lives of all of us, is made up of a continuous flow of relevant and irrelevant, affecting and indifferent events, and to trace cause to effect, or external happening to internal mood, is hazardous at best, most often impossible. Biography, these documents seem to say, can never be more than a complex web of speculation, and then quite frequently of the trivial and insignificant.

But though the reader is invited to become Emily's biographer, he must still stay within the restrictions imposed by the conditions of a life and by the editor's selections. Of all the hours and minutes of Emily's life, only that small portion which became verbalized and then placed on paper and then survived the succeeding years and then was discovered and then was considered somehow pertinent—only this tiny, tiny portion of her life is spread forth here for our prying eyes. We cannot but conclude that the poetry, with all its cryptic statement and mysterious hints, reveals more than Mr. Leyda's massive selection of facts. By printing the documents without comment, Mr. Leyda designedly abdicates, in favor of his reader, the responsibility of judgment and imaginative extension of fact—the usual function of a biographer. It seems a pity that, after poring over all the voluminous material related to Emily to count her *Years and Hours,* he does not relate the full wisdom of his search. He does reveal some of his speculation, however apologetically, in an introductory section entitled "The People around Emily Dickinson." Here he deals summarily with the three persons most frequently proposed by previous biographers as the objects of Emily's mysterious amorous attachments. In the case of her father's law student, Benjamine F. Newton, Mr. Leyda flies in the face of the scarcity of his own facts ("but the bareness of these mementos cannot hide. . . .") to affirm the young man's importance in her emotional and intellectual development. Catherine Turner Anthon is dismissed as the sexual solution to Emily's riddle, but Mr. Leyda guesses at the importance of her influence in Emily's dedication to poetry. And, most surprising of all, the Reverend Charles Wadsworth is, in Mr. Leyda's view ("If I [too] may speculate. . . .") no more than spiritual counselor to Emily—not the unaware, or half-aware, beloved as most biographers believe. It is somewhat startling to realize that in these important, generally negative judgments, Mr. Leyda seems uninhibited by the absence of conclusive "accretions of detail."

If Mr. Leyda demonstrates how little can be really known of Emily's important life, Charles R. Anderson shows, in *Stairway of Surprise,* how much can be made of Emily's poetry by generally ignoring her biography. Of course he has absorbed all that has been said and guessed about Emily, but he assigns himself the task of critic, to deal with the reality of the poetry, not the reality of the life. Although there have been critical works before, none has had the advantage of the complete and accurate text of her poetry nor the chronological arrangement of her poems. Like the unsettled biographical problems, however, there remain unsettled poetic problems. What is a manageable and critically valid grouping of her poems, what are her major subjects and themes, what is the best point of departure, what the best perspective? What, indeed, are the finest and lasting poems? Mr. Anderson tries his hand at answering all these questions. He rejects the chronological approach, although it is newly available to him. He begins, instead, with an analysis of Emily's theory of art as revealed in the poems, and he then examines her various attitudes toward nature, continues with an exploration of the poems of ecstasy and despair, and concludes with a survey of her poems on death and immortality. All along the way he is constantly making value judgments, pointing out the successful, laying aside the defective.

Although the Leyda volumes are biographical and the Anderson work critical, it is the latter which gives a greater sense of reality to Emily Dickinson as a living being. She lies inert and enigmatic and almost insignificant behind the multitude of documents in Leyda; but in Anderson she springs to life from the first and breathes, sheds tears, feels agony, cries joy, knows death. By the time we have finished the Anderson volume, we feel that we know a human being intimately by sharing a life's pains and pleasures as measured forth in art. For biography to dehumanize and criticism to enliven is a paradox that Emily would have understood and enjoyed. How could anyone expect (she might well exclaim) a newspaper clipping of a public event to contain the pulse of life stirring in a poem shaped from the depths of a soul?

When we turn from Anderson to the one-volume *Complete Poems*, we are ready to say with Whitman in *Leaves of Grass*, ". . . this is not a book,/Who touches this touches a man." And we recognize before we read far that, for all the order that Mr. Anderson imposed on Emily's work to allow a systematic treatment, there remain the ragged edges, the inexplicable tangents, the unexplored depths of actual life. For example, we come upon poem 1670, which opens—

> In Winter in my Room
> I came upon a Worm
> Pink lank and warm
> But as he was a worm
> And worms presume
> Not quite with him at home
> Secured him by a string
> To something neighboring
> And went along.

As we read on in fascination, we learn that this extraordinary worm turns into a snake "ringed with power," fair as well as fearsome—

> He fathomed me—
> Then to a Rhythm *Slim*
> Secreted in his Form
> As Patterns swim
> Projected him.

Our first impulse is to say, "Is this our Emily?" But of course it is, and this poem suggests symbolic depths of her poetry yet unplumbed. It teasingly concludes, "This was a dream." In the future lies the challenging task of a deep-diving biographical-critical study which, while cognizant of dream psychology and psychoanalytical symbols, will maintain a respect for poetic genius and the integrity of art. This demanding work might bring together the massive labor of the Leyda volumes, the critical insight of the Anderson book, and set about deliberately taking some calculated risks in imaginative plunges to the depths of Emily's poetry. In exploring the worm-turned-snake, for instance, this study might first be led to the personal unconscious and Freud, and then beyond to the collective unconscious and the snake of the Garden—to myth and the Mother of us all.

It may not seem so strange to discover childless Emily comprehending such a basic female role. Her progeny are her poems, born of her marriage with her Lexicon. Mr. Anderson was certainly right to get her dictionary and trace her meanings back to their source. When she wrote to T. W. Higginson, "Soon after, my tutor died, and for several years my lexicon was my only companion," she was revealing a sublimation and a substitution that ran deep and lasted long. Whatever the future biographer will discover, we know now that the real lover between her sheets was her dictionary, and it disturbed her dreams more than any man:

(Poem 276):   Many a phrase has the English language—
I have heard but one—
Low as the laughter of the Cricket,
Loud, as the Thunder's Tongue—

Murmuring, like old Caspian Choirs,
When the Tide's a' lull—
Saying itself in new inflection—
Like a Whippowil—

Breaking in bright Orthography
On my simple sleep—
Thundering it's Prospective—
Till I stir, and weep—

Not for the Sorrow, done me—
But the push of Joy—
Say it again, Saxon!
Hush—Only to me!

Never before was a love affair with language so intimate, the "push of Joy" of the masculine linguistic so transporting. It is this ecstasy of language that makes Emily a modern poet: she fondles a phrase until it is aroused and seized with a stiffening desire that ambushes the attention: where the reader expects the softness of feminine sentimentality, he is surprised by the toughness of masculine vigor.

Tough-textured and contemporary, Emily's poetry leaps across time to the present and on to the edge of Immortality. Her brilliance, essentially timeless, derives from her linguistic libido; her genius, essentially modern, sparkles in her bright Orthography. The scholars and critics who take up where Leyda and Anderson leave off, who begin with the fine ground-breaking of the Johnson editions, must next penetrate the placid surface of the life and the "slant" surface of the poetry to the instinctual life below, down into the teeming sub-levels of visionary consciousness, down into the timeless pools of deepest knowing. There, in the secret recesses of her inmost being, Emily may yet yield her profoundest meanings.

Emily Dickinson:
The Thunder's Tongue

Emily Dickinson published only seven poems during her life-time; since her death, some 1775 of her poems have been published, many for the first time as recently as 1955. Grad-ually her reputation has risen during this century until now she takes her place with Whitman to rank as one of the two greatest nineteenth-century American poets. Because she was a "non-professional," because she wrote no single masterpiece nor any piece sustained much beyond forty or fifty lines in length, because her poetry was made up of a multitude of brief, frequently "faulty" lyrics in simple metrics and conven-tional stanzaic forms, it was long thought that she was a tal-ented amateur limited by a poor ear, a defective sense of form, and an imperfect grasp of language.

It is only recently that we have come to realize that the "faults" and the "imperfections," the "defects" and the "er-rors," were an inseparable part of her way of seeing, an essential element of her imagination, and lay at the very heart of her genius, constituting, indeed, a kind of linguistic poetics.[1]

Although Emily never undertook to formulate—or rather to intellectualize—her theory of poetry, the scattered references in her letters and poems indicate that she had little doubt about

[1] Charles R. Anderson's *Emily Dickinson's Poetry: The Stairway of Surprise* (New York: Holt, Rinehart & Winston, 1960) is the most useful and perceptive critical work on the poet to appear thus far. It has had the advantage of all the recent bibliographical and textual scholarship. Professor Anderson makes brilliant use of Emily's lexicon itself in analyzing the unusual language of the poetry.

the fundamental nature of poetry as well as its impenetrable mysteries. Her comments both prose and poetic, as well as her practice, reveal that there were in her view three basic elements of poetry—or rather, two parodoxical ingredients which were held in suspended tension by the third. In their simplest terms, these elements might be defined as *surprise*, the *familiar*, and *language*. And the theory might be formulated: The surprise of discovery in the familiar issues from the shock of language.

Underlying this theory is the simple psychological assumption that startling juxtapositions in language bestow an intensified awareness that penetrates beneath the commonplace: The language jars us into seeing deeply where the eye merely glanced before. It is precisely this psychological insight that relates Emily more closely to our time than her own. When she wrote, the prevailing poetry was a lulling verse of predictable diction, more likely to soothe than to startle; since her time, there has been a revolution in the language of poetry—in which she played no small part.

When asked how she was able to recognize poetry, Emily returned a simple, surprised answer: "If I read a book and it makes my whole body so cold no fire ever can warm me, I know *that* is poetry. If I feel physically as if the top of my head were taken off, I know *that* is poetry. These are the only ways I know it. Is there any other way?"[2] Although the modern critic has tended to brush aside this test of poetry as impressionistic and emotional, Emily undoubtedly meant it as serious and certain, a basic tenet, indeed, of her poetics. That her vivid definition was not the generalization of a fanciful mood is attested by the many recurrences of the basic belief in her poetry:

(Poem 1247): To pile like Thunder to it's close
              Then crumble grand away
              While Everything created hid
              This—would be Poetry—

              Or Love—the two coeval come—
              We both and neither prove—
              Experience either and consume—
              For None see God and live—[3]

[2] Thomas H. Johnson, ed., *The Letters of Emily Dickinson* (Cambridge: Harvard Univ. Press [Belknap Press], 1958), pp. 473–74.

[3] Thomas H. Johnson, ed., *The Poems of Emily Dickinson* (Cambridge: Harvard Univ. Press [Belknap Press], 1955). All Dickinson quotations are from this text and are identified by poem numbers.

This small lyric, in comparing the structure of poetry with the "piling" and then "crumbling" of Thunder, introduces a favorite metaphor in describing the powerful impact of true poetry on the reader. But the poem concludes with more than emotion: it is the privilege of the thunderstruck to "see God." Although the central image of this poem is the Thunder, it takes only a little ingenuity to see the symbolic suggestions of all three elements of Emily's poetics in the poem—if the Thunder is thought of as linguistic, and the view of God as insight penetrating the commonplace.

The problem for the poet, then, is to create thunder, but his job is made infinitely more complex by limitations—this thunder cannot be the artificial rumble of the stage-prop, nor an echo of the real thing captured from the sky in a divine frenzy. The thunder must be human, and must originate from the common human experience:

(Poem 448): This was a Poet—It is That
                Distills amazing sense
                From ordinary Meanings—
                And Attar so immense

                From the familiar species
                That perished by the Door—
                We wonder it was not Ourselves
                Arrested it—before—

                Of Pictures, the Discloser—
                The Poet—it is He—
                Entitles Us—by Contrast—
                To ceaseless Poverty—

                Of Portion—so unconscious—
                The Robbing—could not harm—
                Himself—to Him—a Fortune—
                Exterior—to Time—

The materials out of which the thunder must be piled are not grandiose visions or cosmic schemes but the common and the everyday. Out of "ordinary Meanings" the poet "distills amazing sense"—like the perfumer who extracts the powerful essence from a familiar flower that we pass daily with scant notice.

In sum, Emily Dickinson's poet must amaze with the ordinary, surprise with the familiar—or create "thunder" out of the human sounds in the next room. The means for this achievement are the only means at the poet's command—language. Emily felt that the possibilities for creation with language were limitless:

(Poem 276):   Many a phrase has the English language—
I have heard but one—
Low as the laughter of the Cricket,
Loud, as the Thunder's Tongue—

Murmuring, like old Caspian Choirs,
When the Tide's a' lull—
Saying itself in new inflection—
Like a Whippowil—

Breaking in bright Orthography
On my simple sleep—
Thundering it's Prospective—
Till I stir, and weep—

Not for the Sorrow, done me—
But the push of Joy—
Say it again, Saxon!
Hush—Only to me!

This simple tribute to language suggests not merely an obsession but the source of poetic inspiration itself—the "bright Orthography" and the "thundering . . . Prospective" of English. One can envision the lonely and withdrawn Emily restless in her bed at night as the words and phrases of unwritten poems flood the uninhibited imagination of her "simple sleep." In the closing stanza, language becomes personified ("Saxon" in a former version was "English language") and fulfills, with its "push of Joy," the intimate role of the lover. Emily's acute sensitivity to language, here transfigured into romantic terms, is the secret of her poetic genius, the source of her "Thunder's Tongue." For her, words are charged with meanings both limitless and unfathomable:

(Poem 1409):   Could mortal lip divine
The undeveloped Freight
Of a delivered syllable
'Twould crumble with the weight.

In asserting the impossibility of verbalizing all the "meaning" of a poem ("delivered syllable"), Emily was anticipating the modern critic's obsession with ambiguity and irony, with detailed explications and minute analyses of multiple levels of meaning.

Thunder, the commonplace, and language—these are the simple ingredients of Emily's singular poetics. But they do not tell the whole story of her method of composition. As she did not have a publisher during her lifetime, she in a sense became her own publisher: that is, she wrote her poems on sheets which she fastened together into little booklets.[4] Whenever she wanted a poem (and she frequently sent poems to relatives and friends), she would copy suitable verses from the booklets into her notes and letters. Usually on the pages in the booklets, copied neatly beneath the poems, were alternate readings for the text—words or phrases that could be substituted in certain lines of the poem. Sometimes there were several words jotted down offering several choices for a single word in the poem. These booklets, which held the multitude of poems in suspended incompletion, suggest that Emily's method in word-choice was intuitive and instinctive. Some words and phrases must have flashed forth for her inevitable and unchangeable, but others must have seemed imprecise and dubious. By recording alternate choices and leaving the poem, but not abandoning it, she could hope for another intuitive flash that would assure her of a right selection.

Indeed, that this method was the one she followed is borne out by one of her poems describing the poet in the process of selecting a word:

(Poem 1126): Shall I take thee, the Poet said
To the propounded word?
Be stationed with the Candidates
Till I have finer tried—

The Poet searched Philology
And was about to ring
For the suspended Candidate
There came unsummoned in—

That portion of the Vision
The Word applied to fill
Not unto nomination
The Cherubim reveal—

It was belief in this mysterious process of the poetic inspiration—an inspiration primarily linguistic—that no doubt

[4] Thomas H. Johnson gives a vivid description of Emily's writing habits in his introduction, "Creating the Poems," in *The Poems of Emily Dickinson.*

prompted Emily, on first writing this poem, to jot down for "finer" in line 4 two competing candidates, "vainer" and "further"; for "searched" in line 5, "probed"; for "was" in line 6, both "just" and "when"; and for "There came" in line 8, "Advanced." Since the only copy of this poem known is the penciled draft, we might assume that Emily never went back to it to make her final choices in the light of later Cherubim revelations. But a subsequent editor (in *Bolts of Melody*, 1945) decided some of Emily's candidates offered superior readings—"further" in line 4, "probed" in line 5, and "when" in line 6.

This willingness of an editor to aid Emily in the writing of her poetry has been the rule rather than the exception in the history of her publication. When she died in 1886, her sister Lavinia discovered the great mass of her poems and set about the difficult task of finding an editor. The story is fascinating as it becomes apparent that some minor accident, some insignificant obstacle, could quite easily have deprived the world of Emily's poems—they were for a time in the care of frail forces indeed. And moreover, when they began to appear in 1890 (subsequent volumes were published in 1891 and 1896), the two editors, Mabel Loomis Todd and Thomas Wentworth Higginson, felt compelled to alter and change, to modify and regularize, not to suit their own taste so much as that which they conceived as the public's. For example, one poem which utilizes as a central image a room (the speaker's, who is undergoing the sensations of death) was begun by Emily:

> (Poem 465):   I heard a Fly buzz—when I died—
> The Stillness in the Room
> Was like the Stillness in the Air—
> Between the Heaves of Storm—

Ignoring the effect of the peculiar and jarring off-rhyme of "Room" and "Storm" (the initial rumble of the piling Thunder), the editors changed the second line to the flat and contrived, "The Stillness round my form." In her second stanza, Emily persisted in her image of the Room, giving it the final emphasis:

> The Eyes around—had wrung them dry—
> And Breaths were gathering firm
> For that last Onset—when the King
> Be witnessed—in the Room—

Here of immense but indefinable value is the distorted echo of the off-rhyme of the first stanza—"firm" and "Room," the latter now beginning to be haunted by an eerie and dissonant music, to turn out finally to be the buzz of a fly. But the editors would still have none of the domestic scene of the death, the Room. They meddled:

> The Eyes *beside*—had wrung them dry—
> And Breaths were gathering *sure*
> For that last Onset—when the King
> Be witnessed—in *his power*—

It is ironic that even in their shifting the editors failed to regularize the rhyme; and *their* eyes do not stare hauntingly all *around*, but they gathered the haunting eyes from *around* the bed and placed them primly *beside*.

This editorial tampering might seem insignificant with many a writer, but with Emily Dickinson it appears vital, somewhat like bloodletting—meant to cure the patient but actually weakening him, sometimes killing. For a poet like Emily whose genius is in her language, minor word changes can be major blundering. Her electric clap of Thunder can easily be diminished to a faint rumble or an effete rap. But of course, all blame does not lie with Emily's editors; indeed, their credit in rescuing the poetry from oblivion far outweighs their debit in tampering with the text. But is it almost unforgivable to find a minor talent like Thomas Bailey Aldrich condescendingly manhandling Emily's fine opening stanza—

> (Poem 214):   I taste a liquor never brewed
> From Tankards scooped in Pearl—
> Not all the Frankfort Berries
> Yield such an Alcohol!

Emily herself thought that sometime she might want to change "the Frankfort Berries" to "the vats upon the Rhine." Aldrich not only decided on the alternate reading, but nonchalantly "improved" the other lines as well:

> I taste a liquor never brewed
> In vats along the Rhine;
> No tankard ever held a draught
> Of alcohol like mine.[5]

---

[5] Quoted in George F. Whicher, *This Was a Poet* (New York: Charles Scribner's Sons, 1938), p. 230, from *The Atlantic Monthly* of 1892 (Jan.).

In this instance, the life has bled away and the Thunder silenced entirely! But Aldrich's arrogant revision serves an excellent purpose in pointing up the effervescent magic of Emily's uncommon, uncanny language. To compare the two versions is to discover some (not all) of her secrets: who can measure what is lost in the disappearance of the Pearl and in the de-emphasis (by shifting) of the Alcohol, and who can say what died with the sing-song rhythm and the jingly rhyme. Clearly Aldrich's alcohol has nothing of the power of Emily's. Perhaps he did not know that when the poem he revised was published during Emily's lifetime, the editor of the *Springfield Daily Republican* similarly felt compelled to change the first stanza:

> I taste a liquor never brewed,
> From tankards scooped in pearl;
> Not Frankfort berries yield the sense
> Such a delicious whirl.[6]

Although the pearl is saved, the "delicious whirl" is sufficiently artificial in tone to derail the poem completely. Emily was not enough impressed by this surgery on her defenseless progeny to record the "improvements" in her booklet.

The editorial compulsion to rewrite Emily's poetry, to compel it to conform, to suppress the quaint and inject the predictable, is particularly fascinating when viewed in the light of Emily's own revisions of her poems. Clearly her editors and critics were off in one direction while she intuitively plotted her route in another. Although it is doubtful that any of her lyrics "came" to her in as bad a form as they were made by her emendators (as exemplified above), if they had she would have set about immediately transfiguring them into the irregular, cryptic, non-conformist lyrics that we recognize now and at once as her singular, startling style.

A brief look at a couple of instances of Emily at work will bear out the unusual and unpredictable nature of her revisions. One short poem exists only in a penciled worksheet draft:

> (Poem 1452):　1 Your thoughts dont have words every day
> 　　　　　　　2 They come a single time
> 　　　　　　　3 Like signal esoteric sips

[6] Quoted in Thomas H. Johnson, ed., *The Poems of Emily Dickinson*, p. 150.

4 Of the communion Wine
5 Which while you taste so native seems
6 So easy so to be
7 You cannot comprehend its price
8 Nor it's infrequency

It is an interesting exercise to pause for a moment and search for those weak spots in the poem which might have tempted Emily to select alternate candidates. For example, the opening line seems a bit awkwardly turned, perhaps too long and a little clumsy around the "don't." But apparently the line never bothered Emily: and on a little reflection we realize that the line's heaviness and slight stumble are actually a re-enforcement of the meaning, a breathing demonstration of the strange obstacles to the true marriage of thoughts and words.

In line 4, Emily thought that she might sometime want to drop "the communion" and replace it with "sacramental." No doubt the loss of an unconnotative article appealed to her, as well as substituting one word for two; and perhaps she was not sure in her own mind as to the word of richer connotations. In line 5, where we might have expected "so natural" but got instead "so native," we might eventually have had "adjacent" had Emily returned to restudy her poem—"Which while you taste adjacent seems." Surely "adjacent" is the least expected candidate, and it has just that jolt of unusual sense that jars the reader to attention; also it singly replaces two words, one of which is auxiliary. There are other considerations: the original "so" offers the advantage of alliteration with the nearby "seems," but it carries also the perhaps slight disadvantage of its exact repetition twice in the immediately following line: "So easy so to be." Clearly this line gave Emily her greatest problem. The structure itself is precisely right, its cryptic series of single-syllable two-letter words contrasting with the long flow of the preceding line, its two "so's" functioning in conflicting capacities, one intensifying, the other saying "thus."

But the crucial word, as Emily recognized, is "easy"—it stands out in brilliant illumination and must carry the weight of meaning of the line, which stands or falls with it. Probaby it is the obviousness of "easy"—wine which is easy, words which are easy—that gives Emily pause. Anything so obvious will not signal the attention sufficiently. Emily searched philology for nine additional candidates: *kindred; fully; free; so ample seems;*

bounteous; intimate; affable; Affluent; gracious. But, as in the rest of the poem, Emily's Cherubim never made their final revelation. Emily's editors (*Bolts of Melody*, 1945), however, made their choice, rendering the line "So bounteous, so free," and thereby abandoning its fragilely balanced structure, substituting flaccidity for tautness, triteness for surprise. For the remainder of the poem, Emily questioned "price" in line 7 with "worth"—the one instance in which she might have been considering substituting the usual for the unusual, even at the sacrifice of the alliteration of the "p" in "comprehend." And she noted an entirely new line for line 8: "The stint nor the divinity." It is doubtful that any editor would have meddled with the untroublesome line 8—"Nor it's infrequency"; and it is not at all sure that Emily would have used unchanged her alternate candidate. But we can feel immediately her attraction to the slightly offbeat "stint" and her feeling for the metaphorically compatible "divinity."

But Emily more frequently than not progressed from the worksheet stage to the semi-finished or completed poem, and it is useful to conclude with observation of this progression in one of her familiar poems:

POEM 609

1862		1872
I—Years had been—from Home—	1	I Years had been from Home
And now—before the Door—	2	And now before the Door
I dared not *open*—lest a face	3	I dared not *enter*, lest a face
I never saw before	4	I never saw before
Stare *vacant* into mine—	5	Stare *stolid* into mine (or "horrid")
And ask my Business there—	6	And ask my Business there—
My Business—*just* a Life I left—	7	"My Business *but* a Life I left
Was such—*still dwelling* there?	8	Was such *remaining* there?"
I *fumbled at my nerve*—	9	I *leaned upon the Awe*—
I *scanned the Windows o'er*—	10	I *lingered with Before*
The *Silence*—like an Ocean rolled—	11	The *Second* like an Ocean rolled
And broke against my Ear—	12	And broke against my ear—
I laughed a *Wooden* laugh—	13	I laughed a *crumbling* Laugh
That I—could fear a Door—	14	That I could fear a Door
Who *Danger—and the Dead—had* faced—	15	Who *Consternation compassed*
But never *shook*—before—	16	And never *winced* before.
I fitted to the Latch—*my Hand*—	17	I fitted to the Latch

With trembling care—	18	*My Hand,* with trembling care
Lest back the Awful Door should spring—	19	Lest back the awful Door should spring
And leave me—in the Floor—	20	And leave me in the Floor—
I moved my fingers off, *as cautiously as Glass—*	21 22	*Then* moved my Fingers off *As cautiously as Glass*
And held my Ears—and like a Thief	23	And held my ears, and like a Thief
Stole—gasping—from the House	24	*Fled* gasping from the House—

8. still dwelling there] Remaining there
12. broke] smote—
16. shook] quaked—
24. Stole] fled

In the first column is the original draft, with possible changes jotted down below; in the second column is the revised version, worked out some ten years later, with adoption of only two of the original alternates (in lines 8 and 24), but with many new changes (italics have been used to signal revisions). Beside the second version is one new alternative ("horrid") left hanging in the margin for possible future use.

Emily's editors, without benefit of her revision, adopted two of her original alternates (the "quaked" for "shook" of line 16 and the "fled" for "stole" in the last line), passed over one that she did adopt (line 8, "remaining" for "still dwelling"), and introduced a few of their own. In her third stanza, Emily originally and characteristically rhymed "o'er" and "ear," achieving a dissonance that superbly underscores the ominous silence of the verse; her editors neatly excised this tension by introducing "near" as a true rhyme with "ear": "I scanned the Windows near—" And similarly in the fifth stanza, uncomfortable with Emily's rhyming "care" with "floor," as well as her quaint use of preposition in "And leave me—in the Floor—," solved both "problems" by rewriting the line: "And leave me standing there." This line in its original form never gave Emily doubts, and she left it intact in her revision of the poem. She instinctively understood, as her editors did not, that the pulsing life of the line dwelt in that strange, tiny "in": "And leave me—in the Floor—" "On the floor" might be expected—but why "in"? But of course—the fright of the "Awful Door" springing open would precipitate the visitor *into*, not just on, the floor—he would be so scared that he would "sink into the floor." That innocent "in" is working harder and with greater intensity than any other word in the line.

As we might expect, Emily Dickinson's revisions, in contrast with her editors', show not only a contempt for restraint but also a real sensitivity toward language. No doubt some deep instinct, sounding on the inner ear, led her to a number of minor changes, such as "enter" for "open" in line 3 (the dilemma for the visitor goes beyond merely opening), or "but" for "just" in line 7 (which achieves alliteration with "Business"), or "Then" for "I" in line 21 (which renders a greater and more suspense-filled continuity spanning the stanza-break). "Stolid" for "vacant" in line 5—"Stare stolid into mine"—not only gives two strong, steady "st's" in succession, but hints at a touch of hostility missing in the original. The change from "still dwelling" to "remaining" in line 8 not only condenses but also smooths. In the last line, it seems more appropriate, and certainly offers more vivid contrast, for the vistior to flee than to steal from the house. The excessive caution in letting go the latch would surely be followed by an act of controlled hysteria—flight; and besides, to *steal*, after the simile "like a Thief," extends the metaphor in a distracting and pointless pun.

The middle two stanzas of Emily's poem were the objects of her severest surgery. And these were the stanzas which might well have appeared unimpeachable. The most drastic revisions were made in stanza 3:

I *fumbled at my nerve*—	I *leaned upon the Awe*—
I *scanned the windows o'er*—	I *lingered with Before*—
The *Silence*—like an Ocean rolled—	The *Second* like an Ocean rolled
And broke against my Ear—	And broke against my ear—

The "fumbling" and "scanning" shifting to "leaning" and "lingering" is clownish exterior nervousness giving way to stunned interior terror. Both revised lines link more readily the intensity of the emotion felt with its cause in the past association with the house. And they both suggest an attempt to put on an appearance of casual disengagement. But the activities are inherently impossible—one can't lean on insubstantial Awe, nor can one linger with forever-gone Before. To assert the deeds is merely to put on a brave front. And time breaks through the front, even so insignificant a unit as a Second, to flood the

visitor with the reality of the present. It was a fine talent that
had the Silence breaking through the nervous fumbling and
compulsive scanning; but it was a genuine poet who had the
Second "rolling" to reality the pretended leaning and the
imaginary lingering. We might envision Emily's emendators
trying to move her revised version back to the original, but
never the reverse.

The fourth stanza did not require such drastic surgery, but
the revisions were in sensitive and vital spots:

I laughed a *Wooden* laugh—	I laughed a *crumbling* Laugh
That I—could fear a Door—	That I could fear a Door
Who *Danger—and the Dead—had faced—*	Who *Consternation compassed*
But never *shook*—before—	And never *winced* before.

The Wooden laugh, together with the shaking, the Danger and
the Dead—all have a slightly hollow ring to them. And moreover, such a laugh, in addition to ludicrously and irrelevantly
linking with a door, surely wooden, suggests a stiffness at a
point where dissolution is expected. As the reality of the present breaks through the artificially composed exterior, the laugh
must *crumble* with the terror. The abstract "Danger," followed by the lame (if alliterative) "Dead," seems randomly
and not inevitably chosen, and not really pertinent to the
present terror, which is concerned not so much with personal
safety as with personal knowledge, or self-awareness. The ambiguity of "Consternation," which has been not just faced but
"compassed," seems more immediately relevant and ultimately
more challenging: it could generate from self-dislike within, or
it could be the stern disapproval of someone terrifyingly near
and dear. In either case it seems more real and more
intimate—more closely related to the fear of the door (or of
one's own past)—than the "Danger and the Dead." And in this
shift to a more familiar fear, it seems appropriate to reduce the
exaggerated "Shook" to the restrained (and more probable)
"winced." It is curious that, although the third line of every
other stanza in the poem has four stresses (in contrast to three
stresses in all the other lines—some of the revisions in the last
two stanzas were made to bear out this pattern), in the third
line of this fourth stanza, Emily moved from four stresses to
three. Apparently the compactness of diction and precision of
imagery, strong attractions always, overrode the need to conform to a predetermined metrical pattern.

It is impossible to look closely at Emily in her craft without concluding that she was working within both the restrictions and freedom of an intuitive but complex poetics. In "I Years had been from Home," the materials are familiar and domestic, the quite unspectacular hesitation of a visitor at the front door of a house—and his hasty departure. Such material would seem to promise little with which to develop emotional impact. But out of these ordinary materials, Emily knows that she must give voice to thunder's tongue or the poem itself will remain ordinary, unworthy of serious notice. And the thunder must not be the synthetic variety, the crumpling of tin off stage. With the tempting possibilities of a haunted house, a lesser talent might well have settled for the sheeted ghosts and rattling skeletons of a halloween horror. But Emily will have more—and her Thunder rumbles from psychological depths that speak a genuine terror: this man at the door is Everyman searching his haunted past for a self he has lost, for an identity that has departed—and frightened more at confrontation than at failure. And it is Emily's language, so simple yet so profound, that creates as well as probes the depths! In changing her poem, she did not alter its basic nature, but made it more intensively and effectively what it started out to be from the beginning. The sharpening of the language does not alter what happens in the poem, but rather gives deeper glimpses and keener insight into the significance beneath the surface. Language rumbles from the tongue of Thunder, transfiguring the familiar into the indelibly rare—like a bolt of lightning instantly and vividly reshaping a landscape, surprising our tired eyes into new and deeper sight.

III

JOURNEYS INTO UNCHARTED INTERIORS

Dreams! dreams! golden dreams: endless, and golden, as the flowery prairies . . . my dreams herd like buffaloes, browsing on to the horizon, and browsing on round the world; and among them, I dash with my lance to spear one, ere they all flee.

HERMAN MELVILLE

II

Melville's Quest
in Life and Art

Herman Melville's life has received careful scrutiny from a number of distinguished biographers and scholars for a period now approaching half a century. Indeed, the excessive attention of the twentieth century seems to have compensated amply for the shameful neglect of the nineteenth. Beginning with Raymond Weaver's *Mariner and Mystic* in 1921, Melville has had the concentrated attention of such writers as Lewis Mumford (1929), Richard Chase (1949), and Newton Arvin (1950). This attention culminated in 1951 in the publication of Jay Leyda's two-volume "documentary," *The Melville Log*, on which Leon Howard based his extremely full biography (1951). It may be doubted that additional facts about Melville's life will shed additional light on his genius, but it is certain the biographers will continue their endless search.

In every man's life there are public, private, and subterranean elements. Biographers use publications and public records to reconstruct the first; personal letters, diaries, and acquaintances' memoirs to reconstruct the second; and whatever insight they can muster to suggest the nature of the last. Some writers, such as Longfellow, seem to stand most fully revealed in their public character; some, such as Poe, excite more curiosity by their private life; while others—a few—seem to retreat into the labyrinths of their own souls and there to defy the curious to follow. Melville must be placed in this last rare group. And the writer who would reveal something of the real Melville must take the risk of becoming lost in the labyrinth.

I. Is This Then a Man's Life?

The major known facts of Melville's life may be outlined in a few brief paragraphs. There are a limited number of incidents of major importance around which a great many minor facts tend to huddle. These factual clusters contain the essence of what is known of Melville's life. Allan Melville, Herman's father, Unitarian, New York merchant-importer, world-traveler, volatile and slightly unstable in character, died in debt in 1832, when he was fifty years of age and when Herman was thirteen. Maria Gansevoort Melville, Allan's widow, descended from solid, respectable, New York Dutch ancestry, member of the Calvinistic Dutch Reformed Church, was left on her husband's death to care for her eight children, the pitied poor relation of her well-to-do kin. In this insecure atmosphere of rootless genteel poverty, borne from town to town—New York, Albany, Pittsfield—Herman was subject to an emotional development that may well be imagined: a growing resentment against the father, an intense passion toward the mother running the gamut from love to hate. His formal education was brief; school was expensive, and there was the pressing matter of earning a living for a large family.

No wonder that in 1839, at the age of twenty, Herman went to sea. On this first voyage he sailed as a ship's boy on a merchantman bound for Liverpool. The voyage may well have marked Melville's initiation into adulthood, but it may also have temporarily soured his taste for life at sea. He turned to other activities for a time, including school teaching, and he made one significant journey into the West, visiting an uncle in Galena, Illinois, on the banks of the Mississippi. In 1841, at the age of twenty-two, Melville shipped out of New Bedford as a sailor on the whaler *Acushnet*. He was gone for nearly four years as the calendars count time, but in the world of literature his voyage is not likely to see an end: the greatest body of his work was shaped out of the experiences of this voyage. The sailor Melville jumped ship with his friend Toby in the Marquesas Islands and lived for a time a captive among the "cannibalistic" Typees. After being rescued he took part in a mild mutiny and was imprisoned on Tahiti. When released he roamed the islands with his vagabond friend, a deposed ship's doctor, Long Ghost, and sailed finally on another whaler which took him to Honolulu. From there he shipped on the man-of-war, the U.S.S. *United States,* as a sailor in the U.S. Navy, and after a fourteen-month voyage was discharged at Boston in October, 1844.

After such high adventure in so few years, the remainder of Melville's life seems tame indeed. Beginning in 1846, the books began to pour out seemingly without end: 1846, *Typee* (life as a captive of the savages in the Marquesas); 1847, *Omoo* (life as a vagabond sailor, on shipboard and in Tahiti); 1849, *Mardi* (voyages in the South Sea Islands transmuted into fantasy and allegory); 1849, *Redburn* (life on a merchantman to Liverpool and return); 1850, *White Jacket* (life on a man-of-war home-ward bound); 1851, *Moby Dick* (life in a whaler on a sea of metaphysics)—the great climax in this furious and sustained outburst of creativity, and, indeed, the climax of Melville's life. The rest was decline.

Melville had largely used up his experiences, as though they were the limited pieces of a jigsaw puzzle which when recon-structed left nothing to do. He seemed incapable of finding new pieces for new puzzles. After his youthful voyages, his experiences seemed no longer to make a primary appeal to his imagination. There were, however, vital events, including two crucial relationships: his marriage to Elizabeth Shaw in 1847 and his friendship with Nathaniel Hawthorne, beginning with the meeting in Pittsfield and Lenox in 1850. There were, too, relationships with numerous intellectual companions— Shakespeare, Milton, Hobbes, Spinoza, Rousseau, Hume, Hegel, Kant.

The works published after *Moby Dick,* though they did not reach its grandeur nor strive for its epic scope, had a classic quality all their own. *Pierre* (1852) made uncharted journeys into the human psyche; and the discoveries still startle. *Israel Potter* (1855) illuminated the national character in an adven-turous excursion into history. *The Piazza Tales* (1856) charmed, alarmed, and portrayed the price of withdrawal from the human scene. *The Confidence-Man* (1857) dramatized in bitter comedy the fantastic drift of America—and man—down the treacherous Mississippi in the streamer *Fidèle.* By 1857, Melville must have felt that even the leftover scraps of his central experiences had been consumed, for he never published fiction during his lifetime again, though in his last years he returned to it for the Christ-like story of *Billy Budd*, first published long after Melville's death, in 1924.

The rest may not have been silence, but it was a retreat to privacy, where the imagination need not strain for a vain popular appeal. There were volumes of verse, and even a long narrative poem, but most of these were privately printed for limited circulation. The narrative poem, *Clarel* (1876), was based on a long voyage of 1856–1857, during which Melville paid Hawthorne a last visit in Liverpool and then journeyed on to the Holy Land to work out alone a personal crisis which neither his wife nor his friend seemed desirous of understanding fully nor capable of mitigating.

The last, long years were lived out in obscurity in New York, where the author of *Moby Dick* worked as District Inspector of Customs. Though these years gave leisure for the reading of innumerable books and for the writing of a quantity of verses, there must have been a residue of restlessness if not of bitterness deep within. Two of his four children preceded Melville in death, Malcolm by a self-administered gun shot at the age of eighteen, Stanwix through illness at thirty-five. Melville himself died without fanfare in 1891. He was seventy-two.

II. External Facts and Internal Mysteries

Melville's biographers have not been content with the material they have assembled. Somehow the bare facts have appeared inadequate, and the longer the critic has looked at them, the odder they have seemed. The facts have been looked at long enough so that by now they have taken on a queer cast indeed. A quick excursion through the biographies will suggest the direction speculation has taken.

Raymond M. Weaver, the first Melville biographer (1921), contented himself with long quotations from various documents, particularly letters, which he pretended to let speak for themselves, but he was at times clearly uncomfortable with some of his facts (Melville "sought personal happiness in the illusion of romantic love"; "Exultant was [Melville's] worship of Hawthorne, absolute his desire for surrender").[1] It was not,

[1] Raymond M. Weaver, *Herman Melville: Mariner and Mystic* (New York: George H. Doran Co., 1921), pp. 227 and 340.

however, until he wrote his introduction to the *Shorter Novels* in 1928 that Weaver gave clearer voice to his misgivings about the bare, external facts:

The whole known record of his [Melville's] life seems insistently to indicate that veiled and deep-seated impulses from his nether-consciousness resolutely blocked the way to singleness of purpose and whole-heartedness of surrender; suppressions the more eloquently be-trayed by his efforts both in his writings and in his life, to conceal them from himself.

Weaver went on to suggest the cause of Melville's evasive nature: "Sex, to him, was not the consummation and dedication of ideality, but its filthy reverse."[2]

Succeeding biographers felt the necessity of touching upon the questions raised by Weaver. Speaking of Melville's "early sexual life," Lewis Mumford (1929) asserted, "We cannot doubt that [Melville] made the usual easy transition to a ma-turer state of sexuality." The very tone suggests that the matter needs to be cleared up, and Mumford readily admitted the inadequacies of Melville's marriage: "Melville was disloyal to the spirit of his marriage in a thousand repugnances or indiffer-ences that far more seriously undermined his relations with Elizabeth than the most outright liaison would have done, had it left Melville poised, collected, refreshed."[3]

By the time Richard Chase wrote in 1949, the entire subject of Melville's sexuality seems to have become fascinatingly com-plex. Chase oversimplified the subject by ignoring the hazards of reading works of art as biography: "In *Redburn* there were two images of the author: Redburn himself, who would sur-vive and mature, and Harry Bolton, the homosexual youth who was doomed. But Harry Bolton lived on in Melville." Chase added: "Melville's strain of homosexuality was entirely inward and subdued."[4] Newton Arvin, writing in 1950 (about the same time as Chase), though he was more reasonably restrained in his speculation, was coming to startlingly similar conclusions. "[Melville] was conscious enough, no doubt, of the ardor and intensity of his feelings for members of his own

[2] Raymond M. Weaver, *Shorter Novels of Herman Melville* (New York: Liveright Publishing Corp., 1928), pp. xlv–xlvi.

[3] Lewis Mumford, *Herman Melville* (New York: Harcourt, Brace & Co., 1929), pp. 36 and 278.

[4] Richard Chase, *Herman Melville* (New York: Macmillan Co., 1949), p. 295.

sex, but the possibility that such emotions might have had a sexual undercurrent can only with the utmost rarity, and then fleetingly, have presented itself to his consciousness."[5]

In a recent essay on American culture entitled "Come Back to the Raft Ag'in, Huck Honey," Leslie Fiedler carries to a sensational extreme the psychological analysis of American works of art. He lists Melville with other American writers (Cooper, Twain, Crane) who treat intense male love with a naïve innocence:

In Melville, the ambiguous relationship is most explicitly rendered; almost, indeed, openly explained. . . . In a step-by-step exposition, the Pure Marriage of Ishmael and Queequeg is set before us: the initial going to bed together and the first shyness overcome, that great hot toma-hawk-pipe accepted in a familiarity that dispels fear; next, the wedding ceremony itself (for in this marriage like so many others the ceremonial follows the deflowering), with the ritual touching of foreheads; then, the queasiness and guilt the morning after the *official* First Night, the suspicion that one has joined himself irrevocably to his own worst nightmare.[6]

What are we to think of this arresting interpretation of *Moby Dick*, especially in the face of the extravagant claim of Henry A. Murray (who describes himself as a "professing psychologist") in his introduction to *Pierre* (1949):

Surely Melville deserves to be commemorated as the literary discoverer [not only of the South Seas but] of another and more important part of nature, namely, the Darkest Africa of the mind, the mythological unconscious. As a depth psychologist he belongs with Dostoevsky and Nietzsche, the greatest in the centuries before Freud.[7]

III. Elizabeth and Nathaniel

Before amateur Freudians, cultural historians, or professing psychologists embroil us in further fruitless controversies about the nature of Melville, it is time that those of us who claim to be no more than close readers and admirers of the master artist speak up. There is not much time, for already

[5] Newton Arvin, *Herman Melville* (New York: William Sloane Assoc., 1950), p. 128.

[6] Leslie Fiedler, *An End to Innocence* (Boston: Beacon Press, 1955), p. 145.

[7] Henry A. Murray, "Introduction," *Pierre* (New York: Farrar, Straus, 1949), p. xxvi.

there are students who vaguely assume that medical or at least psychological scholarship has proved that Melville was a sexual deviant and that somehow such "proof" explains, if it does not invalidate, Melville's work.

The biographers have all stubbed their toes on two crucial relationships: Melville and his wife; Melville and Hawthorne. When Elizabeth Knopp Shaw married Melville in 1847, she was one of four children of Judge Lemuel Shaw, Chief Justice of Massachusetts. She was twenty-five, he twenty-eight. The face that stares solemnly out of the quaint old photographs is sober if not severe, the plain features tending toward grossness rather than delicacy. The chief fact of her emotional constitution appears to be her total lack of imagination. This appalling deficiency has caused extended speculation as to why Herman married her in the first place. The best guess seems to be that he looked upon her with the obligation of an older brother to a sister in possible danger of spinsterhood. Lemuel Shaw had loved, before her early death, Nancy Melville, sister to Herman's father Allan, and had continued his close association with Herman's family before and after Allan Melville died. It is quite likely that young Herman saw the kindly Shaw as a father figure. Melville's sense of gratitude was so strong as to compel him to dedicate his first book, *Typee,* to Shaw. If, in marrying Elizabeth Shaw, Melville felt a sense of duty, of the fulfillment of an obligation, he may also have felt a sense of guilt in the commission of an incestuous sin—at least in his unconscious. If Lemuel Shaw acted like a father, Elizabeth must have seemed a sister.

No amount of biographical detail, however large, could grant the insight into Herman Melville's real relationship with his wife which two simple comments in her letters offer. Indeed, in reading these remarks, we have the uncomfortable feeling that we have probed more deeply into their subterranean feelings than the partners in this unusual union ever did themselves. In 1859 Elizabeth wrote to her mother: "Herman has taken to writing poetry. You need not tell any one, for you know how such things get around."[8] In 1876, in a private note secretly enclosed with an innocent letter which she had shown to Herman, Elizabeth wrote to a relative:

[8] Quoted by Howard P. Vincent in his Introduction to *Collected Poems of Herman Melville* (Chicago: Packard & Co., 1947), p. viii.

If ever this dreadful *incubus* of a *book* [*Clarel*] (I call it so because it has undermined all our happiness) gets off Herman's shoulders I do hope he may be in better mental health—but at present I have reason to feel the gravest concern & anxiety about it—to put it in mild phrase—please do not speak of it—you know how such things are exaggerated. . . .[9]

In spite of "Lizzie's" obsessive concern for appearances, in spite of her failure to understand the creative drive that forced the books out of Herman, in spite of the inevitable and trying tensions of their relationship, the marriage did last and must have had its rewarding moments. But it seems unlikely that Melville's marriage gave him, at any time, the intense spiritual and intellectual companionship for which he yearned. The recurring crises of his life, when both his physical and mental health seemed in jeopardy, were probably most frequently precipitated by an acute, if not overwhelming, sense of the deficiency of his few close relationships among family and friends. Whenever he set off on a search, from the time of his first voyages during the early forties through the 1856–1857 tour of the Holy Land, there seemed to lurk somewhere in his psyche the desperate need for the close bonds of friendship.

Outside Melville's fiction the most copiously documented dramatization of such personal need is his meeting with Hawthorne. The relationship of these two writers is perhaps the most curious in all literature. They met when Melville was thirty-one and Hawthorne forty-six, at a time when the Master had just finished his masterpiece, *The Scarlet Letter*, and when the disciple was struggling to finish off his whale, *Moby Dick*. They enjoyed each other's company for some months during 1850–1851 in the Massachusetts countryside and were then separated, to have only one other major—though brief—meeting in 1856 in Liverpool, England. In this relationship the vigorous young Melville seems the pursuer, while the reserved, retiring Hawthorne appears the reluctant object of pursuit. And at the last the younger man had to confess to himself that he was unable to break down the older man's reserve.

A few remarks extracted from the chief documents of this association will suggest the course it ran and something of its subterranean nature. The first document is Melville's famous review, "Hawthorne and His Mosses," which is extravagant in

[9] Eleanor Melville Metcalf, *Herman Melville: Cycle and Epicycle* (Cambridge: Harvard Univ. Press, 1953), p. 237.

its praise, linking Hawthorne and Shakespeare, and making startling confession:

> But already I feel that this Hawthorne has dropped germinous seeds into my soul. He expands and deepens down, the more I contemplate him; and further and further, shoots his strong New England roots into the hot soil in my Southern soul.[10]

If the metaphor seems embarrassingly intimate and unwittingly revealing, it must be recalled that when the shy New Englander acknowledged Melville's praise in his dedication of *Moby Dick* to him, Melville opened his soul in private letter in a manner only hinted at by metaphor in the public review:

> Whence come you, Hawthorne? By what right do you drink from my flagon of life? And when I put it to my lips—lo, they are yours and not mine. I feel that the Godhead is broken up like the bread at the Supper, and that we are the pieces. Hence this infinite fraternity of feeling.[11]

Melville cannot be denied his genius for striking off the right phrase—his "infinite fraternity of feeling" seems precisely right for what he must have felt at least on the conscious level. But there probably were impulses below this level which compelled him to force on Hawthorne the materials for a story concerning one Agatha, a poor woman deserted by her sailor-husband for seventeen years, returning only to assist and then to disappear again. Why this plot should seize Melville's imagination, and, further, why he should insist on Hawthorne's involvement, is fascinating to contemplate. Melville wrote to Hawthorne on the ambiguous point of motivation: "The probable facility with which Robinson first leaves his wife and then takes another, may, possibly, be ascribed to the peculiarly latitudinarian notions, which most sailors have of all tender obligations of that sort."[12] So said Melville the sailor.

Some five or six years after the first fine flowering of their friendship and parting, Melville and Hawthorne came together briefly in Liverpool. The crisis which both must have felt in their relationship does not stand revealed in the journals of either man. Hawthorne, in a long, discursive entry, remarked on their long talks, and offhandedly concluded: "[Melville] has

---

[10] Herman Melville, "Hawthorne and His Mosses," *The Apple-Tree Table and Other Sketches* (Princeton: Princeton Univ. Press, 1922), p. 79.

[11] Metcalf, p. 129.

[12] *Ibid.*, p. 142.

a very high and noble nature, and better worth immortality than most of us."[13] Melville made an abrupt entry of his seaside ramble with Hawthorne: "At Southport. An agreeable day. Took a long walk by the sea. Sands & grass. Wild & desolate. A strong wind. Good talk."[14] But the meeting had far greater impact on Melville than these cryptic remarks reveal. Some twenty years later, Melville turned Hawthorne into Vine in *Clarel,* and related in verse the sad details of his friend's cool rejection of his proffered intimacy.

Melville's farewell to Hawthorne must have been the short lyric, "Monody," which reveals a depth of feeling and a sense of loss rare in the usual friendships of men:

> To have known him, to have loved him
> After loneness long;
> And then to be estranged in life,
> And neither in the wrong;
> And now for death to set his seal—
> Ease me, a little ease, my song!
>
> But wintry hills his hermit-mound
> The sheeted snow-drifts drape,
> And houseless there the snow-bird flits
> Beneath the fir-trees' crape:
> Glazed now with ice the cloistral vine
> That hid the shyest grape.[15]

Though the poem is undated (it was published in *Timoleon* in 1891), it no doubt marks Melville's final insight into the depths of his feeling for Hawthorne—depths which remained largely unexplored and feelings which were ambiguously rebuffed. It is testimony to the strength of Melville's emotions that they demanded imaginative embodiment in a vivid, lyric poem, even after Hawthorne's death. We may safely assume that this sublimation in art granted at least the "little ease" the poet requested.

IV. Adhesiveness and Friendship

As with most artists of genius, however, we know infinitely more about Melville's imaginative than his real life. When we

---

[13] *Ibid.,* p. 161.

[14] Howard C. Horsford, *Journal of a Visit to Europe and the Levant* (Princeton: Princeton Univ. Press, 1955), p. 63.

[15] *Collected Poems of Herman Melville,* ed. Howard P. Vincent, pp. 228–229.

turn from the life to the work in an attempt to isolate and trace through that element we have been discussing, we must remember at every turn that we are examining the theme not in the neurosis of a distraught personality but in works of art. Many rash conclusions have been reached by readers who have assumed the constructed novels to be inadvertent confessions.

In spite of Melville's distaste for Emerson and his ignorance of Whitman, these two transcendentalists shed more light on the fraternal theme in his work than any of the writers he admired. Emerson and Whitman are but two examples from Melville's own time and country; others could be cited—across the sea, Tennyson's *In Memoriam;* or across the centuries, Plato's *Symposium.* But Emerson and Whitman will serve to illustrate the tradition in which Melville was working when he dramatized close comradeship for thematic purposes.

In his essay on "Friendship," Emerson emphasizes the intensity of genuine friendship, and he frequently uses romantic love metaphorically to suggest the qualities of the love of friendship: "I feel as warmly when he [the friend] is praised, as the lover when he hears applause of his engaged maiden." Emerson comments on the universality of the desire for a friend ("every man passes his life in the search after friendship") and distinguishes between the genuine and the superficial: "I hate the prostitution of the name of friendship to signify modish and worldly alliances." Throughout his essay, Emerson stresses spiritual affinity as the essence of friendship. He speaks of "this alliance with my brother's soul" and the "deep peace between two spirits," and he admonishes: "It is foolish to be afraid of making our ties too spiritual."[16]

As Emerson paired his "Friendship" essay with one on "Love," pointing up the distinguishing features in these two profound and related emotions, so Whitman in *Leaves of Grass* followed "Children of Adam," a celebration of the sexual love of man and woman, with "Calamus," a celebration of the spiritual love of comrades. Like Emerson, Whitman speaks of the intensity and impact of the emotion of what he terms "adhesiveness":

[16] Ralph Waldo Emerson, "Friendship," *Essays: First Series* (Boston: Houghton Mifflin Co., 1903–04), pp. 189–217. The first edition appeared in 1841.

> Ethereal, the last athletic reality, my consolation,
> I ascend, I float in the regions of your love O man,
> O sharer of my roving life.

As Emerson spoke of the universal "search after friendship," Whitman celebrates for all the intense "need of comrades." And Whitman frequently lapses into the metaphor, language, or situation of romantic love, as in the concluding lines of "When I Heard at the Close of the Day":

> For the one I love most lay sleeping by me under the same cover
> in the cool night,
> In the stillness in the autumn moonbeams his face was inclined
> toward me,
> And his arm lay lightly around my breast—and that night I
> was happy.

As Emerson stresses the spirituality inherent in friendship, Whitman envisions repeatedly the social, democratic ideal which can develop in a nation devoted to the "life-long love of comrades":

> Yet underneath Socrates clearly see, and underneath Christ the
> divine I see,
> The dear love of man for his comrade, the attraction of friend
> to friend. . . .[17]

In Whitman's philosophy, friendship—or the "Calamus" emotion—was to be the leavening in the eventual rise of democracy.

Melville, if he is to be understood, must be observed in this old-fashioned Victorian setting before he is viewed through the modern Freudian frame. And after he is fully understood, Melville will be granted an insight into the personality and mind of man as deep as any offered by modern psychology.

V. Buddies, Vagabonds, and Savages

Melville's first six novels—*Typee, Omoo, Mardi, Redburn, White Jacket,* and *Moby Dick*—all have in common their dramatization of Whitmanian "Calamus" relationships. Indeed, throughout these works the adhesive relationship assumes greater and greater importance until in *Moby Dick* it has

[17] For variorum readings see Emory Holloway's Inclusive Edition of *Leaves of Grass* (New York: Doubleday, Doran & Co., Inc., 1926).

moved to center stage and is functioning significantly as a major element of theme. In *Typee* and *Omoo*, the narrator, in quest of man's lost Eden, takes along on all his journeys a companion-vagabond. In *Typee* it is Toby, a young fellow-sailor who is "active, ready, and obliging, of dauntless courage"; like the narrator, Toby "had evidently moved in a different sphere of life, and his conversation at times betrayed this." The narrator confesses that he is drawn toward Toby by his "remarkably prepossessing exterior"—"singularly small," "flexibility of limb," "dark complexion," "jetty locks," "large black eyes." Whereas Toby is a picture of dark melancholy, Dr. Long Ghost, the deposed ship's doctor who becomes the buddy of the narrator in *Omoo*, is all bright gaiety: "His personal appearance was remarkable. He was over six feet high—a tower of bones, with a complexion absolutely colorless, fair hair, and a light unscrupulous gray eye, twinkling occasionally with the very devil of mischief." Like Toby, Long Ghost too was from a superior "sphere of life": "he quoted Virgil, and talked of Hobbes and of Malmsbury, besides reading poetry by the canto, especially Hudibras."

In *Omoo*, Melville treats directly an aspect of savage life which was only suggested dramatically in his first book. In a chapter largely devoted to "friendships in Polynesia," he notes that the natives "are in the habit of making bosom friends at the shortest possible notice": "In the annals of the island [Tahiti] are examples of extravagant friendships, unsurpassed by the story of Damon and Pythias: in truth, much more wonderful; for, notwithstanding the devotion—even of life in some cases—to which they led, they were frequently entertained at first sight for some stranger from another island." The narrator in *Omoo* touches quite briefly on two of his "tayos," or close friends. One was "Poky, a handsome youth," who attached himself to the narrator by securing his canoe to the anchored ship, ready to present gifts and run errands, and who became the narrator's "companion and guide" when he went ashore. This indefatigable and wholehearted devotion contrasts with another native's: "Kooloo was a candidate for my friendship; and being a comely youth, quite a buck in his way, I accepted his overtures." But, alas, the depth of Poky's feeling was matched only by the shallowness of Kooloo's. The narrator confesses painfully: "As for Kooloo, after sponging

173

me well, he one morning played the part of a retrograde lover; informing me that his affections had undergone a change; he had fallen in love at first sight with a smart sailor, who had just stepped ashore quite flush from a lucky whaling-cruise."

In *Mardi*, as the vagabond Taji is about ready to jump ship to escape boredom and seek adventure, he looks about for a companion and decides upon one Jarl, who "hailed from the isle of Skye." This primitive, though no savage, has all of the innocence of one. He is ageless, a descendant of Vikings, a "friendless mariner on the main." Though illiterate, he is "an honest, earnest wight; so true and simple, that the secret operations of [his] soul were more inscrutable than the subtle workings of Spinoza's." Taji describes Jarl's devotion as much like that of the savages in *Omoo*—"his loyalty was extreme." In defining his relationship to Jarl, Taji defines the "chummy" system among sailors much as the narrator in *Omoo* described the "extravagant friendships" of Polynesia: "Now this *chummying* among sailors is like the brotherhood subsisting between a brace of collegians (chums) rooming together. It is a Fides-Achates-ship, a league of offence and defence, a co-partnership of chests and toilets, a bond of love and good feeling, and a mutual championship of the absent one." Taji defines the system to explain elaborately that in this partnership, though Jarl may appear to be "chummy the simple" (the drudge or servant), while Taji himself may appear to be "chummy the cunning" (the lazy ne'er-do-well), such is not really the case. Theirs, Taji protests, is genuine chummying of mutual affection.

One of the factors which intensifies the impact of *Redburn* is the hero's isolated, friendless state on this, his very first voyage. He has no tayo, no chummy, no friend. There is no one in whom he can confide, no one to whom he can turn, as the world exposes itself to him in all its rawness, indifference, hostility, wickedness. On the voyage out, Redburn is indeed an Ishmael, a lonely boy alone in the crew. But in Liverpool he discovers Master Harry Bolton: "He was one of those small, but perfectly formed beings, with curling hair, and silken muscles, who seem to have been born in cocoons. His complexion was a mantling brunette, feminine as a girl's; his feet were small; his hands were white; and his eyes were large, black, and womanly; and, poetry aside, his voice was as the sound of a harp." The resemblance to Toby of *Typee* is striking, though Harry seems to be the most effeminate of all Melville's tayos. Encountered in the midst of the wickedness of Liverpool, Harry appears at first as a high gentleman of great misfortune, but soon after as a clever fellow of immense powers of fabrication. The discovery is a blow to Redburn: "I was very sorry for this; as at times it made me feel ill at ease in his company; and made me hold back my whole soul from him; when, in its loneliness, it was yearning to throw itself into the unbounded bosom of some immaculate friend." But Redburn does not hold back entirely, and his relationship with Harry is a source of much pleasure on the return voyage; and the final pages of the book go far out of their way to relate the subsequent and poignant death of Harry Bolton on a whaling voyage.

In *White Jacket*, the hero discovers in Jack Chase the "immaculate friend" that Redburn sought; and, indeed, White Jacket does not restrain his soul, but allows it to "throw itself" whole into Chase's "unbounded bosom." Chase appears as masculine as Bolton seemed feminine: "He was a Briton, and a true-blue; tall and well-knit, with a clear open eye, a fine broad brow, and an abounding nut-brown beard. No man ever had a better heart or a bolder." Like Toby and Long Ghost, Jack Chase had read widely and remembered much: "Jack had read all the verses of Byron, and all the romances of Scott. He talked of Rob Roy, Don Juan, and Pelham; Macbeth and Ulysses; but, above all things, was an admirer of Camoens. Parts of *The Lusiad* he could recite in the original." White Jacket comments simply, "from the outset Jack and I were fast friends." When, at the end of the voyage, he bids Jack Chase farewell, he does not dismiss him from memory. Indeed, the "matchless and unmatchable Jack Chase" endures a lifetime in Melville's memory, to make a final appearance on the dedication page of the old sailor's last novel, *Billy Budd*.

At the opening of *Moby Dick*, Ishmael, the narrator, confesses his isolation from the human race. With a "damp, drizzly November" in his soul, he decides to go to sea. And it is in the process of obtaining a berth that the friendless Ishmael discovers a comrade—but only after a quite unpromising beginning. At the Spouter-Inn, Ishmael is terror-stricken as he learns that his bedmate is the hideous, cabalistically tattooed savage, Quee-queg. After the first chill of the initial encounter subsides and Ishmael gets a better look at the object of his horror, he decides that Queequeg is, after all, a "clean, comely looking cannibal," and concludes that it is better to "sleep with a sober cannibal than a drunken Christian." The night passes peacefully, and Ishmael wakes the next morning affectionately locked in the "bridegroom clasp" of his savage bedmate.

From this point on the bond between Queequeg and Ishmael broadens and deepens, and after a day together highlighted by Father Mapple's sermon they retire to their room for talk and meditation. In the intimate privacy of their shared room, Ish-mael confesses: "I began to be sensible of strange feelings. I felt a melting in me. No more my splintered heart and maddened hand were turned against the wolfish world." After a "social smoke" from Queequeg's pipe, the savage suddenly proposes a lifelong bond and immediately performs the ceremony: "he pressed his forehead against mine, clasped me round the waist, and said that henceforth we were married; meaning, in his country's phrase, that we were bosom friends; he would gladly die for me, if need should be." After this symbolic marriage, Ishmael and Queequeg lie chatting in bed. Ishmael closes the scene: "Thus, then, in our hearts' honeymoon, lay I and Quee-queg—a cosy, loving pair."

Throughout the development of this remarkable relation-ship, Melville is as consistent in his metaphor and symbolism as a metaphysical poet. He uses the imagery of courtship and romantic love repeatedly to suggest the complexity and pro-fundity of the spiritual tie which binds cannibal and Christian into an ever more intimate knot of understanding. The climax comes with the symbolic marriage and honeymoon. Although the friendship reaches its "sudden flame" early in *Moby Dick*, the reader is constantly aware of its silent, but felt, presence throughout, as the self-isolated Ahab directs his monomaniacal search for the white whale. It comes to the fore in the mon-key-rope scene, in which Ishmael and Queequeg find them-selves and their fates tied together, and, at the very end of the book, it surges to the surface of the sea in the form of a coffin, the dead Queequeg's gift of life to the gasping, floundering Ishmael.

VI. Illusions of Youth, Realities of Age

Melville must have sensed that in *Moby Dick* he had exploited to the limits of meaning the deep and intensely felt attachment of adhesiveness or comradeship. Although he had dramatized such relationships in all of his first books, after *Moby Dick* he never portrayed precisely the same kind of companionship again. It is as though the magnificent construction of the Queequeg-Ishmael symbolism had exhausted his imagination on this once favorite theme.

But though he did not again use the "sudden flame of friendship" symbolically and thematically, he did explore its implications and ramifications, its origin, nature, and effect, more minutely. After *Moby Dick* Melville seems to have shifted his focus from man's knowledge of the universe to man's knowledge of self. In short, beginning with *Pierre*, Melville appears to have become much more of a psychological novelist.

There are in *Pierre*, as evidence of this shift, powerfully convincing treatments of intricate and delicately balanced mother-son and sister-brother relationships. And there appears also, almost casually, an account of the intense "love-friendship" of boys. Pierre and his cousin Glen Stanly "had cherished a much more than cousinly attachment": "At the age of ten, they had furnished an example of the truth, that the friendship of fine-hearted, generous boys, nurtured amid the romance-engendering comforts and elegancies of life, sometimes transcends the bounds of mere boyishness, and revels for a while in the empyrean of a love which only comes short, by one degree, of the sweetest sentiment entertained between the sexes." This boy-love parallels in many of its manifestations the love of man and woman: "Jealousies are felt. The sight of another lad too much consorting with the boy's beloved object, shall fill him with emotions akin to those of Othello's; a fancied slight, or lessening of the every-day indications of warm feelings, shall prompt him to bitter upbraidings and reproaches; or shall plunge him into evil moods, for which grim solitude only is congenial."

After portraying the adult Pierre in the act of destroying the full, voluminous, ardent correspondence of his youthful attachment, Melville describes the gradual subsidence of this adolescent love: "But as the advancing fruit itself extrudes the beautiful blossom, so in many cases, does the eventual love for the other sex forever dismiss the preliminary love-friendship of boys. The mere outer friendship may in some degree—greater or less—survive; but the singular love in it has perishingly dropped away." As Pierre's love for his affianced Lucy grew, so his "ardent sentiment" for Glen had diminished. And likewise, cousin Glen's mature and wandering eye, during his travels in France and Italy, had no doubt lit on feminine loveliness, and Pierre had lingered less and less clearly in his memory. Melville makes it clear that the change, though perhaps natural and inevitable, is a loss: "All round and round does the world lie as in a sharp-shooter's ambush, to pick off the beautiful illusions of youth, by the pitiless cracking rifles of the realities of the age." The rifles crack indeed in *Pierre* as what was once ardent love turns to hot hate between the two cousins, resulting, finally, in death for both.

There seems little doubt that this adolescent love, characteristic of a civilization or society which allows for the "elegancies of life," closely resembles the intense and sudden friendships of the primitive societies of Polynesia. Melville seems, in defining this emotion, to be thus linking the civilized child with the savage adult, two individuals whose unsophisticated feelings have frequently been connected and praised for their refreshing innocence.

Israel Potter, like Pierre, is largely free of the friendship motif, for one of the book's points is that the protagonist lives a long life of loneliness and friendlessness. There is one relationship that develops, however, which is reminiscent of the earlier books. In his Revolutionary War adventures, Israel at one point finds himself serving on John Paul Jones's ship. Jones, who confesses that "number one cannot but be lonely," is attracted to Israel by the very magnitude of his misfortunes: "[Jones's] wild, lonely heart, incapable of sympathising with cuddled natures made humdrum by long exemption from pain, was yet drawn toward a being, who in desperation of friendlessness, something like his own, had so fiercely waged battles against tyrannical odds." But though this scene reminds the reader of Melville's earlier companionships, the John Paul

Jones–Israel Potter relationship never really becomes the central drama of this historical novel. Melville seems, throughout the treatment of Jones, primarily interested in the intricate psychology of a national hero.

Although there is some discussion of the nature of friendship in the Winsome-Egbert scenes of *The Confidence Man*, Melville seems bent more on probing psyches than in exploring the communion of souls. And in his last novel, *Billy Budd* (although he addresses his dedication to Jack Chase), in his development of the characters Melville seems more the psychologist than the dramatist. Although Claggart of *Billy Budd* has as his ancestor the evil master-at-arms of *White Jacket*, Claggart's attitude toward Billy corresponds more closely to Jackson's attitude toward the naïve protagonist of *Redburn* (Redburn explained Jackson's malevolence: "For I was young and handsome . . . whereas *he* was being consumed by an incurable malady. . . ."). In analyzing the masked hostility Claggart holds for Billy, Melville explains that though Claggart is "well moulded," Billy is "heroic" in appearance; and the origin of the antipathy lies in Billy's "significant personal beauty," though ultimately the strange hatred becomes much more complex. In many respects, Billy bears physical resemblance to Harry Bolton of *Redburn:* both are described frequently by feminine metaphor. Billy's complexion is "all but feminine in purity" and he goes by the nickname "Baby Budd."

In probing the personalities of Claggart and Budd, Melville seems to discover the reverse of the primitive phenomenon of the "sudden flame of friendship": the hot fire of hate. The two emotions seem, indeed, similarly complicated and intricate in origin, and not, ultimately, unrelated. That there might be some obscure connection was suggested by Melville in *Pierre*, when he portrayed the friendship of Glen and Pierre transforming itself into violent enmity.

VII. The Soul's Caress

Although after *Moby Dick* Melville largely abandoned the comradeship theme in his fiction, he turned to it in his narrative poem, *Clarel*, that long, sometimes tedious, sometimes fascinating tale of an agonized quest for faith. But in *Clarel*, the search for a comrade seems part of the basic quest, not merely a kind of accidental if fortunate accompaniment, as in *Typee* or *White Jacket*.

In the first book of the poem, a profound depth of understanding develops between Clarel, the young protagonist student who is wandering the streets of Jerusalem, and a young monk, Celio, who is shaken by secret doubts. As they pass on one occasion, an exchange of glances instantly informs them that they are brothers bound by a "tie of spirit." Celio is described:

> Young he was,
> With crescent forehead—but alas,
> Of frame misshaped. Word spake he none,
> But vaguely hovered, as may one
> Not first who would accost, but deep
> Under reserve the wish may keep.
> Ere Clarel, here embarrassed grown,
> Made recognition, the Unknown
> Compressed his lips, turned, and was gone.
> Mutely for moment, face met face:
> But more perchance between the two
> Was interchanged than e'en may pass
> In many a worded interview.

This strangely silent relationship develops throughout Book I of *Clarel* but comes to a sudden stop with Celio's death. Though no word has passed between them, Clarel visits Celio's grave—the grave of a comrade in doubt—for a final farewell.

By the time of Celio's death, another character, Vine, convincingly identified with Hawthorne, has already entered the scene—in a sense to take over Celio's role. Vine is appropriately introduced in a canto entitled "The Recluse." He is apart, isolated, withdrawn:

> Like to the nunnery's denizen
> His virgin soul communed with men
> But thro' the wicket.

As to Celio, Clarel is attracted to Vine's shy, retiring nature. In his self-contained and independent posture appear to exist the long sought faith and wisdom:

> Pure as the rain
> Which diamondeth with lucid grain
> The white swan in the April hours
> Floating between two sunny showers

180

> Upon the lake, while buds unroll;
> So pure, so virginal in shrine
> Of true unworldliness looked Vine.

On the occasion on which Clarel sees him in this state of purity, he suddenly forgets past rebuffs as he longs for some response:

> Ah, clear sweet ether of the soul
> (Mused Clarel), holding him in view.
> Prior advances unreturned
> Not here he recked of, while he yearned—
> Oh, now but for communion true
> And close; let go each alien theme;
> Give me thyself!

Impelled by this strong desire for "communion," Clarel approaches Vine, who rambles on in conversation unaware of Clarel's "thrill/Of personal longing."

Clarel, agitated ("Divided mind knew Clarel here;/The heart's desire did interfere"), though he cannot speak, thinks to himself:

> How pleasant in another
> Such sallies, or in thee, if said
> After confidings that should wed
> Our souls in one: —Ah, call me *brother!*—
> So feminine his passionate mood
> Which, long as hungering unfed,
> All else rejected or withstood.

Finally finding the courage to speak, Clarel lets fall "some inklings." Immediately there is a change in Vine's attitude:

> Here over Vine there slid a change—
> A shadow, such as thin may show
> Gliding along the mountain-range
> And deepening in the gorge below.

Vine rebukes Clarel, first for his inability to live alone with his doubts—

> Lives none can help ye; that believe.
> Art thou the first soul tried by doubt?
> Shalt prove the last? Go, live it out.

Then Vine turns to that deeper yearning in Clarel:

> But for thy fonder dream of love
> In man toward man—the soul's caress—

> The negatives of flesh should prove
> Analogies of non-cordialness
> In spirit.

Thus speaks the aloof and coolly independent Vine. And Clarel, after this rebuff, tells himself in self-reproof—"sick these feelings are." And he begins to feel pangs of conscience that he could have felt such yearnings in his soul when his heart should have been full of his betrothed left behind in Jerusalem:

> How findest place within thy heart
> For such solicitudes apart
> From Ruth?—Self-taxings.

Unlike Ishmael, who does discover the "soul's caress" with his pagan companion Queequeg, Clarel is left to struggle alone in the isolation of his solitary soul with his doubts and his loneliness. But ultimately both Ishmael and Clarel are left alone, Ishmael on Queequeg's coffin in the middle of the wide Pacific, Clarel amidst the nameless throngs on the *Via Crucis* in Jerusalem. After Clarel has received news of the death of Ruth comes the time for parting from the companions on the journey. Vine is the first to make his farewell to the saddened Clarel:

> From Vine he caught new sense
> Developed through fate's pertinence.
> Friendly they tarried—blameless went:
> Life, avaricious, still demands
> Her own, and more; the world is rent
> With partings.

Clarel's knowledge, at the end of his journey cannot be far different from Ishamel's, lone survivor of the *Pequod's* catastrophe. Both have insight into the full significance and high rewards of genuinely deep human relationship, and both know the profound wisdom of loss.

VIII. The Measure of Melville

For the reader who would psychoanalyze the recurring dramatization of close male relationships in Melville, there is much related material scattered throughout his work that must be weighed. There is the shock of young Tommo in *Typee* at the looseness of his fellow-sailors as they sport on board ship with the pagan Polynesian maidens. And there is Tommo's own charming encounter and sexual initiation with the beautiful but unbelievable Fayaway in Typee valley. In *Mardi* there is the desperate Taji torn between the dark, evil, sexually alluring Hautia, and the light, ethereal, spiritually appealing Yillah. Redburn's horror upon witnessing the infinite variety of vice in Liverpool is similar to White Jacket's on discovering the depths of depravity on a man-of-war. White Jacket ventures closer than any of Melville's other Young Seekers to setting forth the shocking details of perverse behavior:

What too many seamen are when ashore is very well known; but what some of them become when completely cut off from shore indulgences can hardly be imagined by landsmen. The sins for which the cities of the plain were overthrown still linger in some of these wooden-walled Gomorrahs of the deep. More than once complaints were made at the mast in the Neversink, from which the deck officer would turn away with loathing, refuse to hear them, and command the complainant out of his sight. There are evils in men-of-war, which, like the suppressed domestic drama of Horace Walpole, will neither bear representing, nor reading, and will hardly bear thinking of. The landsman who has neither read Walpole's *Mysterious Mother,* nor Sophocles's *Oedipus Tyrannus,* nor the Roman story of *Count Cenci,* dramatized by Shelley, let that landsman guardedly remain in his ignorance of even worse horrors than these, and forever abstain from seeking to draw aside this veil.

Ironically enough, Melville was to produce a work of his own—*Pierre*—which would link his name with the Sophocles of *Oedipus* and the Shelley of *Cenci. Pierre's* portrayal of the protagonist's complex attitude toward his mother, Mrs. Glendinning, and his only half-conscious feelings for his half-sister, Isabel, places Melville squarely in the tradition of those authors who have dared to deal with the intricate and agonized aberrations of human behavior.

Indeed, there is much in Melville that the amateur analyst must ultimately take into account. He would certainly not want to leave out some treatment of "The Paradise of Bachelors and The Tartarus of Maids." If there is some ambiguity about the profundity of the pleasures the bachelors enjoy in the first of this pair of sketches, there can be no doubt as to the absurdity and monstrosity of the female reproductive process as symbolized by the strange operations of a paper factory in the second.

And, too, among the works which must be scrutinized by the reader-psychologist is "After the Pleasure Party." This poem presents a middle-aged woman, who, having abandoned love in her youth in order to devote herself to intellectual pursuits, suddenly realizes that sex cannot be suppressed:

> Now first I feel, what all may ween,
> That soon or late, if faded e'en,
> One's sex asserts itself. Desire,
> The dear desire through love to sway,
> Is like the Geysers that aspire—
> Through cold obstruction win their fervid way.

In her meditations the woman conceives of the origins of sex in somewhat the same terms as Aristophanes in Plato's *Symposium:*

> Could I remake me! or set free
> This sexless bound in sex, then plunge
> Deeper than Sappho, in a lunge
> Piercing Pan's paramount mystery!
> For, Nature, in no shallow surge
> Against thee either sex may urge,
> Why hast thou made us but in halves—
> Co-relatives? This makes us slaves.
> If these co-relatives never meet
> Self-hood itself seems incomplete.
> And such the dicing of blind fate
> Few matching halves here meet and mate.
> What Cosmic jest or Anarch blunder
> The human integral clove asunder
> And shied the fractions through life's gate?

Regardless of the woman's eloquent plea for freedom from passion, she knows, finally, that she must endure the ignoble resurgence of her suppressed emotions: "Nothing may help or heal/While Amor incensed remembers wrong."

All of these elements in Melville's work, and many more too, allow for a multitude of conclusions about Melville's personality—many of them already quickly reached by easygoing amateur analysts who have read their Freud in haste and spun their theories in leisure. In receiving this curious scrutiny, Melville takes his place in an honored company—Poe, whose Oedipus complex any child can detect; Whitman, whose sexual ambivalence is common gossip; Emily Dickinson, now vying with Sappho in reputation, and not through her poetry alone; Henry James and Mark Twain, the secret of whose work is easily explained away, the first by his "obscure hurt," the second by his prudish wife.

It is time, however, to insist that the work of these writers, and Melville's, be read as they wrote it—as art, not as neurosis; as fiction, not as biography. All of the themes that Melville treats, whether involving the relationships of man and man, man and woman, or man and God, whether embracing matters material, sexual, or celestial, are testimony to the complexity of his vision. We should attempt to measure the scope and profundity of that vision by deep diving, not splatter it with the sediment scraped from the bottom of our own shallow souls.

12

Hawthorne and Melville:
No! in Thunder

With Hawthorne and Melville, questions of religion have usually—and unfortunately—been resolved into questions of belief. And any number of critics have attempted to summarize the religious convictions of the two novelists. Like the philosophy of Shakespeare, the credos of Hawthorne and Melville have been extracted from imaginative writing that is by its nature non-philosophical and uncreedal. As a result, there has been little agreement about their religious belief.

In the case of Hawthorne, for example, Malcolm Cowley has written:

Out of his inner struggles and his sense of guilt, Hawthorne evolved a sort of theology that was personal to himself, but was at the same time deeply Christian and on most points orthodox. He believed in original sin, which consisted, so he thought, in the self-centeredness of each individual. He believed in predestination, as the Calvinists did; but at the same time he had a faith in the value of confession and absolution that sometimes brought him close to Roman Catholicism. He believed in his own unworthiness and in the universal brotherhood of men, based on their weakness before God. He believed in Providence, to which he submitted himself humbly, and he believed in a future life where the guilty would be punished, if only by self-knowledge of their sins.[1]

Mr. Cowley bases his claims for this detailed outline of Hawthorne's theological beliefs on a reading of the "symbols" of his stories and novels. Because Hawthorne expressed himself

[1] Malcolm Cowley, *The Portable Hawthorne* (New York: Viking Press, 1948), p. 13.

not philosophically but "in terms of symbols," he was "closer to the modern mind," Mr. Cowley concludes.

Two more recent writers, Hyatt H. Waggoner and Hubert Hoeltje, reduce Cowley's claims considerably. Mr. Waggoner writes of Hawthorne:

He had no church, though his family had been Unitarian, and he never formulated his religious thought in precise doctrines. Indeed, as an antirationalist he resisted, for reasons both temperamental and principled, the theologian's efforts to achieve clarity in such matters. Nevertheless, Hubert Hoeltje is undoubtedly right so far as he goes in his summary of the religious beliefs that Hawthorne consciously held: "His . . . religious beliefs were limited to a few points, never systematically stated. He had a sure faith in Providence. . . . He thought of Jesus as the Redeemer of mankind, though in what sense explicitly he seems not to have recorded. . . . He had, finally, an unwavering belief in the immortality of the soul."[2]

After presenting his outline of Hawthorne's theology, Waggoner hastens to point out that it does little to aid an understanding of Hawthorne's work, and, indeed, serves well to illustrate that "art has other sources besides conscious belief."

In the case of Melville, the controversy over religious belief has been more violent. The body of Melville's work does not seem to have the consistency that Hawthorne's has: different books yield different theologies. In *Melville's Religious Thought* (1943), William Braswell said that Meville's "inherited theological cast of mind and the religious atmosphere that he was reared in would have made indifference [to religious matters] on his part out of the ordinary."[3] He then attempted to trace Melville's fluctuating religious beliefs, from his early orthodoxy through his doubt and skepticism to an uneasy peace. Ronald Mason, by assuming the centrality of the conclusion of *Clarel*, argued in *Spirit above the Dust* (1951) that Melville's views did not, ultimately, vary in any radical way from the conventionally Christian. Lawrence Thompson, by digging deep beneath the surface of Melville's bland prose, claimed in *Melville's Quarrel with God* (1952) that although

[2] Hyatt H. Waggoner, *Hawthorne: A Critical Study* (rev. ed., Cambridge: Harvard Univ. Press, 1963), p. 14. Quoted is Hubert Hoeltje, *Inward Sky: The Mind and Heart of Nathaniel Hawthorne* (Durham, N.C.: Duke Univ. Press, 1962), pp. 460–1.

[3] William Braswell, *Melville's Religious Thought* (Durham, N.C.: Duke Univ. Press, 1943), p. 4.

Melville attempted to hide his meaning from the heresy hunters, he was actually in violent rebellion (like Ahab) against the injustices of a Calvinistic God. Milton R. Stern, by demonstrating in Melville's books a belief in an absolute naturalism, claimed in *The Fine Hammered Steel of Herman Melville* (1957) that Melville (unlike Ahab) had no impulse to rebel against a God that is a "zero thing" or "nothing itself."

Although these theological accounts of Hawthorne and Melville tend to differ fundamentally, there is good reason for bringing these two major authors together in a discussion of religion. Their personal encounter in 1850 when they discovered they were living near each other in the Berkshires (in Massachusetts) resulted in an intense friendship that revealed more to themselves and each other (and to us) than any other relationship in the lives of either. From the happy time of picnics and parties, afternoons and evenings of hearty and serious talk, during the early 1850's, until the time of their apparently strained last encounter in Liverpool in 1856, they sounded each other's beings to depths never before plumbed. Hawthorne was the master, and Melville the ardent disciple, but each found in the other a way out of the labyrinths of his own reticence and shyness. In the meager record that they left of this relationship, what they said of each other is both puzzling and penetrating.

In the most important book review in American literature, "Hawthorne and His Mosses," 1850, Melville wrote of the Puritanic gloom in Hawthorne—"this great power of blackness in him derives its force from its appeals to that Calvinistic sense of Innate Depravity and Original Sin, from whose visitations, in some shape or other, no deeply thinking mind is always and wholly free."[4] As the key example of this blackness, Melville cited "Young Goodman Brown," a story which, he said, will yield its profundities only to the deep diver. The perceptive reader discovers his own plight reflected in Young Goodman Brown's: ". . . with Young Goodman, too, in allegorical pursuit of his Puritan wife, you cry out in your anguish: ' "Faith!" shouted Goodman Brown, in a voice of agony

---

[4] This review has been reprinted in innumerable volumes. The text is taken here from *Herman Melville, Billy Budd and Other Prose Pieces* (New York: Russell & Russell, Inc., 1963), pp. 123–143.

and desperation; and the echoes of the forest mocked him, crying,—"Faith! Faith!" as if bewildered wretches were seeking her all through the wilderness.'" Melville's capsule statement of the effect of Hawthorne's story is important as a gloss on his sweeping view of Hawthorne's major meaning—his dark power. In short, Melville suggests, Hawthorne's pervading gloom is summed up in the image of mankind wandering in a wilderness, crying out for faith but continually confronted and confounded by his own and the universal wickedness.

Some months after publishing "Hawthorne and His Mosses," after coming to know Hawthorne as a friend, Melville read *The House of the Seven Gables* (1851) and wrote Hawthorne a letter that sounds like an extension of his review:

> There is a certain tragic phase of humanity which, in our opinion, was never more powerfully embodied than by Hawthorne. We mean the tragedies of human thought in its own unbiassed, native, and profounder workings. We think that into no recorded mind has the intense feeling of the visible truth ever entered more deeply than into this man's. By visible truth, we mean the apprehension of the absolute condition of present things as they strike the eye of the man who fears them not, though they do their worst to him,—the man who, like Russia or the British Empire, declares himself a sovereign nature (in himself) amid the powers of heaven, hell, and earth.[5]

The remarkable thing about this letter is that it attributes to Hawthorne a kind of transcendental position beyond theological commitment. And the letter goes on with remarkable impertinence to divinity: "We incline to think that God cannot explain His own secrets, and that He would like a little information upon certain points Himself. We mortals astonish Him as much as He us." Here, of course, Melville has identified himself with Hawthorne's thought so closely that he falls easily into the first person plural. The "grand truth" of Hawthorne, concludes Melville, is that "He says No! in thunder; but the Devil himself cannot make him say *yes*."

Just what is it that Hawthorne thunders *No!* to? Does Melville mean that Hawthorne is defying—or denying—God? Not quite, I think. "All men who say no . . . cross the frontiers into Eternity with nothing but a carpet-bag,—that is to say, the Ego. Whereas those yes-gentry, they travel with heaps of baggage, and, damn them! they will never get through the

[5] Merrell R. Davis and William H. Gilman, Eds., *The Letters of Herman Melville* (New Haven: Yale Univ. Press, 1960), pp. 124–125.

189

Custom House." The difference appears to be, then, not between atheist and Christian, but between the searching man of inquiring faith and the satisfied man of dogmatic faith. The atheist would be committed to dogma as much as the complacent Christian. No dogmatist, whatever his commitment, would wish to explore the "visible world" to discover the "absolute condition of present things" as does Hawthorne. He would look at the world through the reflecting fog of his dogma. Hawthorne sees the visible world in all its darkness, and, like Goodman Brown, cries out in the wilderness for faith.

At least so Melville believes. It would be valuable to have Hawthorne's response to this analysis of himself, but his side of the correspondence does not survive. Although it has been the custom to read Melville's remarkable letter as more revelatory of Melville than of Hawthorne, I would like to suggest that Melville ferreted out Hawthorne's deeper meanings more perceptively than later critics have granted. And in addition to Hawthorne's work, Melville had the advantage of those long conversations with his friend—conversations that must have offered insights available to no other critic.

When Melville made his last brief visit with Hawthorne in Liverpool in 1856, the two friends took a long walk along the sandy coast. Hawthorne recorded the incident in his journal in a well-known passage that has been read as an acute analysis of Melville. In this case, I would like to suggest that the account reveals as much about its author as it does its subject:

Melville, as he always does, began to reason of Providence and futurity, and of everything that lies beyond human ken, and informed me that he had 'pretty much made up his mind to be annihilated'; but still he does not seem to rest in that anticipation; and, I think, will never rest until he gets hold of a definite belief. It is strange how he persists—and has persisted ever since I knew him, and probably long before—in wandering to-and-fro over these deserts, as dismal and monotonous as the sand hills amid which we were sitting. He can neither believe, nor be comfortable in his unbelief; and he is too honest and courageous not to try to do one or the other. If he were a religious man, he would be one of the most truly religious and reverential; he has a very high and noble nature, and better worth immortality than most of us.[6]

If Hawthorne were as orthodoxly faithful as some modern critics have said, it is strange that he did not attempt to per-

[6] Newton Arvin, *The Heart of Hawthorne's Journals* (Boston: Houghton Mifflin Co., 1929), pp. 230–231.

190

suade his friend of the virtues of the way of belief. The tone of the passage, however, suggests not so much a commitment in Hawthorne as a kind of theological neutrality between belief and unbelief. And his use of the image of the desert, "dismal and monotonous," for the grounds in between the poles of commitment—barren grounds over which Melville has spent his life wandering—reveals much of Hawthorne's distaste for fruitless theological debate.[7]

In short, Hawthorne seems to be critical of Melville for not being able to achieve what Keats called *Negative Capability*— "capable of being in uncertainties, mysteries, doubts, without any irritable reaching after fact and reason."[8] Hawthorne himself seems suspended between commitments—and comfortable in his suspension. Melville, also suspended, can find no rest. Herein lies the essential similarity and difference in the two men—the magnet that drew them together, and the irritant that kept them apart.

The commitments historically and biographically available to the two writers were clear enough. Hawthorne in delving into his family's past in Salem found staring back at him the Calvinistic dogmas of his ancestors. Melville inherited through his mother the Calvinistic beliefs of her Dutch Reformed faith. But at their moment in history, faith of every kind was in flight before rationalism and science. The intellectual trend was away from the Calvinistic past to the Unitarian present, with a Transcendental cloud suspended like the Oversoul over the theological battleground. Hawthorne and Melville could see, imprisoned in the dogmas of Calvinism, profound truths which they felt they must free. But they found in the Unitarianism and Transcendentalism everywhere around them many useful, even indispensable, concepts submerged in the cloudy rhetoric and fuzzy vision. And, to further complicate their choices,

[7] Hyatt H. Waggoner has also suggested that Hawthorne's comment revealed much of his own attitude: "Apart from the value of this as a wonderful revelation of Melville, there are in it, it seems to me, both overt and covert revelations of Hawthorne's own religious commitments. . . . But does one whose religious faith is firm consider discussion of ultimate questions of faith to be like wandering over 'deserts' that are 'dismal' and 'monotonous'?" (*Hawthorne: A Critical Study*, p. 242).

[8] Maurice Buxton Forman, *The Letters of John Keats* (4th ed.; New York: Oxford Univ. Press, 1952), p. 71.

they had available to them the "visible truth" of the "absolute condition of present things" by simple observation of themselves and their worlds—the psychological truth waiting in everyman merely to be mined, truths which no theology (or social science) had yet definitively explored. It was the genius of both writers, in their work if not in their lives, to suspend belief and follow truth wherever it led.

Randall Stewart seems to oversimplify the matter when, in *American Literature and Christian Doctrine*, he says of the "counter-romantics" Hawthorne and Melville (and Henry James), "They side with the orthodox, traditional Christian view of man and the world." In this assertion, Stewart does not posit some subtly sophisticated definition of the orthodox. His outline of Christian belief is both refreshingly frank and useful:

Whether one's standpoint is Calvinist or Arminian, Puritan or non-Puritan, Protestant, Anglican, or Catholic, there are the following basic assumptions: (1) the sovereignty of God (God is infinitely wise, powerful, loving, and just, and is truly sovereign in His world); (2) the divinity of Christ (Jesus is the only begotten Son of God); (3) Original Sin (the natural man is imperfect, fallible, prone to evil); (4) the atonement (natural man is redeemed through faith in the efficacy of Christ's atoning death; (5) the inspiration of the Scriptures (the Bible is God's revealed Word). Surely these doctrines broadly considered, constitute an unimpeachable Christian orthodoxy.[9]

There is not one of these points of doctrine to which the work of Hawthorne or Melville yields an unqualified, open, and clear affirmation. Perhaps the most directly applicable to their fictions is Original Sin—but it is by no means certain that theirs was an orthodox view of this complex idea. The other points are, in the main, simply not relevant to the conflicts and tensions central to their work. Hawthorne and Melville, then, were not religious or theological writers so much as psychological writers. They did not portray belief in order to convert readers; on the contrary, they asked the readers to observe with them the astonishing way characters of a variety of beliefs (or unbeliefs) behaved in a variety of circumstances. By this essentially dramatic method they were able to explore the subterranean depths of religious allegiances of all kinds and intensities.

[9] Randall Stewart, *American Literature & Christian Doctrine* (Baton Rouge: Louisiana State Univ. Press, 1958), p. 14.

Had Hawthorne and Melville really been conventional in religious belief, surely their work would have borne the unmistakable stamp of orthodoxy. Instead, the critics have been all too uncertain in interpreting their work—and for good reason. Both writers developed strategies to veil their doubts, uncertainties, and dissents: Hawthorne spun out his plots in mystifying ambiguities and Melville enveloped his prose in multiple ironies. At times both writers seem to be playing games with the reader, but at other times their ambiguities and ironies become the very heart of their meaning. For example, Hawthorne never brushes back the curls of Donatello in *The Marble Faun* to let the reader find out for himself whether his ears are pointed and hairy. But much more fundamental to his meaning, he poses through Kenyon a key question explored by the novel's action: "Is sin, then,—which we deem such a dreadful blackness in the universe,—is it, like sorrow, merely an element of human education, through which we struggle to a higher and purer state than we could otherwise have attained?" When Hilda expresses shock at the suggestion, Kenyon cries out, "I never did believe it!" (Chapter L).[10] And the question hovers over the novel's closing pages, unanswered. It is clearly the paradoxical question, in all its ambiguities, that Hawthorne meant as his meaning—not some simple answer that he or his characters can provide.

Similarly Melville runs the gamut of ambiguity in a novel like *Pierre* (whose subtitle is *The Ambiguities*). On the very opening page, when Pierre emerges from his house, "dewily refreshed and spiritualized by sleep," he beholds a veritable paradise: "The verdant trance lay far and wide; and through it nothing came but the brindled kine, dreamily wandering to their pastures, followed, not driven, by ruddy-cheeked, white-footed boys." The very diction (*verdant, kine*) signals the reader that there is more there than meets Pierre's eye—that beneath the placid bliss lies some sinister element ready to erupt. But these verbal ironies are merely a prelude to the book's titanic moral ironies that are soon to proliferate. Pierre, the fool of virtue, throws over his own and the happiness of all those dear to him in order to adhere to an ideal morality—but

[10] Quotations from the novels of Hawthorne and Melville are identified by chapter number in the text in order to simplify reference to any of the many editions of both writers.

in the very sacrifice he is enabled to glut himself on his incestuous lust. The self-sacrifice is transfigured in Pierre's unconscious into the most repulsive and horrible of self-indulgences. What *is* the way of virtue? Where *is* the escape from self? These questions hover mockingly over the book's conclusion—and remain unanswered.

In Hawthorne and Melville, ambiguity and irony are elevated from method into meaning. Neither writer writes from a posture of certainty or a position of dogma. Both are witness to puzzles and enigmas at the heart of life. Their work is more an articulation of the significant moral questions of existence than a formulation of original answers or a restatement of received belief. Their insistence is on the complexity of those questions for which easy answers have all too frequently been provided—by a muddled theology or a sentimental morality. Their masterpieces, *The Scarlet Letter* and *Moby Dick*, may serve to illustrate these generalizations—and may serve not in spite of but because of the critical traditions, in the case of each, of strongly conflicting interpretations. Had Hawthorne and Melville provided easy answers in these central works of their career, there would now be, in all probability, critical unanimity as to their meaning.

Critics of *The Scarlet Letter* have divided into partisans of Hester Prynne and partisans of Arthur Dimmesdale; and there have even, on occasion, been partisans of Roger Chillingworth. It was, of course, Chillingworth who was the original victim, or casualty, of the scarlet sin. But it is generally agreed that, though wronged, he persists in a pursuit of vengeance which makes him the greatest sinner of the lot. Arthur Dimmesdale compounds his sin by concealing his guilt, thereby exhibiting a weakness that makes some readers contemptuous of his manhood. There can be no doubt that he is weak, but his ultimate act of public confession requires a kind of rare courage that commands respect. Orthodox interpretation finds the central meaning of the novel in Dimmesdale's final refusal to run away with Hester, and his turning instead to the public scaffold for baring his scarlet letter and for expiation in death. For after all, had he run away he would simply have been delivering himself and his soul into the hands of Satan in the form of Chillingworth (who pleaded with him not to confess). In this view most of the demands of orthodox Christianity seem met.

But there remain some puzzling problems. For example, there is the strange efficacy of Dimmesdale's sin on his ministry. His spiritual influence on his flock is intensified and his ability to sway his parishioners in the path of good is increased. Paradoxically, evil begets good. But perhaps even more strange is the sympathy the reader feels for Hester's suffering and the admiration he feels for her strength. It is a rare reader who does not sympathize when she exclaims to Dimmesdale— "What we did had a consecration of its own." And her proposal to escape the mean little puritan community makes eminent sense to the modern audience, especially when she bases her proposal largely on the good that Dimmesdale still has in his power to do:

Begin all anew! . . . There is happiness to be enjoyed! There is good to be done! Exchange this false life of thine for a true one. Be, if thy spirit summon thee to such a mission, the teacher and apostle of the red men. . . . Preach! Write! Act! Do anything, save to lie down and die! (Chapter XVII)

Is Hester to be doubly condemned—once for her original sin, and yet again for her willingness to be the instrument of Dimmesdale's total damnation? But, then, Hester never does genuinely repent her sin: her strength lies in the certain knowledge that the act had a "consecration of its own." Through the strength of her character, the act itself was transfigured into the sacrament of marriage: it *was* no sin.

This view is, naturally, religiously unorthodox—but not unusual in an age of transcendentalism, which located divinity within as well as without the individual. But was it Hawthorne's view? The book provides no answer. But the fact remains that our sympathies are stirred by both Hester and Dimmesdale, and our contempt is aroused for the community and for Chillingworth. There is no need, then, finally, to choose between hero and heroine. Both are true to their beings, as they must be, but they differ radically in their psychological identities. Perhaps the best gloss on Hester is found in *The Marble Faun*, in Miriam's comment on Donatello's psychological reaction to *his* sin (the murder, at Miriam's bidding, of her evil persecutor):

Alas! it was a sad mistake! He might have had a kind of bliss in the consequences of this deed, had he been impelled to it by a love vital enough to survive the frenzy of that terrible moment,—mighty enough to make its own law, and justify itself against the natural remorse. (Chapter XXII)

Such was the strength of Hester's love, but not Dimmesdale's. In Hester and Dimmesdale, Hawthorne presents authentic psychological portraits rather than a theological solution to a problem of behavior. The ambiguity—the alternate moralities of the two central characters—*is* the meaning of *The Scarlet Letter*. Either morality alone is a distortion. Together they mirror the moral complexity of the human psyche in encounter with the visible world.

Like *The Scarlet Letter*, *Moby Dick* (dedicated, it should be recalled, to Hawthorne) has inspired contradictory interpretations. There have been partisans of Ahab and partisans of Ishmael, with lesser defenses of Queequeg, Starbuck, and Pip. The most startling misreading, but one that recurs, is the identification of Melville with Ahab. It is true that Ahab's wound is great, and that he has his humanities. But it seems just as true that, by the time Ahab makes his final monomaniacal commitment to Fedallah and the pursuit of Moby Dick to the death, he has forfeited the reader's sympathies. Over against Ahab are set Starbuck and Pip, each achieving some measure of success in dissuading Ahab from his mad pursuit—but each finally failing, and out of some significant weakness. In the case of Starbuck, who is "mere unaided virtue," it is fear for the damnation of his own soul that prevents his stopping Ahab by force when the opportunity with the musket arises—a fear that paralyzes even in the sure knowledge of Ahab's madness leading to the destruction of the *Pequod* and its crew. In the case of Pip, it is a divine insight that has displaced all earthly sense that becomes both his strength and his weakness. Abandoned by Stubb, Pip sinks to the sea's depths, and there: "He saw God's foot upon the treadle of the loom, and spoke it; and therefore his shipmates called him mad. So man's insanity is heaven's sense" (Chapter XCIII). Pip's madness complements Ahab's, and arouses his humanities. But the black boy's possession of "heaven's sense" proves too much of an antithesis to Ahab's deepening commitment to the diabolism of Fedallah and the hellish world he represents.

While both Starbuck and Pip represent, in some sense, the orthodox religious position in the novel, Queequeg and Ishmael are the book's pagans. If Ahab is in rebellion against God while Starbuck and Pip are in league with Him (in one way or another), Queequeg and Ishmael have achieved a neutrality that somehow transcends the battleground. Ishmael both opens and closes the novel; what happens to him in between, though it has little effect on the fate of the *Pequod*, is of the highest significance. On the opening page of the book, Ishmael appears with a "damp, drizzly November" in his soul. His alienation from the world and the universe is as severe as Ahab's will appear later. But the encounter with Queequeg, at first implicit with terror, ultimately transfigures the wanderer Ishmael; he is converted from "Christianity" to paganism—or humanity. His soul restored to a conciliatory, receptive state, he is ready for a voyage of discovery—discovery of the terms of the human condition. Ishmael's education proceeds through the monkey-rope and mat-making episodes to reach a climax in the spermacetti-squeezing scene:

Would that I could keep squeezing that sperm forever! For now, since by many prolonged, repeated experiences, I have perceived that in all cases man must eventually lower, or at least shift, his conceit of attainable felicity; not placing it anywhere in the intellect or the fancy; but in the wife, the heart, the bed, the table, the saddle, the fire-side, the country; now that I have perceived all this, I am ready to squeeze case eternally. (Chapter XCIV)

Ishmael's knowledge, deriving ultimately from his transfiguring love for Queequeg, is not far different from Hester's, growing from her transcendent love for Dimmesdale: it derives from humanity within rather than deity without; it is self-created and self-nourished. Fundamentally existential, it is a human knowledge of human relationships in a world of humanity.

The central tension of *The Scarlet Letter*, developed between the two moralities of Hester and Dimmesdale, is echoed in *Moby Dick* in the two discoveries of Ishmael and Pip. Just as Hawthorne refuses to choose between his two characters, Melville withholds his own judgment from Ishmael and Pip. The reader's sympathies are drawn toward both, and his awareness is enlarged by participation in the newfound knowledge of each. But in both *The Scarlet Letter* and *Moby Dick*, it should be carefully noted, two characters survive: Hester and Ishmael. Chillingworth and Ahab are both destroyed, victims of their own monomania. Dimmesdale and Pip (and Starbuck) die, victims of the subtle weakness that lies hidden in the center of their very strength. Only Hester and Ishmael survive, and in their endurance enact, perhaps, their own somber commentary on what they have discovered in their tragic encounter with experience.

But though Hester and Ishmael call into question any commitment of Hawthorne and Melville to orthodox religious belief, they certainly offer no demonstration that the two authors were committed to Emersonian transcendentalism or Whitmanian optimism. Indeed, critics have long noted in the work of both writers strong satiric thrusts at transcendentalism. Hawthorne in "The Celestial Railroad" and Melville in "Cock-A-Doodle-Doo" offer incisive criticism of the characteristic attitudes of the popular Emersonian philosophy which dominated American thought in the early nineteenth century. But a major error in judging Hawthorne and Melville has been the recurrent reduction of their choices to two: as they were not transcendentalists, at least in the conventional sense, then they must have been Calvinists, at least in some modified sense. In their fables the vivid portrayal of evil as a vital principle in man and the universe seemed to substantiate the hasty conclusion. After all, a cardinal principle of Calvinism was the universality of evil and the innate depravity of man.

It will be recalled that Melville's review of Hawthorne emphasized his "blackness"—"that Calvinistic sense of Innate Depravity and Original Sin, from whose visitations, *in some shape or other*, no deeply thinking mind is always and wholly free." The key modifying terms here I have italicized: *in some shape or other*. The suggestion is clear: there is truth in man's predisposition for evil, but it is a truth which no more confirms than it is confirmed by the religion that asserts it. Hawthorne and Melville have come upon this truth by their independent observation of mankind—by their "deeply thinking" minds. For them, the truth has psychological validity—this is their discovery and the object of their dramatizations. In short, their commitment to the reality of evil may be more a psychological than a religious commitment. They may be looked upon not so much as affirming a religious truth as freeing a psychological truth from its religious imprisonment.

"And though all evils may be assuaged; all evils can not be done away. For evil is the chronic malady of the universe; and checked in one place, breaks forth in another" (Chapter CLXI). This is the great lesson the pilgrims of Melville's *Mardi* learn in Vivenza (the fictional name for the United States). "How sad a truth, if true it were, that man's agelong endeavor for perfection had served only to render him the mockery of the evil principle, from the fatal circumstance of an error at the very root of the matter! The heart, the heart,—there was the little yet boundless sphere wherein existed the original wrong of which the crime and misery of this outward world were merely types." This is the agonizing lesson of Hawthorne's "Earth's Holocaust," in which the bonfire's voracious flames fail to consume all the world's wickedness. These direct statements about the ubiquity of evil may be multiplied from either author; and more important, the theme may be traced through major works by both writers—for example, Melville's *The Confidence Man* or Hawthorne's *The Marble Faun.*

Although Hawthorne and Melville never present the universality of evil as merely a religious truth, but always as a realistic psychological phenomenon of human behavior, both authors make constant use of religious metaphors and symbols in the portrayal of their sinning or wicked men. Satanic imagery abounds. Hawthorne writes in *The Scarlet Letter:* "Had a man seen old Roger Chillingworth, at that moment of his ecstasy [on discovering the scarlet letter on Dimmesdale's breast], he would have had no need to ask how Satan comports himself when a precious human soul is lost to heaven, and won into his kingdom" (Chapter X). And in "Egotism; or, The Bosom Serpent," Hawthorne introduces the dominant image of his story—the Satanic snake—in his title. Melville writes in *Moby Dick,* in preparation for the awesomeness of Fedallah's presence on board the *Pequod,* that on a whaler of that day "Beelzebub himself might climb up the side and step down into the cabin to chat with the captain" (Chapter L) without creating a great stir among the crew—but Fedallah remained "a muffled mystery to the last." And in Melville's *The Confidence Man,* regardless of the various guises in which the title character appears, he recurringly betrays his nature by his gliding and hissing.

The close relationship of the fictional strategy of the two writers is witnessed by the ease with which Melville, in *Billy Budd,* cites Hawthorne's "The Birthmark" as a precedent for his own symbolism: "Though our Handsome Sailor had as much of masculine beauty as one can expect anywhere to see;

nevertheless, like the beautiful woman in one of Hawthorne's minor tales, there was just one thing amiss in him. . . . In this particular [his stutter], Billy was a striking instance that the arch-interpreter, the envious marplot of Eden still has more or less to do with every human consignment to this planet of earth" (Chapter II). There can be little doubt that Billy's stutter and Georgiana's birthmark (the shape of a hand on her cheek) are different manifestations of the same truth; they are the "visible mark of earthly imperfection." In some sense or other, all the characters in Hawthorne and Melville have their birthmarks or their stutters; and these weaknesses and imperfections are frequently attributed to the "arch-interpreter" or Satan: but this does not mean that the two writers automatically believed in the Christian doctrine of Original Sin. What they were dramatizing was the psychological validity of their perception of human nature and the human condition. Convenient at hand was the Satan myth and metaphor; familiar to their readers was the ancient doctrine of original sin. Hawthorne and Melville were not merely substantiating Christian dogma; they were exploring psychological labyrinths and discovering fundamental elements of human nature. The Christian myth, Satan as the serpent, made translation into dramatic action simple and immediately meaningful.

The greatest of all sins in both writers was what Hawthorne called the unpardonable sin. But whereas the orthodox Biblical definition of the sin for which there is no forgiveness is the sin "against the Holy Ghost," Hawthorne and Melville portrayed the sin primarily in secular terms—that is, in terms of human relationships rather than man-God relationships. Hawthorne's Ethan Brand, prototype of the unpardonable sinner in both Hawthorne and Melville, set the pattern: "He had lost his hold of the magnetic chain of humanity. He was no longer a brother-man, opening the chambers or the dungeons of our common nature by the key of holy sympathy, which gave him a right to share in all its secrets; he was now a cold observer, looking on mankind as the subject of his experiment, and, at length, converting man and woman to be his puppets, and pulling the wires that moved them to such degrees of crime as were demanded for his study." Ethan Brand, Roger Chillingworth, Taji, Ahab—these are but a few of the characters who commit the unpardonable sin by breaking the "magnetic chain of humanity" and deliberately violating the hearts of their fellows. In effect what Hawthorne and Melville have done is take the principle Christian sin out of its highly abstracted context and render it in intensely human terms. In short, they have revealed once again the basic psychological validity of a religious truth.[11]

In Randall Stewart's outline of Christian belief, the "sovereignty of God" probably stands next to original sin as a theme of major consideration in the work of Hawthorne and Melville. If Randall Stewart's explanatory gloss on this doctrine is accepted—that "God is infinitely wise, powerful, loving, and just, and is truly sovereign in His world"—it is surely open to question as to whether Hawthorne and Melville may be labeled orthodox in their belief. Here as in other areas of their work touching on religion, there are more questions posed than answers given. And the questions are couched not in metaphysical but relentlessly human terms.

In Melville's remarkable commentary on *The House of the Seven Gables*, in which he praised Hawthorne for saying *No!* in thunder, he linked Hawthorne with himself in saying: "We incline to think that God cannot explain His own secrets." It is important to recall that it is Hawthorne's Clifford, victimized by his own kin and deprived in effect of all normal human happiness, that most deeply engages Melville's sympathy and triggers his wide-ranging speculation about Hawthorne's blackness and its meaning. An examination of *The House of the Seven Gables*, especially in the portrayal of Clifford's tragically and senselessly wasted life, reveals a good many thematic currents that substantiate Melville's interpretation.

As a kind of preparation for the somber note that is going to be struck when Clifford is to enter the novel, Hawthorne writes in an early passage (touched off, in fact, by the oddity in the mean fate of the good Hepzibah):

. . . if we look through all the heroic fortunes of mankind, we shall find this same entanglement of something mean and trivial with whatever is noblest in joy or sorrow. Life is made up of marble and mud. And, without all the deeper trust in a comprehensive sympathy above us, we might hence be led to suspect the insult of a sneer, as well as an immitigable frown, on the iron countenance of fate. What is called

[11] For a full treatment of this subject see "Hawthorne and Melville: The Unpardonable Sin," chapter 13 in this volume.

poetic insight is the gift of discerning, in this sphere of strangely mingled elements, the beauty and the majesty which are compelled to assume a garb so sordid. (Chapter II)

We are likely to be lulled by the conventional and expected, not to say reassuring, reference to the "deeper trust in a comprehensive sympathy above us," a phrase that lubricates the mind so as to propel it smoothly forward over the rocky qualifiers that are immediately placed in its path. But pause and look at those qualifiers: ". . . we might hence be led to suspect the insult of a sneer, as well as an immitigable frown, on the iron countenance of fate." "Sneer"? "Iron countenance of fate"? Is this the vocabulary of a man comfortable in his belief? There is equivocation or irony in the passage, of just the kind that Melville would relish. And in the light of the fate of the characters in the novel, Melville would have assigned the irony to that "comprehensive sympathy" which appears notable for its absence.

And it seems most absent in the fate of poor Clifford. After he is released from prison, the gap between his childish pleasures and his advancing age emphasizes the depth of his deprivations. His past is lost, his future is "blank," and his "Now" seems like a parody of life in its triviality. And there is a vast gulf between his genuine innocence and the terrible blows dealt him by fate—aided by the wickedness of his kinsman. How well does he comprehend his own tragedy:

Clifford saw, it may be, in the mirror of his deeper consciousness, that he was an example and representative of that great class of people whom an inexplicable Providence is continually putting at cross-purposes with the world: breaking what seems its own promise in their nature; withholding their proper food, and setting poison before them for a banquet: and thus—when it might so easily, as one would think, have been adjusted otherwise—making their existence a strangeness, a solitude, and torment. (Chapter X)

This "inexplicable Providence" is not far different from the "iron countenance of fate" which seems to insult with its sneer. But though the judgment here seems both steady and severe, it must be noted that it is introduced with uncertainty—"it may be." However accurate Clifford's inward vision was, it is certain that Melville looked in that interior mirror with him, and generalized from it to Hawthorne's blackness.

Another example of this dark, turbulent undercurrent from *The House of the Seven Gables* will suggest the stoutness of its grip on Hawthorne's imagination. As Clifford whiles away his days in simple pleasures, he watches the passing scenes on the streets. Among these is the procession of the young Italian boy with his monkey and his hand organ. What attracts Clifford's—and Hawthorne's—attention is the company of dancing figures in the organ case. All of life in all its varied activities seems represented in the dance, a blacksmith, a cobbler, a soldier, a drunkard, a scholar, a milkmaid, a miser, and a lover:

Possibly some cynic, at once merry and bitter, had desired to signify, in this pantomimic scene, that we mortals, whatever our business or amusement,—however serious, however trifling,—all dance to one identical tune, and, in spite of our ridiculous activity, bring nothing finally to pass. For the most remarkable aspect of the affair was, that, at the cessation of the music, everybody was petrified, at once, from the most extravagant life into a dead torpor. (Chapter XI)

The bleakness of this scene is unmistakable. The vision penetrates to the essential absurdity of the human condition, the essential meaninglessness of man's activity and man's fate: death is his only end and certainty. Hawthorne seems here on the brink of articulating his most bitter theme—that Melvillean blackness in all its dark despair. But Hawthorne has by no means backed himself into a thematic corner. The passage characteristically opens with an escape—"possibly some cynic" had constructed this amusing showpiece. And further along on the page, Hawthorne shuts off the flight of grim fancy: "Saddest of all, moreover, the lover was none the happier for the maiden's granted kiss! But, rather than swallow this last too acrid ingredient, we reject the whole moral of the show." With this airy dismissal, Hawthorne commits himself to nothing. But the vivid image of the mechanical and grotesque dance of life haunts the remainder of the novel with an intensity and effect not unlike those of the ancestral curse on the Pyncheon mansion.

The bleakness which surges repeatedly to the surface in *The House of the Seven Gables* reappears at a critical moment in Hepzibah's frantic attempt to shield Clifford from old Judge Pyncheon. She tries to pray:

Her faith was too weak; the prayer too heavy to be thus uplifted. It fell back, a lump of lead, upon her heart. It smote her with the wretched conviction that Providence intermeddled not in these petty wrongs of one individual to his fellow, nor had any balm for these little agonies of a solitary soul; but shed its justice, and its mercy, in a broad, sunlike sweep, over half the universe at once. Its vastness made it nothing. (Chapter XVI)

This entire passage is calculated to remind the reader of that macabre dance scene which Clifford had so perceptively witnessed—indifferently controlled by a single hand and motivated by a single tune. But of course Hawthorne does not let Hepzibah's despairing vision stand alone. He adds: "But Hepzibah did not see that, just as there comes a warm sunbeam into every cottage window, so comes a lovebeam of God's care and pity for every separate need." The sentimentality of this view, somewhat sticky in its expression, hints at the ironic. And it is certainly true that the bitter view which it opposes tends to overwhelm it and reduce its meaning to a vague abstraction. One might well ask where God's lovebeam of care and pity was during the long period of Clifford's wasted and suffering years—when he seemed abandoned to his fate by an "inexplicable Providence."

And it is worth noting that Hepzibah's dark thoughts are echoed in *The Marble Faun*, when, near the end of the novel, Kenyon is searching for the lost Hilda. She is so innocent and pure, he thinks, that surely God will protect her:

Providence would keep a little area and atmosphere about her as safe and wholesome as heaven itself, although the flood of perilous iniquity might hem her round, and its black waves hang curling above her head! But these reflections were of slight avail. No doubt they were the religious truth. Yet the ways of Providence are utterly inscrutable; and many a murder has been done, and many an innocent virgin has lifted her white arms, beseeching its aid in her extremity, and all in vain; so that, though Providence is infinitely good and wise,—and perhaps for that very reason,—it may be half an eternity before the great circle of its scheme shall bring us the superabundant recompense for all these sorrows! (Chapter XLV)

Clearly there are two Providences in Hawthorne, one inexplicable and inscrutable, the other manifesting "care and pity for every separate need." The first appears dominant, not only in the exposition but in the action of the drama—where it really counts. In this scene from *The Marble Faun*, Kenyon acknowledges the two Providences, but he finds no comforting reassurance in the "religious truth." Apparently the practical truth is the inscrutability of Providence, and one must act in the light of this practical truth—as Kenyon does.

In view of the prominence of the inexplicable Providence in Hawthorne, Melville's "No! in thunder" comment becomes more comprehensible. Perhaps in his exuberance Melville exaggerates, but he seems to hit his mark accurately when he says of himself and Hawthorne: "We incline to think that God cannot explain His own secrets." Little space need be devoted here to demonstrating this view in Melville's own work. It runs all through such novels as *Moby Dick, Pierre,* and *The Confidence Man.* As Kenyon decides that he must act by a practical rather than a religious truth, so the major characters throughout Melville's novels discover that to live singlemindedly by a religious truth is to court disaster: to live in this world they must, like Kenyon, discover a lower, more immediate truth (in *Pierre,* the Plinlimmon pamphlet labels the two truths the chronometrical and the horological). In *Mardi,* the inscrutability of Providence (or Oro, the Mardian term for God) is made explicitly clear in Babbalanja's vision near the end of the voyage. When Babbalanja puts the paradoxical, almost mocking question that lies at the heart of the work of Hawthorne and Melville,—why does Oro "create the germs that sin and suffer, but to perish," his celestial guide answers: "That . . . is the last mystery which underlieth all the rest. Archangel may not fathom it; that makes of Oro the everlasting mystery he is; that to divulge were to make equal to himself in knowledge all the souls that are; that mystery Oro guards; and none but him may know." (Chapter CLXXXVIII)

In the light of the closeness of attitudes in Melville and Hawthorne, it is perhaps understandable why Melville saw Hawthorne as saying *No!* in thunder. Both writers were saying *No!* in their different ways to easy religious belief which falsified the "visible truth" of worldly experience. Neither writer placed his faith—or the faith of his perceptive characters—in an easy and comfortable and shielded relationship with an "infinitely wise, powerful, loving, and just" God— explicable or inexplicable. But both writers placed their strongest and ultimate faith—and that of their wisest characters—in love, a word curiously omitted from Randall Stewart's outline of fundamental Christian belief. As the greatest—or unpardonable—sin was, according to Hawthorne and Melville, a violation of human relationships (cutting of the "magnetic chain of humanity"), so the greatest good or highest virtue was the obverse—the sanctification of human relationships through a selfless and purifying love. This theme is so strong in both writers that a single example from each should suffice to recall its nature.

In Hawthorne's short story, "The Procession of Life," the author rearranges the categories of mankind according to the kinds of evil they have perpetrated. But when the procession seems to have been completed, including the whole of the human species, Hawthorne turns to one other category—the Good. In this category he brings together all the disparate individuals who have only in common their service to their fellow man. He then generalizes:

We have summoned this various multitude—and, to the credit of our nature, it is a large one—on the principle of Love. It is singular, nevertheless, to remark the shyness that exists among many members of the present class, all of whom we might expect to recognize one another by the free masonry of mutual goodness, and to embrace like brethren, giving God thanks for such various specimens of human excellence. But it is far otherwise. Each sect surrounds its own righteousness with a hedge of thorns. It is difficult for the good Christian to acknowledge the good Pagan; almost impossible for the good Orthodox to grasp the hand of the good Unitarian, leaving to their Creator to settle the matters in dispute, and giving their mutual efforts strongly and trustingly to whatever right thing is too evident to be mistaken.

In this vision, morality is placed above religion. And, indeed, sectarianism is seen as divisive and blinding, even among the good and the worthy. It is notable that Hawthorne includes the Pagan in his category of the good. Love and goodness are not the property of any institution or any belief. Like evil, they are universal—or at least a universal potential. As Hawthorne's principle of evil cannot be narrowed to the Original Sin of Christianity, so his principle of goodness cannot be assigned simply to the New Testament doctrine of brotherly love.

The most explicit dramatization in Melville of this purifying love that pervades all goodness appears in *Moby Dick*—in, significantly, the relationship between a pagan and a Christian, Queequeg and Ishmael. Queequeg is the instrument of the transfiguration, in Ishmael's soul, from a "damp, drizzly November" to a tranquil summer. In the presence of this good savage, Ishmael feels himself change: "I felt a melting in me.

No more my splintered heart and maddened hand were turned against the wolfish world. This soothing savage had redeemed it. There he sat, his very indifference speaking a nature in which there lurked no civilized hypocrisies and bland deceits" (Chapter X). Later in the book, after Ishmael has passed through a number of enlightening experiences, he finds himself—in that crucial scene already cited—squeezing spermacetti and meditating on mankind: "Such an abounding, affectionate, friendly, loving feeling did this avocation beget; that at last I was continually squeezing their hands, and looking up into their eyes sentimentally; as much as to say,—Oh! my dear fellow beings, why should we longer cherish any social acerbities, or know the slightest ill-humor or envy! Come; let us squeeze hands all round; nay, let us all squeeze ourselves into each other; let us squeeze ourselves universally into the very milk and sperm of kindness" (Chapter XCIV). There follows the vision in which Ishmael discovers "attainable felicity" not in the "intellect or the fancy" but "in the wife, the heart, the bed, the table, the saddle, the fire-side, the country." In effect, Ishmael's vision is a vision of Hawthorne's "magnetic chain of humanity," its necessity and its possibility. Man's highest good, as his greatest happiness, derives from love and can be located only in human—not divine—relationships.

The ways of orthodoxy were open to both Hawthorne and Melville during their lifetime, but they avoided these well-beaten roads for the obscure lanes and bypaths. It was the human drama, not theological speculation, that fired their imagination. The truth they discovered and explored in all its labyrinthine complexity was a concrete truth of the human mind and heart, not the abstract truth of theological dogma. That their concrete—or "visible"—truth sometimes paralleled the received truth of Christian doctrine—they themselves often noted. Indeed, they called attention to the parallel through dramatic use of religious myth. Both Satan and Christ figure prominently in the work of both writers, but always as metaphor, never as doctrine. As a matter of fact, it could be cogently argued that Hawthorne's melodramatic Satan, with his horns and fiery eyes, and Melville's saccharine Christ, with his feminine grace and disastrous innocence, are grotesques which owe more to folklore than to genuine Christianity.

Through these and other religious metaphors, Hawthorne and Melville were enabled to question—rather than merely confirm—Christian doctrine.

In sum, it would be closer to the truth of their fiction to call Hawthorne and Melville *psychological* rather than *religious* writers. In their exploration of the incredible complexities of the human mind, they made discoveries which sometimes seemed to confirm such ancient doctrines as original sin—but these confirmations did not lead to the broadside reinstitution and reaffirmation of religious dogma. On the contrary, they inspired further and deeper exploration, leading ultimately to the mapping of heretofore uncharted psychological terrain. Thus "Young Goodman Brown" and *Pierre*, in their different ways, represent Hawthorne and Melville delving deeply into man's unconscious—before Freud and Jung had pronounced its existence. The American writers were pioneers, breaking paths into the interior wilderness that is the human psyche. The truth that they discovered there, though often embodied in symbol and extended in metaphor, was in concrete terms a human, rather than a divine, truth, lending itself more readily to expression in psychological rather than theological terms. Although religious belief shaped their modes of thinking, Hawthorne and Melville readily pushed beyond the bounds of doctrine or dogma. As Melville said of Hawthorne, both writers "cross frontiers into Eternity," not with "heaps of baggage," but "with nothing but a carpet-bag."

13

Hawthorne and Melville:
The Unpardonable Sin

The Scarlet Letter explores the effects, on the transgressors, of three distinct types of sin—the revealed sin of Hester, the concealed sin of Dimmesdale, and the unpardonable sin of Chillingworth. The complexity of these effects is suggested when Hester, outwardly penitent, exclaims to Dimmesdale that their deed had a consecration of its own, or when Dimmesdale, spiritually tormented by his hidden guilt, finds his power for good in the community increased as a result of his transgression, or when Chillingworth becomes, through his demonic pursuit of revenge, the greatest sinner of them all, and is assigned, finally, to eternal damnation in Hawthorne's special hell reserved for those of his villains who commit the sin for which there is no forgiveness.

Hawthorne dealt with these and other aspects of sin throughout his novels and stories: the initiation into sin ("Young Goodman Brown"), the discovery of the omnipresence of sin ("Egotism; or, the Bosom Serpent"), the tortures of concealed sin ("Roger Malvin's Burial"), the beneficial results of sin (*The Marble Faun*). But he explored no ramification of this favorite theme more deeply than that which he called the unpardonable sin. The most explicit and direct treatment is in "Ethan Brand," which was published in 1850 but whose genesis is found in two 1844 entries in the *American Notebooks*. The first entry contains only the brief but germinal idea of an investigator searching for the unpardonable sin, discovering it, finally, in "his own heart and practice." In the second entry, such a sin is tentatively defined as "a want of love and reverence for the Human Soul" resulting in a "separation of the intellect from the heart."[1] A large number of Hawthorne villains are embodiments of this supreme evil and constitute a searching study of the unpardonable sin: Ethan Brand, Chillingworth, Lady Eleanore in "Lady Eleanore's Mantle," Aylmer in "The Birthmark," Rappaccini in "Rappaccini's Daughter," Roderick Elliston in "Egotism; or, the Bosom Serpent," Judge Pyncheon in *The House of the Seven Gables*, Hollingsworth and Westervelt in *The Blithedale Romance*, the Capuchin Monk in *The Marble Faun*.

From this extensive treatment of the unpardonable sin emerges a pattern which has significance not only for Hawthorne's fiction but also for that of writers who followed and were, perhaps, influenced by the master. For example, the theme of isolation, so important in the fiction of a later day, may be illuminated by a study of this pattern. In the following pages I wish to explore the motives of Hawthorne's characters in committing the unpardonable sin, the fateful steps which constitute its commission, and the existence of these identical motives and steps in *Moby Dick*, a work in progress at the height of the Melville-Hawthorne friendship.

I. The Shadowy Scope of Time

It has not been sufficiently noted that Hawthorne invariably envisioned the unpardonable sin as originating in a seemingly justifiable cause, in an apparent good. The experience of Ethan Brand is typical. On that fateful night of his return, after the others have gone away and he is left alone to stare into the blazing lime kiln, he recalls the past when he was "a simple and loving man," and he remembers with "what pity for human guilt and woe, he had first begun to contemplate those ideas which afterwards became the inspiration of his life" (III, 494).[2] But it seems to be the intensity of his goodness, the overbounding passion with which he contemplated the unhappy predica-

---

[1] *The American Notebooks by Nathaniel Hawthorne*, ed. Randall Stewart (New Haven: Yale Univ. Press, 1932), p. 106.

[2] Numbers following all quotations from Hawthorne indicate volume and page in *The Works*, ed. George Parsons Lathrop (Cambridge, Mass.: Riverside Press, 1883).

ment of mankind, that leads him to commit the unpardonable sin. It is not surprising to find Hawthorne dramatizing the greatest evil as originating from good in view of his fascination with the converse of this process—that is, the genuine benefits which result from sin. Ethan Brand's ruling passion springs from his concern for the existence of guilt and misery in the world. He searches too deeply for causes, and in his search he loses that very pity which had originally motivated his search.

Aylmer, in "The Birthmark," like Ethan Brand, seeks perfection and finds, instead, eternal damnation. His desire to remove the birthmark in the form of a small human hand on the cheek of his wife, Georgiana, becomes an obsession and turns him, too, into a fiend. His failure, like Ethan Brand's, is a failure of vision: "The momentary circumstance was too strong for him; he failed to look beyond the shadowy scope of time, and, living once for all in eternity, to find the perfect future in the present" (II, 69). All of Hawthorne's major villains are, like Aylmer, acutely aware of "this dim sphere of half development," the "momentary circumstance," in which there are sin, evil, imperfection. And, with all of their intellectual development, they have not the vision to see beyond this "shadowy scope of time"; too much obsessed with the ills of the present, they are blind to eternity, which also exists in the present—that eternity in which alone resides perfection. It is clear that they do not see because they attempt to understand solely with their keenly developed intellects what can be perceived only with the heart. Convinced of the non-existence of what they cannot perceive, they attempt to supply the imagined deficiency; in their attempt to assume the role of God they naturally give their allegiance to Satan, and subsequently find themselves contributing to that very imperfection which they had originally wished to eliminate.

Chillingworth has devoted his entire career to study, to the pursuit of that particular knowledge which is most concerned with the alleviation of human suffering—medical science: "But all my life had been made up of earnest, studious, thoughtful, quiet years, bestowed faithfully for the increase of mine own knowledge, and faithfully, too, though this latter object was but casual to the other,—faithfully for the advancement of human welfare" (V, 208). And it is these very studies, altruistic as they seem to be, that lead him, finally, to hold in contempt the spiritual values of life. Even his intense scrutiny of Dimmesdale's soul is, at first, undertaken because he is "desirous only of truth" (V, 158). Hollingsworth, in *The Blithedale Romance*, becomes an intellectual machine in the attempt to realize his "scheme for the reformation of the wicked by methods moral, intellectual, and industrial, by the sympathy of pure, humble, and yet exalted minds" (V, 469). Like Chillingworth, Aylmer, and Ethan Brand, he demands perfection in "this dim sphere of half development," and, in his demand, becomes over-intellectualized and evil, wreaking havoc among his fellow-humans. Unlike the rest, however, he comes to understand, through Priscilla, the human heart, and, retiring from the world, humbly seeks his salvation.

Rappaccini, in "Rappaccini's Daughter," like Aylmer and Chillingworth, has devoted his life to science. His daughter, Beatrice, is the subject of his most terrible scientific experiment, the attempt to render a human being immune to poison through the gradual and systematic administration of poison. But Rappaccini's original motive, although perverted, is not blameworthy. Confronted with his daughter's accusing cry of anguish, he exclaims: "What mean you, foolish girl? Dost thou deem it misery to be endowed with marvellous gifts against which no power nor strength could avail an enemy. . . . Wouldst thou, then, have preferred the condition of a weak woman, exposed to all evil and capable of none?" (II, 147). Rappaccini, too, saw the evil in time's shadowy scope, and the only solution of his warped intellect was to confront evil with evil, poison with poison. But, like the rest of Hawthorne's villains, he succeeds not in eradicating imperfection but in creating more and greater evil. It is Beatrice who has the vision that Rappaccini lacks, that vision of the perfect future, of eternity. Just before her death she exclaims: "I am going, father, where the evil which thou hast striven to mingle with my being will pass away like a dream—like the fragrance of these poisonous flowers, which will no longer taint my breath among the flowers of Eden" (II, 147).

Roderick Elliston, in "Egotism; or, the Bosom Serpent," along with Hollingsworth of *The Blithedale Romance*, is one of the few Hawthorne villains who escape committing the unpardonable sin by finding their way, before it is too late, to salvation through an understanding and rejection of their error. Elliston, burdened with a snake in his bosom which bestows the ability to discover the sins concealed in the hearts of his fellow men, is obsessed with the revelation of evil in all human beings. It is this obsession that almost drives him to commit the unpardonable sin. It is understandable that the community should be alarmed: "It was not to be tolerated that Roderick Elliston should break through the tacit compact by which the world has done its best to secure repose without relinquishing evil" (II, 314). It is not the community, however, which succeeds in changing Elliston; it is Rosina, his wife, who is able to turn him from his passion to reveal all evil, to deflect him from his consuming egotism. After the serpent has fled his bosom, Elliston asks Rosina, "Can a breast, where it has dwelt so long, be purified?" "Oh yes," she replies. "The serpent was but a dark fantasy, and what it typified was as shadowy as itself. The past, dismal as it seems, shall fling no gloom upon the future. To give it its due importance we must think of it but as an anecdote in our Eternity" (II, 320–321). Elliston learns from Rosina what Ethan Brand, Chillingworth, Rappaccini, and Aylmer never learned, that the evil of the present is but a "dark fantasy," "an anecdote in Eternity." Unlike the others, he is endowed through Rosina with insight of the heart to see beyond the shadowy scope of time.

Near the end of *The Blithedale Romance*, Miles Coverdale reflects on this strange paradox of so great an evil originating in the desire for good, and concludes that philanthropy, when it becomes a ruling passion, although it might be of some value to the world, is dangerous to the individual, because it destroys the "heart, the rich juices of which God never meant should be pressed violently out, and distilled into alcoholic liquor, by an unnatural process, but should render life sweet, bland, and gently beneficent, and insensibly influence other hearts and other lives to the same blessed end." Hollingsworth's fate is "an exemplification of the most awful truth in Bunyan's book of such,—from the very gate of heaven there is a by-way to the pit!" (V, 595).[3] This byway is the path that all of Hawthorne's

---

[3] Hawthorne's reference here is to *The Pilgrim's Progress*, at the end of which Bunyan, after describing Christian's entrance into the celestial city, notes that Ignorance, ferried across the river by Vain-hope, is not

great sinners take. Inflamed with the knowledge of the imperfections of this world, unable to reach the higher vision of eternity, they enter, at first perhaps unwittingly, the service of the devil to do battle against God.

II. The Byway to the Pit

Once consumed with a passionate desire to set the world aright, to correct the vast imperfections of the universe, Hawthorne's men of little vision start down that byway to the pit, a byway whose route is marked by a number of clearly defined stages. The sinner first elevates his intellect to a triumphant position over his heart, an act which invariably results in a consuming passion, or monomania, in which all values are sacrificed to a single overruling purpose; the sin then manifests itself in pride, or egotism, which deprives the sinner of the common human sympathies, thereby bringing about his isolation from humanity; the transgressor, intent on accomplishing his one single purpose, imposes his will, without regard for the sanctity of the human heart and soul, on others, diabolically forcing them to do his bidding; at some point along this path, the sinner reveals his allegiance to the devil, his devotion to evil, and, conversely, his hatred of good, his revolt from God: in his monomania he attempts to usurp the role of God.[4]

Ethan Brand, obsessed with the desire of discovering the unpardonable sin, cultivates his intellectual powers until he

---

only denied entrance but is carried away to a door in the side of a hill: "Then I saw that there was a way to hell, even from the Gates of heaven" (John Bunyan, *Grace Abounding and The Pilgrim's Progress,* Cambridge Univ. Press, 1907, ed. John Brown, p. 279). Hawthorne's indebtedness to Bunyan is the subject of W. Stacy Johnson's "Hawthorne and *The Pilgrim's Progress,*" *Journal of English and Germanic Philology,* L, 156–166. It is possible that Hawthorne's interest in the unpardonable sin was stimulated by Bunyan's autobiographical *Grace Abounding to the Chief of Sinners,* in which Bunyan describes his search for such a sin, his anguished despair when he assumes that he has committed it, and his ebullient rejoicings upon his discovery that he did not commit it after all. The unpardonable sin is also the subject of the sermon-tract, *The Jerusalem Sinner Saved; or, Good News for the Vilest of Men.*

[4] Too frequently, studies of Hawthorne, referring to the notebooks or to Ethan Brand's own brief description of the transgression, have assumed only some one of these aspects to be the unpardonable sin.

rises from an unlettered laborer to stand "on a starlit eminence, whither the philosophers of the earth, laden with the lore of universities, might vainly strive to clamber after him." But so high a position had been attained only through the awful sacrifice of the heart; it "had contracted,—had hardened,—had perished! It had ceased to partake of the universal throb" (III, 494–495). The fate of Ethan Brand's heart is made dramatically clear at the end of the story when its shape is maintained in spite of the intense fire of the lime kiln to which Ethan Brand consigns himself.

Like Ethan Brand, Chillingworth, Aylmer, Rappaccini, and Hollingsworth devote their lives to the development of their minds. Chillingworth has studied intensively the "human frame," and in the process has "lost the spiritual view of existence amid the intricacies of that wondrous mechanism, which seemed to involve art enough to comprise all of life within itself" (V, 146). Aylmer has "devoted himself . . . too unreservedly to scientific studies ever to be weaned from them by any second passion" (II, 47). Rappaccini cares "infinitely more for science than for mankind," and his countenance wears a "cold, and purely intellectual aspect" (II, 116–117). Hollingsworth, in the pursuit of his once noble aims, becomes "a monster! A cold, heartless, self-beginning and self-ending piece of mechanism!" (V, 566).

In the process of developing such monstrous intellects, these doomed men become the victims of a ruling passion, a monomania; they become insane in their desire to accomplish some great, single purpose. To the fulfillment of this high aim they devote all of their energies, all of the ruthless cunning of their madness. In Ethan Brand it is the search for the unpardonable sin itself. In Chillingworth it is revenge: "as he proceeded, a terrible fascination, a kind of fierce, though still calm, necessity seized the old man within its gripe, and never set him free again until he had done all its bidding" (V, 158). Aylmer, in his compulsive desire to remove his wife's birthmark, experiences "the tyrannizing influence acquired by one idea over his mind" (II, 52). Rappaccini "would sacrifice human life, his own among the rest, or whatever else was dearest to him, for the sake of adding so much as a grain of mustard seed to the great heap of his accumulated knowledge" (II, 116). Roderick Elliston's mania is, with "cankered ingenuity," to seek out and reveal the blackest and vilest sins of all his fellow men. Hollingsworth's "overruling purpose," his "rigid and unconquerable idea," is his vast scheme for reformation of the wicked.

Pride is the most obvious of the manifestations of the unpardonable sin, and it is an intense pride, a consuming regard for self, an egotism that knows no bounds. When Hollingsworth exclaims to Zenobia, "Show me one selfish end, in all I ever aimed at . . . " Zenobia cries out, "It is all self! . . . Nothing else; nothing but self, self, self!" (V, 566). Ethan Brand, when he arises to explain the unpardonable sin to his companions, stands erect "with a pride that distinguishes all enthusiasts of his stamp" (III, 485). The snake in Roderick Elliston's bosom seems "the symbol of a monstrous egotism to which everything was referred, and which he pampered, night and day" (II, 309). Rappaccini, when he realizes that his diabolical experiment with Beatrice and Giovanni is successful, gazes on them with "a triumphant expression" as his bent form grows "erect with conscious power" (II, 146). Aylmer's pride is similar to Rappaccini's, a pride in his scientific power over nature; he speaks to Georgiana "in glowing language of the resources of his art" (II, 58). Chillingworth's wounded pride is the source of his desire for revenge, and in the process of wreaking the revenge, he has all of the terrible and implacable pride of Satan, a concern for self that shows no pity whatsoever for the victims of his fiendish pleasure.

Hawthorne's most explicit statement on pride, as an aspect of the unpardonable sin, is, however, "Lady Eleanore's Mantle." Lady Eleanore Rochcliffe is the only woman among Hawthorne's great transgressors, but she is as surely damned as the rest. She is "remarkable for a harsh, unyielding pride, a haughty consciousness of her hereditary and personal advantages." Her pride itself is "hardly less than a monomania" (I, 310). Within the folds of her richly decorated but sinister mantle, which symbolizes this devastating pride, lurks the contagion that rages through the community, killing both high and low, and killing, finally, Lady Eleanore herself. Thus does pride spread its devastation among the human family. It is not until the mantle is destroyed that the pestilence finally subsides.

It is not surprising that all of these foregoing traits (triumph of the intellect over the heart, monomania, and pride) should result in the next—isolation of the sinner. The isolation is, of course, spiritual, but frequently Hawthorne allows physical isolation to symbolize the spiritual withdrawal from humanity. In the ball scene in "Lady Eleanore's Mantle," Lady Eleanore stands "apart from the mob of guests," and as the scene progresses, her circle grows smaller; at the close of the story, her beauty blasted by the dread disease, she secretes herself, alone, behind the curtains of her canopied bed, terrified in her pride that anyone should look upon her ugliness. But Lady Eleanore's is a self-imposed isolation; she withdraws because she no longer has any link with common humanity. At the opening of the story, in one of the finest of Hawthorne's sharply drawn vignettes, Lady Eleanore steps from her coach on to the prostrate form of Jervase Helwyse, who has offered himself as a human footstool: "and never, surely, was there an apter emblem of aristocracy and hereditary pride trampling on human sympathies and the kindred of nature" (I, 312). It is the same Jervase Helwyse who, later on, at the ball, pleads with Lady Eleanore to drink from the goblet which he offers, as "a symbol that you have not sought to withdraw yourself from the chain of human sympathies—which whosoever would shake off must keep company with fallen angels" (I, 317). But Lady Eleanore does not drink, and in the scuffle which ensues, the sacred wine is spilled on the fabulous mantle: compassion is wasted on pride.

All of Hawthorne's villains withdraw, like Lady Eleanore, from the "chain of human sympathies." Ethan Brand's intellect has "triumphed over the sense of brotherhood with man," and he has "lost his hold of the magnetic chain of humanity. He was no longer a brother-man, opening the chambers or the dungeons of our common nature by the key of holy sympathy, which gave him a right to share in all its secrets" (III, 495). Near the end of the story, before his fatal leap, he is left alone, a "lonely man bent forward over this terrible body of fire" (III, 496). Chillingworth completely withdraws from the human family. "And what am I now?" he exclaims to Hester, "A fiend!" And Hester pleads, "hatred . . . has transformed a wise and just man to a fiend! Wilt thou yet purge it out of thee, and be once more human?" (V, 208–209). Aylmer and Rappaccini, in their obsession with their scientific magic, have withdrawn to their dark laboratories to cultivate their sinister powers, willing to sacrifice human life in their diabolical experiments; surely they have removed themselves from the chain of human sympathies. And Hollingsworth, in his single-minded pursuit of his one goal, has abandoned humanity, has become "not altogether human" (V, 399). All of these transgressors, whether or not they live apart from mankind, are spiritually isolated because they do not share that sense of brotherhood which unites the human family.

Closely allied with this lack of human sympathy, yet one more step down the fatal byway, is the loss of respect for the sanctity of the human heart and soul. This characteristic is not simply a passive trait, however; it results in overt action which is not only terrible but frequently fatal. Hawthorne's transgressors are men of powerful will, and invariably they impose their will on others. It is not, moreover, mere physical dominance that these sinners seek; they desire to master the minds, the hearts, the very souls of those about them. They do not hesitate to violate these most precious and divine elements of the individual.

Ethan Brand becomes "a cold observer, looking on mankind as the subject of his experiment, and, at length, converting man and woman to be his puppets, and pulling the wires that moved them to such degrees of crime as were demanded for his study" (III, 495). When the old, white-haired father comes to Ethan Brand to hear tidings of his lost daughter, Ethan recalls that she is the very girl whom he has "made the subject of a psychological experiment, and wasted, absorbed, and perhaps annihilated her soul, in the process" (III, 489). Old Roger Chillingworth, confronted with Hester's refusal to reveal her guilty partner, resolves to seek him out: "Sooner or later, he must needs be mine! . . . Let him live! Let him hide himself in outward honor, if he may! Not the less he shall be mine!" (V, 98–99). And Chillingworth fulfills his pledge; he discovers Dimmesdale's secret guilt: "not merely the external presence, but the very inmost soul . . . seemed to be brought out before his eyes. . . . He became, thenceforth, not a spectator only, but a chief actor, in the poor minister's interior world. He could play upon him as he chose" (V, 171). This spiritual torture of Dimmesdale's soul brings about the transformation of both men: Dimmesdale becomes only a pale reflection of his former self, while Chillingworth slowly takes on all of the sinister characteristics of Satan.

Lady Eleanore, in her pride, has before her arrival at the Province House violated the heart and soul of Jervase Helwyse. Helwyse had been a poor youth, with nothing "save the mind and soul that nature gave him; and . . . it was his misfortune to meet this Lady Eleanore Rochcliffe. He loved her—and her scorn has driven him mad" (I, 313). The lightness with which she takes a deed with such terrible consequences is indicated when she exclaims that she can find in her heart "to do nothing but laugh at him" (I, 317). The power which Aylmer has over his assistant, Aminadab, a "human machine," a "man of clay," seems complete: "While incapable of comprehending a single principle, he executed all the details of his master's experiments" (II, 55). But it is Georgiana that comes under Aylmer's powerful dominance in the progress of the story. Horrified when she first learns of Aylmer's intense dislike of the birthmark, her individuality is gradually subjected to his dominant will and, finally, she demands that the fatal experiment on her be made. "Not even Aylmer now hated it so much as she" (II, 60). Rappaccini, like Aylmer, finds the secret of his power in his "fatal science." It is without the consent of Beatrice and Giovanni—indeed, without their knowledge—that Rappaccini corrupts their innocence into a deadly evil, that he inflicts this "miserable doom."

Judge Pyncheon, in *The House of the Seven Gables*, is willing to go to any lengths in his singular determination to obtain his uncle's hidden wealth. Hepzibah justly exclaims to him, "You have forgotten that a woman was your mother!— that you have had sisters, brothers, children of your own!—or that there ever was affection between man and man, or pity from one man to another, in this miserable world!" (III, 282). It is he who is responsible for Clifford's madness by remaining silent when his knowledge would have declared Clifford innocent of murder and saved him from imprisonment. "Thus Jaffrey Pyncheon's inward criminality, as regarded Clifford, was, indeed, black and damnable; while its mere outward show and positive commission was the smallest that could possibly consist with so great a sin" (III, 370). And it is Clifford's very insanity, brought about, however indirectly, by Judge Pyncheon, that places both Clifford and Hepzibah in Pyncheon's power. Should Clifford refuse him the information he desires, Pyncheon explains to Hepzibah, he will be convinced that Clifford is insane. "And, once sure of the course pointed out by conscience, you know me too well, Cousin Hepzibah, to entertain a doubt that I shall pursue it" (III, 282). Hepzibah knows only too well that Judge Pyncheon, in his greedy pursuit, will not hesitate to damage a human soul beyond repair.

In *The Blithedale Romance*, there are two individuals who ruthlessly "use" their fellow creatures, regardless of the havoc created in heart and soul. Hollingsworth encourages Zenobia's affection when it seems that her supposed wealth might become available for the furtherance of his philanthropic schemes, rejecting her when this possibility vanishes. The burden of guilt for Zenobia's death thus becomes his. But Zenobia accuses him of a viler evil: "foremost and blackest of your sins, you stifled down your inmost consciousness!—you did a deadly wrong to your own heart!—You were ready to sacrifice this girl" (V, 567). Hollingsworth had been willing to allow the innocent and spiritual Priscilla to become the subject of one of Westervelt's devilish experiments. Through mesmerism, Westervelt pretended to demonstrate, with Priscilla as his victim, "the miraculous power of one human being over the will and passions of another" (V, 544).

The Capuchin Monk in *The Marble Faun*, like Westervelt in *The Blithedale Romance*, remains a somewhat shadowy and indistinct embodiment of evil, but it is clear that he, too, like all of Hawthorne's supreme villains, imposes his will on others without care for the resulting wreckage of the heart or soul: "there seemed to be a sadly mysterious fascination in the influence of this ill-omened person over Miriam; it was such as beasts and reptiles of subtle and evil nature sometimes exercise upon their victims" (VI, 115). When Miriam and Donatello look upon the dead Capuchin Monk, their guilt locked within their hearts, they see "the same visage that had glared upon their naked souls. . . ."

But even the extreme wickedness of this desecration of the sacred heart and soul does not complete the pattern of evil in the unpardonable sin. Finding its origin in a revulsion at the imperfection of the world and mankind, it finds its conclusion in wholehearted dedication to that very evil. It is in the portrayal of this fatal step that the witchcraft or satanic imagery recurs throughout Hawthorne's fiction.[5] After detailing the account of Ethan Brand's transformation from a simple, good man to one guilty of the unpardonable sin, Hawthorne states simply: "Thus Ethan Brand became a fiend" (III, 495). Ethan Brand does not fling himself into the fiery furnace of the lime kiln because of the unbearable weight of his guilt; he does so as a defiance of Heaven, a supreme obeisance made to the devil: "O stars of heaven, that shone on me of old, as if to light me onward and upward!—farewell all, and forever. Come, deadly element of Fire,—henceforth my familiar friend! Embrace me, as I do thee!" (III, 496). Ethan Brand's act is not self-destruction at all, but rather a dedication to eternal service in the war of Hell against Heaven.

Of all Hawthorne's villains, Roger Chillingworth exemplifies best "man's faculty of transforming himself into a devil" (V, 205). The transformation is a gradual one, with the external manifestations keeping pace with the accumulation of the evil which he does. One of the infallible signs which develops out of his wicked allegiance is the "glare of red light out of his eyes; as if the old man's soul were on fire, and kept on smouldering duskily within his breast, until, by some casual puff of passion, it was blown into a momentary flame" (V, 205). In characteristic fashion, Hawthorne, without committing himself to belief in witchcraft, fills in Chillingworth's diabolical background by citing rumor and gossip: "According to the vulgar idea, the fire in his laboratory had been brought from the lower regions, and was fed with infernal fuel; and so, as might be expected, his visage was getting sooty with the smoke" (V, 156). Chillingworth's full devotion to Satan is thus carefully drawn so that it comes as no surprise to the reader, when Dimmesdale dies, that Chillingworth, deprived of the

[5] Cotton Mather, in *The Wonders of the Invisible World* (London, 1862), after describing one of the witch trials, comments: "The witches were executed; and confessed nothing; which indeed will not be wondred by them, who consider and entertain the Judgment of a Judicious writer, *that the unpardonable sin, is most usually committed by Professors of the Christian Religion, falling into witchcraft*" (p. 120). The pattern which Hawthorne follows in his accounts of the unpardonable sin may be found, in part, shadowed forth in Cotton Mather's learned disquisition on the abominable art of witchcraft.

object of his consuming desire for revenge, simply withers up, shrivels away: when "there was no more Devil's work on earth for him to do, it only remained for the unhumanized mortal to betake himself whither his Master would find him tasks enough, and pay him his wages duly" (V, 307).

Aylmer, in the process of bringing Georgiana under his sway, performs a series of experiments which succeed in impressing his wife with his awful powers. "Airy figures, absolutely bodiless ideas, and forms of unsubstantial beauty came and danced before her, imprinting their momentary footsteps on beams of light" (II, 56). Whenever Georgiana wished to know what was going on in the outside world, "as if her thoughts were answered, the procession of external existence flitted across a screen" (II, 56–57). Georgiana naturally becomes convinced that her husband possesses "sway over the spiritual world." But after these successes there follow two "mortifying failures." As Georgiana watches a vessel filled with earth, a beautiful flower shoots up and unfolds. Aylmer tells her to pluck and inhale, thus perpetuating in herself a beauty that is soon to vanish; but as soon as Georgiana touches the flower, its leaves blacken "as if by the agency of fire." Next Aylmer attempts to take Georgiana's picture "by rays of light striking upon a polished plate of metal," but the results are frightening: the features of her face are "blurred and indefinable; while the minute figure of a hand appeared where the cheek should have been" (II, 57). If this be science, it is science that man performs only with the aid of the devil. It exhibits an unnatural, or abnormal, control over nature, or God's creation; in short, it is witchcraft. The source of Aylmer's secret powers becomes clear when Georgiana inadvertently intrudes upon him at work in his laboratory: "The first thing that struck her eye was the furnace, that hot and feverish worker, with the intense glow of its fire, which by the quantities of soot clustered above it seemed to have been burning for ages" (II, 63). About the room there are a distilling apparatus, an electrical machine, retorts and crucibles for chemical research, and the atmosphere is close, "tainted with gaseous odors which had been tormented forth by the processes of science" (II, 63). And in the midst of this miniature reproduction of Hell was Aylmer, "pale as death, anxious and absorbed," hanging over the furnace. The image which emerges from the accumulation of this detail is not that of a man of science at work in his laboratory but that of a wizard preparing his black magic or of Satan tending his evil fires in Hell.

In "Egotism; or, the Bosom Serpent," the sustained symbol is that which has traditionally been associated with Satan—the snake, or serpent. Roderick Elliston himself becomes "unhumanized" and takes on some of the external characteristics of a serpent: "the blackest midnight was his chosen hour to steal abroad; and if ever he were seen, it was when the watchman's lantern gleamed upon his figure, gliding along the street" (II, 307). Here the words "gleamed" and "gliding" are perfectly placed to achieve the quality of suggestion desired. But it is the serpent in his bosom to which Aylmer gives his allegiance: "He appeared to imagine that the snake was a divinity,—not celestial, it is true, but darkly infernal,—and that he thence derived an eminence and a sanctity, horrid, indeed, yet more desirable than whatever ambition aims at" (II, 309–10).

The Satan image is not prominent in *The House of the Seven Gables,* but it is there. It was the temptation "by the devil" that caused the young Jaffrey Pyncheon to be searching his uncle's room, and to witness, when the old man returned, his death, brought about by his "alarm and horror" as well as his "hereditary liability." And as the aged Jaffrey Pyncheon sits silently in the old parlor of the darkened house, after the flight of Hepzibah and Clifford, there is seen "the visage of grimalkin, outside the window, where he appears to have posted himself for a deliberate watch. This grimalkin has a very ugly look. Is it a cat watching for a mouse, or the devil for a human soul?" (III, 332). On the metaphorical level the question is rhetorical: there can be no doubt that the figure is Satan, come to claim his own.

In *The Blithedale Romance,* it will be remembered, Hollingsworth had, "from the very gate of heaven" taken a "by-way to the pit!" Men of his kind, cursed with an overruling passion, "have an idol to which they consecrate themselves high-priest, and deem it holy work to offer sacrifices of whatever is most precious; and never once seem to suspect—so cunning has the Devil been with them—that this false deity, in whose iron features, immitigable to all the rest of mankind, they see only benignity and love, is but a spectrum of the very priest himself, projected upon the surrounding darkness" (V, 400). In *The*

Marble Faun, the power which the Capuchin Monk has over Miriam is described as an "iron chain, of which some of the massive links were round her feminine waist, and the others in his ruthless hand . . . [which] must have been forged in some such unhallowed furnace as is only kindled by evil passions and fed by evil deeds" (VI, 115). It could only be, of course, the devil's furnace. The first mysterious appearance of the monk from out the depths of the catacomb of St. Calixtus, "a creature to whom midnight would be more congenial than noonday" (VI, 45), suggests that his true master is Satan.

The recurring image of the unhallowed furnace glowing with the lurid flames of evil is more than mere indulgence in fancy; it is a clear statement of the fate of those who arbitrarily cut themselves off from the great human community, who, in their contempt of the race's destiny to indulgence in petty sin, dedicate themselves heart and soul to the perpetuation of consuming evil. The image serves as a symbol of renunciation of fellowship with humanity and obedience to God, and an entry into an unholy alliance with Satan. In this new alliance, these sinners have not only abandoned God, but have entered into the devil's perpetual attempt to overthrow Him and to usurp His position. In every case we find these great transgressors defiantly asserting their power over some province, human or natural, which belongs properly to God.

Ethan Brand, in his dedicated search for the unpardonable sin, takes upon himself the heavy knowledge which man was not meant to have, the unbearable knowledge of the supreme evil which only God can determine. When Hester exclaims to Chillingworth, "Forgive, and leave his [Dimmesdale's] further retribution to the Power that claims it!" (V, 209), she is striking at the heart of the matter: Chillingworth is attempting to fill the role of God in his punishment of Dimmesdale. Both Aylmer and Rappaccini are probing for the "secret of creative force" and desire "from the investigation of Nature a power above Nature, and from physics a sway over the spiritual world" (II, 61). In short, they are attempting to achieve the power of the Creator. If Georgiana's birthmark (sin, sorrow, decay, and death) is to be removed, it must be left to God; if the beautiful Beatrice is to be made genuinely immune to evil, the immunity must be achieved through divine not devilish power. Lady Eleanore in her pride is attempting to achieve a position like God's, above humanity. Roderick Elliston, in his obsession to reveal the hoarded sin of his fellow creatures, assumes the awful power of God's judgment. Hollingsworth, in his overruling passion to reform the wicked, is obsessed with the solution of a problem that is properly God's. It has already been shown how all of these transgressors, including Judge Pyncheon, Westervelt, and the Capuchin Monk, seek power over that single manifestation of God in all His creatures, the human soul. To tamper with the soul of a fellow creature is to interfere with, perhaps desecrate, that which above all is God's province.

It would be strange indeed were Hawthorne to portray so vividly the supreme sin and ignore entirely its opposite, the supreme good. Brief note should be taken here of his portrayal of such good. In "The Procession of Life," Hawthorne envisions the various classifications into which mankind can be ranked for the "funereal procession" which is life. After calling together all the guilty to rank themselves "in accordance with the brotherhood of crime," he says: "now let us call the Good. . . . But how is this? Does none answer to the call? Not one: for the just, the pure, the true, and all who might most worthily obey it, shrink sadly back, as most conscious of error and imperfection. Then let the summons be to those whose pervading principle is Love. This classification will embrace all the truly good" (II, 244). This identification of love with the greatest good was necessary for one whose eternal vision was that of the entire world stained with sin. The supreme good must, of necessity, be the pervading principle of love.

"The Great Stone Face," which appears in the same volume of stories (*The Snow Image and Other Twice Told Tales*) as "Ethan Brand," is, in most respects, a companion piece for the story of the unpardonable sin. Ernest, like Ethan Brand, spends the greater part of his life in a search, and, at the end, discovers in himself that for which he is looking. But here Ernest's resemblance to Ethan Brand ends. Ernest's search is for "the greatest and noblest personage of his time," whose countenance, legend says, will resemble the Great Stone Face which overlooks the valley. Mr. Gathergold, the rich merchant, old Blood-and-Thunder, the illustrious commander, Old Stony Phiz, the eminent statesman, are each advanced and hailed in turn as the noble personage prophesied in legend, and each is reluctantly but finally rejected. Meanwhile, Ernest continues to live in his native valley, and although he remains a humble, simple-hearted man, he gradually becomes known among the people for his acts of selfless kindness and for his humble wisdom: "Not a day passed by, that the world was not the better because this man, humble as he was, had lived. He never stepped aside from his own path, yet would always reach a blessing to his neighbor" (III, 426). Ernest finally hears of a man whom he believes to be the long-awaited individual, a poet whose songs have a "strain of divinity." The poet comes to the valley and he and Ernest meet and talk, their minds according "into one strain." It is the poet who, as Ernest is delivering his usual discourse to his neighbors, points out his resemblance to the Great Stone Face, and Ernest is then accepted as the fulfillment of the old prophecy.

Ernest's traits appear, in almost every instance, to be the opposite of those which characterize the great sinners. Emphasis is on the heart as against the intellect, and there is no dominating passion but rather a diffusion of good works; humility replaces pride, and the chain of human sympathies is binding, and does not allow isolation; the human heart and soul retain their divinity inviolate; and the service which Ernest enters is God's: "Almost involuntarily, too, he had become a preacher" (III, 426). In almost all of the stories in which are portrayed the supreme transgressors there appear in contrast embodiments of the greatest good. We have already seen that in the two cases in which the sinners are saved from eternal damnation, salvation is brought about by such etherealized or spiritualized characters: Rosina in "Egotism; or, the Bosom Serpent," and Priscilla in *The Blithedale Romance*. Although they are less successful in reforming the transgressors, similar roles are played by Hilda in *The Marble Faun*, Phoebe in *The House of the Seven Gables*, Beatrice in "Rappaccini's Daughter," Georgiana in "The Birthmark," and Hester, in part, in *The Scarlet Letter*.

Jervase Helwyse in "Lady Eleanore's Mantle" is one of the few males whom Hawthorne invests with the qualities of supreme goodness. Helwyse, like Georgiana, Beatrice, and Priscilla, is the direct victim of one of the great sinners—Lady Eleanore. It is her scorn which has driven him mad, but madness in his case seems, ironically, to call forth all of those supreme qualities of goodness in which Lady Eleanore is so deficient. While she is proud, he is humble; while her heart is suppressed, his heart is all that his madness has left him; while she places herself above common human sympathies, he is an inseparable part of the great human family; while she violates his soul, he attempts to save hers. Although he has stolen the sacramental vessel which he offers to Lady Eleanore, it is clear that he has greater right to such a religious symbol than any one else in the story. Helwyse, wise in the ways of Hell, recognizes the unpardonable sin for what it is, and attempts, in the service of Heaven, to bring about the salvation of a lost soul.

III. Ahab's Sin

The central action of *Moby Dick* is Ahab's monomaniacal pursuit of the great white whale, and it is central in the true sense that all of the remainder of the action revolves about it, all of the rest of the characters are subordinate to Ahab. Ahab's character is, then, the key to *Moby Dick*, and the key to Ahab's character is the unpardonable sin.[6] Ahab follows the same fatal byway taken by Ethan Brand, Chillingworth, Ayl-

---

[6] The meeting on 5 Aug. 1850 and the subsequent friendship of Hawthorne and Melville while the latter was in the midst of revising *Moby Dick* have given rise to a good deal of speculation about Hawthorne's influence on the book. A good summary of the relationship between the two writers is contained in Randall Stewart's "Melville and Hawthorne," *South Atlantic Quarterly*, LI (July 1952), 436–446; rptd. in *Moby Dick Centennial Essays*, ed. Tyrus Hillway and Luther S. Mansfield (Dallas, 1953), pp. 153–164. Nathalia Wright suggests specific influences in "*Mosses from an Old Manse* and *Moby Dick:* The Shock of Discovery," *Modern Language Notes*, LXVII (June 1952), 387–392. Although my primary point is not that Melville borrowed from Hawthorne, but rather that a pattern for the commission of the unpardonable sin is common to the work of both, it is true that most of Hawthorne's stories and novels in which I have traced the pattern had appeared before the meeting took place. *Mosses from an Old Manse* (1846), which Melville read just before he met Hawthorne and which he reviewed in *The Literary World*, 17 and 24 Aug. 1850, contains "The Birthmark," "Rappaccini's Daughter," and "Egotism; or, the Bosom Serpent." *The Scarlet Letter* appeared in 1850; "Lady Eleanore's Mantle" appeared in the *Democratic Review* in Dec. 1838; "Ethan Brand" appeared originally in *The Boston Museum*, Jan. 1850, but a letter to Hawthorne in 1851 indicates that Melville did not read it until its appearance in the *Dollar Magazine* in 1851 (see Julian Hawthorne, *Nathaniel Hawthorne and His Wife*, Boston, 1884, I, 404).

mer, Rappaccini, and the rest. He becomes obsessed with the "shadowy scope of time," the evil and imperfection of this world, so that he changes from a simple, "family" man into a man of sharpened intellect but shrunken heart. His normal desire for revenge develops into a monomania, a cunning madness, which allows nothing to stand between him and his gigantic goal. As his desire for revenge has its roots in a personal injury, so it is a personal triumph which he is seeking, an elevation of self, a possessing pride developing into arrogance. Such pride, together with his position of command, naturally isolates him, cuts him off from the common human feelings that bind the crew together. He violates the soul of his crew by imposing his powerful will on theirs, by implicating them in his diabolical schemes. And, as happened with all of Hawthorne's great transgressors, Ahab finds himself, finally, in league with the devil, dedicated to evil, at war with God, attempting to take over God's role in the universe.

Hatred of evil cannot be abhorrent to God, but when the hatred becomes obsessive, when the victim can no longer see sin, evil, and imperfection in their true relation to eternity, when he can no longer see beyond the "shadowy scope of time," he is well on his way down the bypath that leads from the very gates of heaven. Like Ethan Brand, Aylmer, Chillingworth, Rappaccini, and Hollingsworth, Ahab lacks the necessary vision to see through "this dim sphere of half development." In his motivation, Ahab is close to Chillingworth. Both seek revenge for a painful, personal injury, a revenge which transforms both pursuer and pursued, the one into a creature possessed, the other into an all-consuming symbol. But in his obsession, Ahab is closer to Aylmer. Georgiana's birthmark in the shape of a hand became, in Aylmer's eyes, a symbol of man's imperfection, a symbol of the sin, sorrow, decay, and death to which man seemed doomed. Similarly, Moby Dick becomes in Ahab's eyes "that intangible malignity which has been from the beginning; to whose dominion even the modern Christians ascribe one-half of the worlds. . . ." In short, "all evil, to crazy Ahab, were visibly personified, and made practically assailable in Moby Dick" (181).[7]

[7] Numbers after the quotations from *Moby Dick* refer to pages in the edition by Luther S. Mansfield and Howard P. Vincent (New York: Hendricks House, 1952).

Melville is careful to point out that Ahab's intense hatred of the whale did not spring to life instantaneously the moment Moby Dick reaped away his leg: "when he received the stroke that tore him, he probably but felt the agonizing bodily laceration, but nothing more" (182). It was on the homeward journey, necessitated by the injury, that Ahab's "torn body and gashed soul bled into one another; and so, interfusing, made him mad" (182). In other words, Ahab's hatred is no momentary passion of the heart; it is, rather, the deep-seated animosity of a brooding intellect. Ahab is intellectual brother to Chillingworth, Aylmer, and Rappaccini, Hawthorne's villains morbidly devoted to "science." As they sought the inmost secrets of nature in order to establish diabolical control over it, so Ahab uses his knowledge to increase his sway over the crew. Ahab shows contempt for and superiority over ordinary science when he smashes the quadrant to the deck, and confronted shortly after with the failure of the compass, immediately orders materials brought forth and proceeds to construct his own; in the midst of this procedure, he goes "through some small strange motions . . . whether indispensable to the magnetizing of the steel, or merely intended to augment the awe of the crew, is uncertain" (511). It is perhaps noteworthy that the allowance of alternate interpretations of the "small strange motions" made by Ahab is the method of dealing with the supernatural used by Hawthorne throughout his work. But the important point is that Ahab is here pitting his intellect, his power over nature, against God's, and, for the time being, he succeeds.

Just as Ethan Brand singlemindedly sought out the unpardonable sin; just as Chillingworth relentlessly tracked down and fought for Dimmesdale's soul; just as Hollingsworth subordinated all else to the accomplishment of his plan of reformation; and just as Aylmer became obsessed with removing his wife's birthmark; so Ahab pursued, with all the concentration of his being, the great white whale: "his special lunacy stormed his general sanity, and carried it, and turned all its concentrated cannon upon its own mad mark" (182–83). Ahab's overruling passion, like that of Hawthorne's villains, is a madness, but a madness with sense, a madness that sharpens the mind in order the better to fulfill the single purpose. Only by cunning could Ahab so easily have deceived the *Pequod's* owners into trusting his command on another voyage. "Gnawed within and scorched without, with the infixed, unrelenting fangs of some incurable idea" (184), Ahab curiously resembles Roderick Elliston, whose serpent in his bosom gnawed him within, too, and drove him relentlessly in his morbid effort to reveal all secret sin. But Ahab is concerned not merely with the revelation of evil: "with the mad secret of his unabated rage bolted up and keyed in him, Ahab had purposely sailed upon the present voyage with the one only and all-engrossing object of hunting the white whale" (184). The object of the hunt is destruction; nothing less than the annihilation of Moby Dick will satisfy Ahab's terrible internal gnawing.

When Ahab exclaims to Starbuck, "There is one God that is Lord over the earth, and one Captain that is lord over the Pequod" (471), the ease, readiness, and ingenuousness with which he draws such a comparison suggest the height of the position which he conceives as his. It is of a level with Ethan Brand's "starlit eminence." Something of a peak in the intensity of Ahab's pride is reached when, after constructing his compass to replace those destroyed by the thunder, he addresses the crew, "Look ye, for yourselves, if Ahab be not lord of the level loadstone! The sun is East, and that compass swears it" (511). One by one they look, overawed by Ahab's unnatural power over nature, and fearfully slink away. "In his fiery eyes of scorn and triumph you then saw Ahab in all his fatal pride" (512). Like Chillingworth during the times of his greatest triumph, Ahab has difficulty concealing the flames that dart from his eyes, disclosing his wicked allegiance. And Ahab's scorn and "fatal pride" will recall Lady Eleanore's scorn, which drove Helwyse mad, and her "fatal mantle," which devastated the community with its dread disease. Ahab's pride, like Lady Eleanore's, results not only in the death of others, but, finally, in annihilation of self.

Isolation is an important theme in *Moby Dick*. It is introduced on the very first page, not only in Ishmael's anguished meditation, but also in the "insular city of the Manhattoes," with its thousands upon thousands of men "posted like silent sentinels all around the town . . . fixed in ocean reveries." Emphasis is placed on the theme again just before Ahab's first appearance: "Islanders seem to make the best whalemen. They were nearly all Islanders in the Pequod, *Isolatoes* too, I call such, not acknowledging the common continent of men, but each *Isolato* living on a separate continent of his own. Yet now, federated along one keel, what a set these Isolatoes were!" (118). Melville's "common continent of men" might be equated with Hawthorne's "chain of human sympathies." Whereas Ishmael, by the end of the tale, has discovered this common continent, Ahab has cut himself irrevocably adrift from it. Like Ethan Brand, Lady Eleanore, Chillingworth and the rest, Ahab feels none of the bonds that unite, or federate, the human race.

Some kind of isolation is inevitable for one, such as Ahab, in command of a ship at sea, but it is plain that his isolation goes far beyond the necessity of his position. There is first the self-imposed seclusion in his cabin for the first several days of the fateful voyage, and when he does emerge, it is not to mingle or even communicate with the officers or crew, but merely to make himself visible: "moody stricken Ahab stood before them with a crucifixion in his face; in all the nameless regal overbearing dignity of some mighty woe" (122). At the dinner table, that most common of all places for social inter-course, Ahab presides "like a mute, maned sea-lion on the white coral beach, surrounded by his warlike but still deferen-tial cubs" (147). These cabin meals "were somehow solemn meals, eaten in awful silence; and yet at table old Ahab forbade not conversation; only he himself was dumb" (147). In such an indigestible atmosphere, what Flask had a chance to eat "did not so much relieve his hunger, as keep it immortal in him" (148). The scene, humorous though it is, seriously symbolizes the barriers between Ahab and his officers, which make even the most superficial kind of communication impossible. Ahab himself is fully aware of his isolated position. In one of the few instances in the novel in which he discloses a deep sense of the loss entailed by his terrible mission, Ahab confides to Starbuck: "When I think of this life I have led; the desolation of solitude it has been; the masoned, walled-town of a Captain's exclu-siveness, which admits but small entrance to any sympathy from the green country without—oh, weariness! heaviness! Guinea-coast slavery of solitary command!" (534). The image of the green country, in contrast with the walled town, is implicit with suggestions of the vitality of human intercourse; and the image is extended, a few paragraphs later, when Ahab

231

is described as a "blighted fruit tree," casting his "last, cindered apple to the soil." Ahab had deliberately deprived himself of that necessary nourishment which human sympathy alone provides.

Like all of Hawthorne's great transgressors, Ahab gains diabolical dominance over the souls of mortal men: through his "evil magic," he possesses the souls of his crew. After the voyage of the *Pequod* is well underway, Ahab emerges from his seclusion and orders Starbuck to send everybody aft. There follows the quarterdeck scene, in which Ahab pits not only his outward strength but also all of the suppressed power fed him by his monomania against the collective will of his men. The nailing of the Spanish doubloon to the main-mast, the splicing of hands, the drinking of grog from the flagon, and, finally, the crossing of the lances, impart to the crew the fiery intensity of Ahab's monamania. The magic ritual concludes with the drinking of the "fiery waters" from the sockets of the harpoon barbs held forth by Queequeg, Tashtego, and Daggoo as the mesmerized crew raises the universal chant, "Death to Moby Dick."

After the crew's will has been made his, Ahab muses to himself, " 'Twas not so hard a task . . . my one cogged circle fits into all their various wheels, and they revolve. . . . What I've dared, I've willed" (165–166). But there is one who does not revolve so easily. From the first, Starbuck requires "a little lower layer" of Ahab, and the deeper revelation ("All visible objects, man, are but as pasteboard masks" [161]) simply confirms Starbuck in his disquiet. Alone, he cries out: "My soul is more than matched; she's overmanned; and by a madman! Insufferable sting, that sanity should ground arms on such a field!" (166). Starbuck alone has recognized Ahab's violation of his soul, and realized the damage done: "I plainly see my miserable office,—to obey, rebelling; and worse yet, to hate with touch of pity! . . . Yet is there hope" (167). Out of this faint hope derives the uneven conflict of wills which provides the action with tension and suspense. The final issue of the conflict is determined when Ahab, seemingly persuaded for the moment by Starbuck's determined appeal to memory of home, hearth, wife, and child, turns at the apparent height of his response and deliberately crosses the deck to Fedallah, while Starbuck, "blanched to a corpse's hue with despair," steals away. Starbuck had long before assured himself that entreaty or reasoning would not sway Ahab, and his will to overt action had been sapped by a stronger will. Starbuck's soul had, indeed, been overmanned.

When Ahab leaves Starbuck, crosses the deck, and looks down into the water, he finds himself gazing into "two reflected, fixed eyes"; Fedallah is "motionlessly leaning over the same rail" (536). Implicit in the scene is the rejection of good, as represented by Starbuck, and allegiance to evil, as represented by Fedallah. Following the method of Hawthorne, Melville avoids committing himself to belief in the supernatural origins of Fedallah through use of the crew's superstition and speculation. Like the devil in Cotton Mather's day,[8] Fedallah appears in black, and his shadowy companions are natives of the Manillas, "a race notorious for a certain diabolism of subtilty, and by some honest white mariners supposed to be the paid spies and secret confidential agents on the water of the devil, their lord, whose counting-room they suppose to be elsewhere" (215). Stubb's theories about Fedallah are, as on all things, outspoken and to the point: "I take that Fedallah to be the devil in disguise. . . . the old man is hard bent after that White Whale, and the devil there is trying to come round him, and get him to swap away his silver watch, or his soul, or something of that sort, and then he'll surrender Moby Dick" (323–324).

At times, Fedallah is made to appear simply a projection of Ahab: "Ahab chanced so to stand, that the Parsee occupied his shadow; while, if the Parsee's shadow was there at all it seemed only to blend with, and lengthen Ahab's" (327). At other times, Fedallah appears so thin and insubstantial that he seems but a "tremulous shadow cast upon the deck by some unseen being's body" (527). Whatever he is, it is clear that Fedallah's evil power over Ahab matches Ahab's over the crew: "even as Ahab's eyes so awed the crew's, the inscrutable Parsee's glance awed his" (527). In the final scene before the chase begins, when Ahab spurns Starbuck and crosses the deck to gaze in Fedallah's reflected eyes, the accumulated references to and

[8] Cotton Mather, pp. 80–81: "The *Devil*, exhibiting himself ordinarily as a small *Black man*, has decoy'd a fearful knot of proud, froward, ignorant, envious and malicious creatures to lift themselves in his horrid Service by entering their names in a *Book* by him tendred unto them."

descriptions of the Parsee make quite clear that the Captain has at last irrevocably committed himself to do the devil's bidding. Although "Ahab seemed an independent lord, the Parsee but his slave" (528), Fedallah, like Aminadab in "The Birthmark," who appeared to be Aylmer's lowly servant, is in triumphant control of his master.

There are other scenes in *Moby Dick* which indicate Ahab's unholy alliance. When he fashions for himself the harpoon intended for the white whale, he insists on the use of blood from the three pagan harpooners for tempering the steel: " 'Ego non baptizo te in nomine patris, sed in nomine diaboli,' deliriously howled Ahab, as the malignant iron scorchingly devoured the baptismal blood" (484). Upon the appearance of the corposants, in the midst of the lurid light cast by the flames of the burning masts, Ahab seizes the main-mast links in order to cast the pulse of his blood against the alien fire, places his foot on prostrate Fedallah, and shouts his defiance to the heavens. The scene is climaxed with the mysterious appearance of a forked fire at the tip of Ahab's wickedly forged harpoon. Starbuck recognized the omen as ill: "God, God is against thee, old man; forbear!" (501). But Ahab does not forbear; he seizes the harpoon, brandishes it about to quiet the panic-stricken crew, and then, in a final gesture of defiance, blows out the flame with one mighty blast of his breath. Ahab for the moment becomes Satan, extinguishing the light of God.

Like Chillingworth in his consuming desire for revenge, like Aylmer in his obsession to rid the world of imperfection, like Rappaccini in his mad passion to protect his own from evil, Ahab invades the province of Heaven and attempts to assume God's role in the universe. When Starbuck cries out to Ahab, "To be enraged with a dumb thing . . . seems blasphemous," Ahab replies, "Talk not to me of blasphemy, man; I'd strike the sun if it insulted me" (161–162). In seeking revenge against the "Inscrutable malice" of Moby Dick for having reaped away his leg, Ahab is attempting, in his own right, to deliver divine justice which becomes, as a result, neither divine nor just. When, further, Ahab takes into his own hands the task of ridding the world of all evil through the destruction of Moby Dick, he is directly challenging the purposes and the power of God, purposes whose inscrutability he finds intolerable, power which maddens him because it is not his own. As Hawthorne had dramatized in his tales over and over again, such purposes and power may be understood not with the intellect but only with the heart, not in the momentary circumstance but only in eternity.

Although Ahab is cast in the central role in *Moby Dick*, his attitude is not Melville's.[9] Like Hawthorne, Melville carefully places in contrast to his great sinner a number of characters who suggest or symbolize the supreme good. Ishmael, Starbuck, Queequeg, and Pip function in a number of scenes to point out the virtuous way, a way in notable contrast to the fatal bypath taken by Ahab. As in Hawthorne, the greatest good lies not in the total absence of sin, an impossibility with mortal man, but rather in an all-engrossing love. As Ishmael sits hour after hour, squeezing lumps of sperm into fluid, he gradually begins to feel "divinely free from all ill-will, or petulance, or malice, of any sort whatsoever," until he is overcome with a "strange sort of insanity" (414). He finds himself inadvertently squeezing the hands of his companions, and is overcome with an "abounding, affectionate, friendly, loving feeling" that causes him to cry out to his fellows, though not aloud, "Come; let us squeeze hands all round; nay, let us all squeeze ourselves into each other; let us squeeze ourselves universally into the very milk and sperm of kindness" (414–415). Love, affection, kindness—these are the qualities which both Hawthorne and Melville found the essence of all good.

In Melville, as in Hawthorne, the reverse of all those traits characteristic of the greatest of sinners is portrayed as virtuous.

[9] In *Melville's Quarrel with God* (Princeton: Princeton Univ. Press, 1952), Lawrance Thompson has attempted to identify Ahab's attitude with Melville's: "Baldly stated, then, Melville's underlying theme in *Moby Dick* correlates the notion that the world was put together wrong and that God is to blame; that God in his infinite malice asserts a sovereign tyranny over man and that most men are seduced into the mistaken view that this divine tyranny is benevolent and therefore acceptable" (pp. 242–243). In order to arrive at such a reading of *Moby Dick*, Thompson has relied heavily on "insinuated" meaning which is "quite contrary to the superficial sense of the overt statement" (p. 7), and he claims that Melville deliberately obscured his meaning to protect himself from heresy hunters. Such an approach is, it seems to me, highly speculative and frequently misleading, and results, as the body of this chapter indicates, in what I consider incredible conclusions. Although Melville's point of view, like Hawthorne's, is not orthodoxly Christian, neither, surely, is it, as Thompson would have it, anti-Christian.

Ishmael at one point in *Moby Dick* presents the sum of all his knowledge: "I have perceived that in all cases man must eventually lower, or at least shift, his conceit of attainable felicity; not placing it anywhere in *the intellect* or the fancy, but in the wife, *the heart,* the bed, the table, the saddle, the fireside, the country" (415—italics added). Ishmael thus elevates the heart over the intellect, in a statement of philosophy which is the basis for Starbuck's final, almost hysterical appeal to Ahab: "grand old heart, after all! . . . Why should any one give chase to that hated fish! . . . Let us home! Wife and child, too, are Starbuck's—wife and child of his brotherly, sisterly, playfellow youth; even as thine, sir, are the wife and child of thy loving, longing, paternal old age! Away! let us away!" (535). But Starbuck has been deceived by the momentary lapse of Ahab's iron will. The appeal fails because it is an appeal to a heart that has too long been dominated by intellect. Both Ishmael and Starbuck recognize the fatality of such dominance.

In contrast with Ahab's determined, single-minded pursuit of Moby Dick stands Pip's intent but gentle search for himself. Pip's loss of his mind is a greater loss than Ahab's leg; yet the event, instead of transforming him into a monomaniac like Ahab, fills him, as Ahab recognizes, "full of the sweet things of love and gratitude" (515). Pip comes closer to success than Starbuck in changing Ahab's course. When Pip protests his desire to remain with Ahab, the Captain exclaims, "If thou speakest thus to me much more, Ahab's purpose keels up in him" (525). Pip's humility contrasts sharply with Ahab's arrogant pride. After the powerful quarterdeck scene, in which Ahab mesmerizes his crew with his evil magic, Pip cries out, "Oh, thou big white God aloft there somewhere in yon darkness, have mercy on this small black boy down here; preserve him from all men that have no bowels to feel fear!" (175). As Lady Eleanore's scorn had driven Helwyse mad, so his shipmates' indifference to his fate when he jumps overboard drives Pip to idiocy. But in each instance, "man's insanity is heaven's sense" (413). This insanity is the same "strange sort of insanity" that seizes Ishmael in the midst of the sperm-squeezing scene, at the moment of his greatest lucidity. It is insanity only because it is insight into, and encompasses, those supreme virtues which are as rare as they are divine.

When Ahab says to Pip, "Thou touchest my inmost centre, boy; thou art tied to me by cords wove of my heart-strings" (514), he is admitting that the thick cover of his self-imposed isolation has been, for the moment, penetrated. And when Pip, feeling Ahab's "kind" hand, exclaims, "Oh, Sir, let old Perth now come and rivet these two hands together" (514), he is expressing the strong pull of what Hawthorne termed the "magnetic chain of humanity." Ahab's deliberate severance of that chain is balanced by Ishmael's discovery and acceptance of it. To demonstrate the compelling magnetic pull of the chain, Melville throws together two extremely disparate individuals and links them fast together. When Ishmael first sees Queequeg, the Christian is terrified and repelled by the pagan. But after a brief period of "courtship," during which mutual understanding and respect grow, Queequeg declares to Ishmael that they are henceforth "married." The marriage imagery used throughout the development of this relationship aptly suggests the strength and depth of those human sympathies which bind man, regardless of superficial differences, to his fellow man. A different imagery touches upon the same theme in the scene of the monkey-rope. While Queequeg grapples with a whale down in the sea, Ishmael, fastened to the pagan by the monkey-rope, clings to the ship's side. Ishmael muses: "Queequeg was my own inseparable twin brother; nor could I any way get rid of the dangerous liabilities which the hempen bond entailed" (318). It is these very liabilities, entailed by the bonds of brotherhood, that Ahab disowns, but which Ishmael, upon their discovery, accepts.

At the opening of *Moby Dick*, Ishmael intensely feels a "damp, drizzly November" in his soul, and he is ready to disinherit the human race. But instead of following his morbid instinct to commit suicide, he goes to sea. Significantly, among the "wild conceits" that sway him to his purpose, there floats into his "inmost soul . . . one grand hooded phantom, like a snow hill in the air" (6). In short, Ishmael at the opening of *Moby Dick* is Ahab in miniature—isolated, defiant, obsessed. But, unlike Ahab, Ishmael changes in the course of the novel; the experience of the sea becomes for him an experience of purgation, purification. Ishmael alone escapes the catastrophe, and the source of his salvation is Queequeg's coffin life buoy, a single symbol uniting death and birth, descent and resurrection. Ishmael survives not because someone must remain to tell the tale, but rather because, unlike Ahab or the rest of the crew, he experiences a rebirth on the voyage of the *Pequod*. His is a voyage of discovery—discovery of the "pervading principle of love."

14

Poe's "Ulalume" Resurrected

Mr. Yvor Winters has stated the case against Edgar Allan Poe about as well as it can or need be stated. Mr. Winters' condemnation is as sweeping as it is severe:

> I am about to promulgate a heresy; namely, that E. A. Poe, although he achieved, as his admirers have claimed, a remarkable agreement between his theory and his practice, is exceptionally bad in both. I am somewhat startled, moreover, to awaken to the fact that this is a heresy, that those who object to Poe would do well to establish their position now if ever. Poe has long passed casually with me and with most of my friends as a bad writer accidentally and temporarily popular; the fact of the matter is, of course, that he has been pretty effectually established as a great writer while we have been sleeping.[1]

Following this opening shotgun blast, Mr. Winters first takes a few random shots at Poe's defenders and then settles down to the job of leveling Poe's reputation with the rapidity and methodicalness of a machine gun.

Mr. Winters is not isolated in his view of Poe. What has come to be called, loosely, the New Criticism, when it has chosen to acknowledge Poe at all, has found far more to condemn than to praise.[2] Indeed, the situation which Mr. Winters describes seems very nearly reversed: Poe has been pretty

---

[1] Yvor Winters, *In Defense of Reason* (New York: Swallow-Morrow, 1947), p. 234.
[2] See, for example, Allen Tate, "Our Cousin Mr. Poe," *Partisan Review*, XVI (Dec., 1949), 1207–19.

effectually established as a *bad* writer while those of us who have taken his position for granted have been sleeping.

Surely no one can quarrel with Mr. Winters' point that no amount of biographical, historical, or textual scholarship can establish Poe's or anybody else's greatness as a writer. The quantity of such scholarship in the case of Poe is staggering, and underlying all of it is the assumption that Poe is a major figure to be reckoned with in our literature. Too often we are tempted to believe that the scholarship proves the assumption. Such is never the case, and we should always be prepared to defend the assumption; indeed, we should always convince ourselves of the assumption before ever engaging in the scholarship. If Mr. Winters is right in his charges against Poe, this vast body of scholarship stands as a monument to wasted effort; if Poe is not worth reading (and certainly he is not if he is as bad as Mr. Winters thinks), surely the scholarship is less so.

If Poe's reputation is to be sustained or reestablished, it must be by the painful and slow process of complete critical revaluation. Such a large undertaking is, of course, outside the scope of this essay. But something in the nature of a first step is attempted here. Mr. Winters includes "Ulalume" among six poems on which, he says, "Poe's reputation as an important poet must rest. . . ."[3] I have concentrated attention on this one poem in the hope that, if it can be resurrected from the critical tomb to which it has been relegated, there will be increased interest in rescuing the rest.

When asked by a friend for an explanation of "Ulalume," Poe remarked: "I would endeavor to explain to you what I really meant—or what I really fancied I meant by the poem, if it were not that I remembered Dr. Johnson's bitter and rather just remark about the folly of explaining what, if worth explanation, should explain itself."[4] But "Ulalume" has not explained itself, as the various conflicting interpretations which have been made since the poem's first publication will testify. In the many attempts to derive consistent meaning from the poem, three general approaches may be distinguished: the biographical, the psychoanalytical, and the "purely" critical. Those who

[3] Winters, p. 251.

[4] Quoted in Arthur Hobson Quinn, *Edgar Allan Poe: A Critical Biography* (New York: D. Appleton-Century Co., 1941), p. 534.

have analyzed the poem with either of the first two methods have usually seemed satisfied that their results are conclusive, and that the value of the poem as a personal revelation of Poe's life or psychology is sufficient. Those who have attempted a critical analysis have usually reached a negative verdict, but, as I shall attempt to show, without giving sufficient attention to the evidence which a thorough reading of the poem yields.

Mrs. Sarah H. Whitman suggested the possibility of biographical interpretation when she pointed out that the lost Ulalume was Poe's wife, Virginia, who had died a few months before the poem was written—or so Mrs. Whitman believed.[5] This theory proved attractive to subsequent biographers, and the matter seemed settled. As one writer put it:

> The simplest interpretation of the poem is the best: It is the anniversary night of the burial of Mrs. Poe. The poet is in communion with himself, with his subconscious or subliminal self. He wanders along the well-worn pathway to the grave and, momentarily forgetful of his grief, feels the call of peace and morning. But Psyche, his deeper soul-nature, sees an omen of ill. Hardly has he allayed the foreboding of Psyche when he comes abruptly upon the grave. Memory returns now with an added pang because of the interim of forgetfulness.[6]

The psychoanalytical readings of "Ulalume" are in a sense simply an intensification of the biographical interpretations, with Poe's mind and personality subjected to a much more rigorous, albeit speculative, scrutiny. One doctor of medicine has stated offhandedly, ". . . such a poem as *Ulalume* might have been formulated in a brain which was somewhat diseased, but whose capacity for rhythm and euphony remained unim-

[5] Arthur H. Quinn and Richard H. Hart, eds., *Edgar Allan Poe: Letters and Documents in the Enoch Pratt Free Library* (New York: Scholars' Facsimiles & Reprints, 1941), p. 49. In a letter to Maria Clemm, Mrs. Whitman says: "I have heard Edgar speak of the circumstances under which he composed the poem of Ulalume. It purports to have been suggested by a midnight walk on the Anniversary of a burial—and it is my impression that he told me it *was* so written. But Virginia died in January did she not?—And the poem was professedly written in *October*—Perhaps the correspondence in *time* was purely *ideal*—I know he described the emotions themselves as *real*." For evidence that the poem may have been written before the death of Virginia, see Killis Campbell, *The Poems of Edgar Allan Poe* (New York: Ginn and Co., 1917), p. 266.

[6] C. Alphonso Smith, *Edgar Allan Poe: How to Know Him* (Indianapolis: The Bobbs-Merrill Co., 1921), pp. 225–26. It is difficult to see how the critic here can say that the poet "feels the call of peace," in view of the fact that his heart is described as "volcanic."

paired."[7] The most exhaustive study of this kind is that by Marie Bonaparte, who diligently probes Poe's poetry in search of unintended meanings and implications:

Psyche is thus, on the one hand, Poe's mother, to whom he unconsciously remained faithful through life and, on the other, the educative mother who, by moral injunctions, protects her developing child from incest and sexual indulgence. . . . But it seems to me that Psyche's drooping, trailing wings in this poem symbolize in concrete form Poe's physical impotence. We know that flying, to all races, unconsciously symbolizes the sex act, and that antiquity often represented the penis erect and winged. In this poem, Psyche's trailing wings symbolize the fact that, however ardent his "ethereal" passions, Poe was impotent sexually.[8]

Mr. Yvor Winters, in his treatment of the poem, points out at the beginning the dangers inherent in the foregoing approaches:

In examining this poem, we must confine ourselves strictly to what Poe offered us, namely, the poem, and refrain from biographical entanglements, which are both gratuitous and uncertain. If the poem is not self-sufficient, it is obscure; and, as critics of art, we are bound to rest with the assumption that the obscurity was satisfactory to Poe.

After a close reading of the poem, Mr. Winters concludes, "In other words, the subject of grief is employed as a very general excuse for a good deal of obscure and only vaguely related emotion."[9]

In a similar but more extended analysis of "Ulalume," Messrs. Brooks and Warren, after a summary of the "elements of incident" in the poem, seem uncertain that any conclusion can be drawn:

This is, apparently, an *allegorical* way of saying that love (or the semblance of love, for the crescent is defined as "the spectre of a planet") only leads him to the door of the tomb where Ulalume is buried. But all of this leaves a great many questions, even questions that should have factual answers, without answer.

These questions revolve about the use of place names which "have no historical or geographical existence" (Auber, Weir),

---

[7] John W. Robertson, M.D., *Edgar A. Poe: A Psychopathic Study* (New York: G. P. Putnam's Sons, 1923), p. 70.

[8] Marie Bonaparte, *The Life and Works of Edgar Allan Poe: A Psycho-Analytic Interpretation* (London: Image Publishing Co., Ltd., 1949), pp. 150–51.

[9] Winters, *op. cit.*, pp. 252–53.

the seemingly arbitrary and unjustified use of the ghouls in the last stanza, and the "emphatic beat of rhythm that becomes monotonous."[10]

Mr. Winters is surely right in demanding that the poem be self-sufficient, that we not go outside the poem to explain it; and the questions raised by Messrs. Brooks and Warren are certainly valid—unless the monotonous rhythm, the mythical place names, and the ghouls have some function in the poem, their use constitutes a major defect. I wish to emphasize that I accept, in my examination of the poem, the critical framework within which both of these analyses have been written, although I reach somewhat different conclusions.

It seems self-evident now that those who were concerned with establishing Poe as the protagonist in the poem were not dealing with a relevant critical problem. However, these writers have, though perhaps accidentally, placed the emphasis where it belonged: on the emotional state of the speaker not as he exists inside the poem but rather as he exists in the act of conceiving the experiences related in the poem. One should not go, of course, to Poe's biography to reconstruct this emotional state; the poem itself should and does give sufficient material for such a reconstruction.

"Ulalume" presents the protagonist in three different and distinguishable emotional states, in three different places at three different times. There is, first, the protagonist as he conceives himself at the opening of the poem, wandering through a death-suggestive landscape with Psyche, his soul:

> These were the days when my heart was volcanic
>> As the scoriac rivers that roll—
>> As the lavas that restlessly roll
> Their sulphurous current down Yaanek
>> In the realms of the Boreal Pole.

There is, next, the protagonist as he conceives himself at the end of the poem, in a sadly familiar setting, at the tomb of Ulalume:

> Then my heart it grew ashen and sober
>> As the leaves that were crispèd and sere—
>> As the leaves that were withering and sere;

---

[10] Cleanth Brooks and Robert Penn Warren, *Understanding Poetry* (New York: Henry Holt and Co., 1938), pp. 358–62.

And finally, there is the protagonist as narrator, as he in actuality *is,* whose imagination has created the experience of the poem in which he has involved himself.

It is in the protagonist as *narrator* that the dramatic key to the poem resides, and it is a *dramatic,* not a biographical, psychoanalytical, or allegorical key. Curiously enough, this neglected narrator is the only reality in the poem; all else is filtered through his mind in its singular mental state. The reader is not asked to believe in the incredible events, or even to make sense of them, except inasmuch as they relate to or define the emotional state of the speaker.

The experience described in the poem is not, then, in its own terms a coherent experience. Critical attempts to impose coherence have ended either in failure, and condemnation of the poem, or in strange distortions and a glossing over or ignoring of glaring difficulties. It is, perhaps, because of the immediacy of the description in the first stanza that the assumption has usually been made that the events which follow represent an immediate experience, described by the man as he is at the end of the poem. But in the second stanza, a distance in time, as important as the distance in place, is indicated:

> Here once, through an alley Titanic,
>> Of cypress, I roamed with my soul—
>> Of cypress, with Psyche, my soul.
> These were days . . .

The time references here ("Here once . . ." "These were days . . .") imply that the speaker is recalling the past, the distant past, perhaps even an imagined past. In any event, there is no reason to assume that the speaker, at the time of the recreation of his experience, is in the same psychological condition as that which he conceives for himself at either the beginning or the end of the poem.

The reality which the imagination of the reader must reconstruct is the reality of the speaker, as he is while conceiving the experience of the poem; the unreality of the experience, the "rather disorderly use of suggestion,"[11] and the monotony of the rhythm, all contribute richly to this reconstruction. Indeed, one can contend that the poem has not been really understood unless the imagination has performed this reconstruction. The

[11] *Ibid.,* p. 360.

disorder of the images at the opening of the poem is significant: from skies, to leaves, to night, to the "dim lake of Auber" and the "misty mid region of Weir." This arrangement is not a logical one, nor is that which follows in the second and third stanzas: from external situation, to internal personal feeling, back to external situation, and, finally, a return to the somber setting which is in essence a recapitulation of much of the first stanza. This disorder underscores the abnormal or dream-like state of mind of the speaker, from which images, ideas, phrases emerge, are repeated, disappear, and then recur. The almost exact repetition of certain lines, such as

> The leaves they were crispèd and sere—
> The leaves they were withering and sere.—

point also to a mind in a trance-like state which lingers almost sensuously over certain images, releasing them only reluctantly.

The monotonous rhythm, the repetitious but slow beat, beat, beat, with its lulling, hypnotic effect, emphasizes the non-rational state of the speaker's mind. He is in that twilight of the mind where the real and the unreal intermingle and become indistinguishable. It is a point midway between waking and sleeping, sanity and insanity. It is only when the narrator is conceived in some such state or situation as this, and placed in the dramatic center of the poem, that the incoherence of the stated experience becomes coherent. For the experience flows from the non-rational mind of the narrator, has existence only in that mind, and is significant only in terms of it.

The torment in the mind of the narrator has its roots in a deep-seated frustation: the inability to achieve sexual fulfillment because of its inevitable association with death. This frustration has precipitated the narrator into a state of mental suspension between the real and the unreal, a state in which an imagined experience abounds with images and symbols reflecting the frustration.

In these terms, it is important that there *not* be any geographical locations of Auber and Weir except in the imagined world of the narrator. The value of these place names must exist solely in their associations and their sounds: Auber—awful; Weir—weird. These associations fit admirably the setting, in which symbols of death abound: the skies are ashen (burnt-out, dead); the leaves are crispèd and sere (dried out, dead); it is October, the traditional month of the death of nature; the adjectives, "dim," "misty," "dank," "ghoul-haunted," lend their force to the prevalence of death; and the cypress tree has associations with graveyards.

In this setting of death, in the midst of death, the narrator sees himself filled with a passionate life: his heart is described as "volcanic," an image of explosive movement, heat, and light which is in dramatic contrast with the setting. And the image, as it is expanded, takes on sexual overtones, in the "scoriac rivers," in the word "restlessly," and in "sulphurous currents." It is a strong, perhaps overwhelming, sexual impulse that the narrator feels, and the connotations of death resulting from the impulse are not noted by him. The predominance of death which has been caused by excessive heat, suggested by "ashen," "crispèd," and "sere," should be noted; the connection between the sexual feeling (turbulent heat) and death (brought about by intense heat) is thus made direct.

Psyche is a projection of the narrator's mind, born of his soul, but gradually evolving into the sex object. She progresses from phantom to physical reality. At the opening of the poem, although their talk had been "serious and sober," their thoughts were "palsied and sere." Upon the appearance of Astarte, Psyche is described in physical terms, "uplifting her finger," "letting sink her wings till they trailed in the dust." And at the height of his passionate feeling, intensified by the "Sibyllic splendor" of Astarte, the narrator kisses Psyche, and conquers her "scruples." Psyche's transition from insubstantial soul to a separate being capable of physical love takes place, of course, only in the unstable mind of the speaker.

But as Psyche is derived from the narrator's realized sexual impulse, so the ambiguous Astarte springs from a deeper, a suppressed knowledge:

> At the end of our path a liquescent
> And nebulous lustre was born

The narrator immediately assumes that Astarte will lead to sexual fulfillment, but Psyche draws back in mistrust. Psyche sees the pallor of death; the narrator sees the Sibyllic splendor of love. And just as the narrator is on the verge of fulfillment, just as he has overcome the scruples of Psyche, they come upon the "legended tomb." Death intrudes. And there is the dramatic climax in which Psyche, the sex object, points to the tomb, symbol of death:

> " 'Tis the vault of thy lost Ulalume!"

It is the narrator's discovery of his deep-set frustration; it is the full realization of the inevitable link between sexual love and death, the realization that sexual love ends with death, is in itself a kind of death.

What does lie in the tomb? The references are few and obscure:

> " 'Tis the vault of *thy lost Ulalume!*"
>
> "That I brought *a dread burden* down here."
>
> "From *the secret* that lies hidden in these wolds,
> From *the thing* that lies hidden in the wolds."

The assumption that Ulalume is the dead wife or love of the narrator seems to me hasty, and difficult to reconcile with "a dread burden," "the secret," and "the thing," hardly terms to describe a beloved. Is it not rather the terrible knowledge of the connection between sexual love and death, which the narrator has attempted to forget, and which, in the course of the poem, he rediscovers? The narrator sees all death, even his own, more especially his own, in the tomb. Ulalume, then, is Death itself, a personification of turbulent sexual impulse combined with its inevitable destruction. The discovery of the tomb, remembrance of death, causes the narrator's heart to become

> ashen and sober
> As the leaves that were crispèd and sere—
> As the leaves that were withering and sere;

The live sexual instinct has been killed, and the narrator is no longer in conflict with his environment. He has accepted death into his heart; he has acknowledged the dreaded link.

The poem closes with the narrator and Psyche speaking together, wondering whether the ghouls have attempted to keep them from the discovery. Why should they think so? The ghouls have a morbid interest in death; therefore, they represent the unrealized desire for death created by the sexual impulse. They would have drawn up the "sinfully scintillant" Astarte in order to encourage the sexual impulse and its concomitant compulsion toward death. They are, therefore, "pitiful" and "merciful" in that they naturally would have encouraged the narrator in the fulfillment of his passionate desires. But the revelation of the morbid link has banished the sexual feeling and, at the same time, the compulsion toward death. The ghouls, then, succeed only in accomplishing the reverse of their purpose. But, of course, all of these symbols have their origin in the mind of the narrator, a mind in conflict with itself; they represent, therefore, the conflicting desires which the narrator feels.

What is, then, the essential experience of "Ulalume"? It is not the incoherent experience as it is described independently in the poem. It is, rather, this experience in symbolic terms as it is related to the pervading intelligence of the narrator—an intelligence in a suspended state, in static conflict with itself. It is an intelligence in trance, in dream. This intelligence is not just at the center of the poem—it is, in a very real sense, the poem in its entirety.

15

Uncharted Interiors: The American Romantics Revisited

As any graduate student knows, American literature is schizophrenic. It is held paralyzed between hope and despair, between the affirmative and negative, between illusion and fact, between optimism and pessimism, between the ideal and the real. The split is down the middle and the major writers may be divided: Emerson, Thoreau, and Whitman on the one side; Poe, Hawthorne, and Melville on the other. The origins of a divided taproot have been traced back incredible distances, but in America itself there are, for the sons of light, eighteenth-century rationalism, deism, and Quakerism, and for the sons of darkness, seventeenth-century puritanism and Calvinism. Our own twentieth century has looked back on this split personality in American literature, and has declared the chasm unbridgeable. Indeed if we would be frank, we should acknowledge that the twentieth century has most frequently found its own dark features best reflected in Hawthorne and Melville, and even in Poe when he sounds most like Kafka. And the contemporary critic of Emerson and Whitman has found himself apologizing for the smiling countenance of his subject, and the commentator on Thoreau has had to stress that the woodsdweller is not a hermit permanently committed to his pond-side solitude.

In short, modern criticism, whatever its protestations, has judged the American Romantics not on their art but on their attitudes. The bad guys are those who embraced life with a gusto, vigor, and virility that jar the anxiety-ridden modern sensibility; the good guys are those who held life at a distance because of its horror, hostility, and evil—the twentieth century's view of its own predicament. No one writer can be cited as the cause of the shift in critical view, but one can be named as pivotal: T. S. Eliot. After "Tradition and the Individual Talent" (1920), few critics seemed able to take seriously Emerson's call for the American to establish his own original relation with the universe. After *The Waste Land* (1922), few poets seemed able to listen seriously to the barbaric yawp of Whitman. And it is, surely, no accident that it was precisely at this period that American criticism discovered it had been overlooking perhaps its greatest writer, Herman Melville.

Whatever the causes—and they surely run deep in political, social, philosophical, and religious undercurrents—the fact remains, there was a massive shift in American critical outlook between the 1850's and the 1920's. The benign optimism of one prince of American letters, Ralph Waldo Emerson, was transmogrified into the scowling gloom of his successor to the crown, T. S. Eliot. And even now, after our precarious entry into the second half of the tentative twentieth century, we have not escaped the shadow of that long scowl. We accept as our own, too often without question, judgments that hardened into dogma almost a half-century ago. We have been timid in questioning the established gospel; we have been afraid to see the world anew with our own eyes.

It is time that we reexamined the schizoid character of American literature and set about discovering those elements that would make it an integrated personality. But at the outset of such a search, we should agree that writers of genius—and this category would include Emerson, Thoreau, Whitman, Poe, Hawthorne, and Melville—are distinguished by their uniqueness, by their separateness from all that has come before or after. To make categorical and inflexible groupings is false; to make rigid alignments and alliances is phony. If we explore relationships of these American Romantics, we are not seeking a single pool from which they all sipped, but a subterranean torrent that quenched their varied thirsts.

What I propose is not a conclusion but a beginning, not a discovery but an exploration. As a context for a new perspective, a number of quotations from twentieth-century psychology may best be introduced forthwith.

Uncharted Interiors: The American Romantics Revisited

I cannot but think that the most important step forward that has occurred in psychology since I have been a student of that science is the discovery, first made in 1886, that, in certain subjects at least, there is not only the consciousness of the ordinary field, with its usual centre and margin, but an addition thereto in the shape of a set of memories, thoughts, and feelings which are extra-marginal and outside of the primary consciousness altogether, but yet must be classed as conscious facts of some sort, able to reveal their presence by unmistakable signs . . . generalizing this phenomenon, Mr. Myers has given the name of *automatism*, sensory or motor, emotional or intellectual, to this whole sphere of effects, due to 'up-rushes' into the ordinary consciousness of energies originating in the subliminal parts of the mind.[1]

A more or less superficial layer of the unconscious is undoubtedly personal. I call it the *personal unconscious*. But this personal unconscious rests upon a deeper layer, which does not derive from personal experience and is not a personal acquisition but is unborn. This deeper layer I call the *collective unconscious*. I have chosen the term 'collective' because this part of the unconscious is not individual but universal; in contrast to the personal psyche, it has contents and modes of behavior that are more or less the same everywhere and in all individuals. It is, in other words, identical in all men and thus constitutes a common psychic substrata of a suprapersonal nature which is present in every one of us.[2]

Heaven, hell, the mythological age, Olympus and all the other habitations of the gods, are interpreted by psychoanalysis as symbols of the unconscious. The key to the modern systems of psychological interpretation therefore is: the metaphysical realm = the unconscious. Correspondingly, the key to open the door the other way is the same equation in reverse: the unconscious = the metaphysical realm. "For," as Jesus states it, "behold, the kingdom of God is within you."[3]

Additional quotations could be cited, especially from Sigmund Freud or D. H. Lawrence, but these from William James, Jung, and Joseph Campbell should serve our purposes. The hypothesis I wish to offer, with no hope of testing it in this short space, derives from the kind of thinking, with its strong psychoanalytic drift, embodied in the foregoing quotations. In brief it runs as follows: the meeting ground of Emerson, Thoreau, and Whitman is in their transcendental mysticism—spirit; while the meeting ground of Poe, Hawthorne,

[1] William James, *The Varieties of Religious Experience* (New York: Doubleday Dolphin Book, n.d.), pp. 215–16.

[2] C. G. Jung, *The Basic Writings* (New York: Random House, Modern Library, 1959), p. 287.

[3] Joseph Campbell, *The Hero with a Thousand Faces* (Cleveland: The World Pub. Co., Meridian Book, 1956), p. 259.

and Melville is in their psychological drama—mind; when the one group leaps high enough in the spirit, and the other delves deep enough in the mind, they find themselves on the same enigmatic, symbolic landscape. Whether exploring the hills of heaven or the pits of hell, the landscape lies within. In short, what all these American Romantics knew and explored together was what the modern psychologists think they have newly discovered—the unconscious. The vocabulary has shifted, but the fundamental visions remain.

Emerson's thought has so long been considered derivative, connecting as it does with Plato, with Oriental philosophy, with Kant, with Carlyle, that attention has been deflected from its possible relationship with modern psychological thought. Quotation after quotation might be culled from his essays to show a kind of prophecy of contemporary concepts of the conscious and the unconscious.

But when, following the invisible steps of thought, we come to inquire, Whence is matter? and Whereto? many truths arise to us out of the recesses of consciousness. . . . As a plant upon the earth, so a man rests upon the bosom of God; he is nourished by unfailing fountains, and draws at his need inexhaustible power. (*Nature*)

What is the aboriginal Self, on which a universal reliance may be grounded? . . . The inquiry leads us to that source, at once the essence of genius, of virtue, and of life, which we call Spontaneity or Instinct. We denote this primary wisdom as Intuition, whilst all later teachings are tuitions. In that deep force, the last fact behind which analysis cannot go, all things find their common origin. ("Self-Reliance")

On my saying, 'What have I to do with the sacredness of traditions, if I live wholly from within?' my friend suggested,—'But these impulses may be from below, not from above.' I replied, 'They do not seem to me to be such; but if I am the Devil's child, I will live then from the Devil.' No law can be sacred to me but that of my nature. Good and bad are but names very readily transferable to that or this; the only right is what is after my constitution; the only wrong what is against it. ("Self-Reliance")

Translated into the modern psychological idiom, this conversation might be conceived as resting on the distinction between Freud's personal unconscious, with all its suppressed sexual emotion, and Jung's collective unconscious, with its universal racial memory.

It is possible, even, to see Emerson's terms of soul and oversoul verging on transfiguration into modern psychology's conscious and unconscious, or the personal as differentiated from the collective unconscious.

The philosophy of six thousand years has not searched the chambers and magazines of the soul. In its experiments there has always remained, in the last analysis, a residuum it could not resolve. Man is a stream whose source is hidden. . . . When I watch that flowing river, which, out of regions I see not, pours for a season its streams into me, I see that I am a pensioner; not a cause but a surprised spectator of this ethereal water; that I desire and look up and put myself in the attitude of reception, but from some alien energy the visions come. . . . We live in succession, in division, in parts, in particles. Meantime within man is the soul of the whole; the wise silence; the universal beauty, to which every part and particle is equally related; the eternal ONE. ("The Over-Soul")

Like Emerson, Thoreau discovered the deepest mysteries of life not without but within, and within those very "chambers and magazines" of the soul which have always baffled philosophy.

I found in myself, and still find, an instinct toward a higher, or, as it is named, spiritual life, as do most men, and another toward a primitive rank and savage one, and I reverence them both. . . . We are conscious of an animal in us, which awakens in proportion as our higher nature slumbers. It is reptile and sensual, and perhaps cannot be wholly expelled; like the worms which, even in life and health, occupy our bodies. Possibly we may withdraw from it, but never change its nature. I fear that it may enjoy a certain health of its own; that we may be well, yet not pure. (*Walden*)

Freud would have no difficulty here in identifying his id, ego, and superego, and Jung would have no trouble in identifying, in the following quotation, his collective unconscious: "Time is but the stream I go a-fishing in. I drink at it; but while I drink I see the sandy bottom and detect how shallow it is. Its thin current slides away, but eternity remains. I would drink deeper; fish in the sky, whose bottom is pebbly with stars" (*Walden*).

As transcendentalism moved closer to the twentieth century and found its finest poetic expression in Walt Whitman, it seemed to become more self-consciously psychological. Whitman himself was a believer in the psychology of his day, phrenology, and prided himself on his own poetically favorable chart of bumps. It is of considerable significance that Whitman saw the attributes of the poet in psychological terms (the words have special phrenological meanings):

Extreme caution or prudence, the soundest organic health, large hope and comparison and fondness for women and children, large alimentiveness and destructiveness and causality, with a perfect sense of the oneness

of nature and the propriety of the same spirit applied to human affairs
. . . these are called up of the float of the brain of the world to be parts
of the greatest poet from his birth out of his mother's womb and from
her birth out of her mother's. (1855 Preface)

"The float of the brain of the world" needs only the slightest
modification to become Jung's collective unconscious, with all
its racial residue of myths and archetypes. In the opening
section of "Song of Myself," the poet says:

> Creeds and schools in abeyance,
> Retiring back a while sufficed at what they are, but never
>   forgotten,
> I harbor for good or bad, I permit to speak at every hazard,
> Nature without check with original energy.

In Jungian terms, the poet seems to be voiding his mind in
preparation for the invading floods from the unconscious. And
later on, fragmentary visions seem to surge to the surface and
flash out in momentary brilliance:

> Urge and urge and urge,
> Always the procreant urge of the world.
>
> Out of the dimness opposite equals advance, always substance
>   and increase, always sex,
> Always a knit of identity, always distinction, always a breed of
>   life.

The very substance of the imagery in such passages as this
suggests a strong affinity with modern psychological thought.
Although the vision is sexual, it appears to drive deeper than
the personal, to that line where levels of the unconscious
mingle, where sex itself begins to generate myth.

In many ways the entire work of Poe can be seen as a
probing of the dark "chambers and magazines" of the soul or
mind. As a foundation stone of his work stands that curious
prose-poem, *Eureka*, with its strange mixture of science, philosophy, religion, and psychology. Observe: "We walk about,
amid the destinies of our world-existence, encompassed by dim
but ever present *Memories* of a Destiny more vast—very distant
in the bygone time, and infinitely awful." Here the Jungian
racial memory lurks in embryo. And more: ". . . that nothing
is, or can be, superior to any one soul; that each soul is, in part,
its own God—its own Creator;—in a word, that God—the material *and* spiritual God—*now* exists solely in the diffused Matter and Spirit of the Universe; and that the regathering of this

diffused Matter and Spirit will be but the re-constitution of the *purely Spiritual* and Individual God." The whole tendency of such a passage is to throw the individual back into himself— the soul is "its own Creator"—in the search for the profund- ities of being. All of Poe's imaginative writing represents in some sense an exploration of hidden labyrinths of the interior; hence his recurring use of the dream as dramatic structure. In "Dream-Land":

> By a route obscure and lonely,
> Haunted by ill angels only,
> > Where an Eidolon, named NIGHT,
> > On a black throne reigns upright,
> > I have reached these lands but newly
> > From an ultimate dim Thule—
> From a wild weird clime that lieth, sublime,
> > Out of SPACE—out of TIME.

The poem is filled with a bizarre symbolism—vales, caves, mountains toppling, seas surging, lakes outspread—that begins to make sense only in terms of psychoanalytic interpretation. And that King of the black throne, "who hath forbid/The up- lifting of the fring'd lid," is surely related, however distantly, to the psychologist's Censor. As has been frequently noted, the house in Poe often becomes the controlling symbol of a work, and is nearly always equated with the mind. Jung him- self could not have discovered a better metaphor for his mean- ings than the school house in "William Wilson":

But the house!—how quaint an old building was this!—to me how veritably a palace of enchantment! There was really no end to its windings—to its incomprehensible subdivisions. It was difficult, at any given time, to say with certainty upon which of its two stories one happened to be. From each room to every other there were sure to be found three or four steps either in ascent or descent. Then the lateral branches were innumerable—inconceivable—and so returning in upon themselves, that our most exact ideas in regard to the whole mansion were not very far different from those with which we pondered upon infinity. During the five years of my residence here, I was never able to ascertain with precision, in what remote locality lay the little sleeping apartment assigned to myself and some eighteen or twenty other schol- ars.

Like Poe's stories, Hawthorne's tales often are basically psy- chological structures with objects, places, or characters func- tioning symbolically, leading the reader not outward into the world of reality but inward into the mazes of the mind. A typical Hawthorne protagonist may be delineated as suffering from a paralysis of the imagination as he fixes his gaze in horror on the personal unconscious, filled as it is with all of the individual's suppressed and unspeakable desires. Unable either to extricate himself from his gaze or to penetrate to the profounder levels of the unconscious, he becomes sick in his obsession with his own and mankind's evil. In "Egotism; or, The Bosom Serpent," Roderick Elliston is such a protagonist who broadcasts to the community that he is being gnawed by a snake in his breast: "The symptoms caused them endless perplexity. They knew not whether ill health were robbing his spirits of elasticity, or whether a canker of the mind was gradually eating, as such cankers do, from his moral system into the physical frame, which is but the shadow of the former. . . . Some thought that their once brilliant friend was in an incipient stage of insanity." In "The Birthmark," the mad scientist, Aylmer, obsessed like Roderick with the world's imperfection, kills his wife in his attempt to remove the disfiguration from her face: "Yet, had Aylmer reached a profounder wisdom, he need not thus have flung away the happiness which would have woven his mortal life of the self-same texture with the celestial. The momentary circumstance was too strong for him; he failed to look beyond the shadowy scope of time, and, living once for all in eternity, to find the perfect future in the present." In Jungian terms, Hawthorne's obsessed heroes have found imprisonment and not freedom in the labyrinths of the unconscious. Theirs is a shallow penetration into the hidden recesses of the mind.

Like Whitman, Melville strikes us as closer to the modern psychological point of view than his predecessors, Poe and Hawthorne. Indeed, in that astonishing chapter called "Dreams" in the middle of *Mardi*, Melville seems to be penetrating and exploring the depths of the unconscious much as Whitman does in his poem, "The Sleepers." Melville: "Dreams! dreams! golden dreams: endless, and golden, as the flowery prairies . . . my dreams herd like buffaloes, browsing on the horizon, and browsing on round the world; and among them, I dash with my lance, to spear one, ere they all flee." And Whitman:

> I wander all night in my vision,
> Stepping with light feet, swiftly and noiselessly stepping and
>   stopping,
> Bending with open eyes over the shut eyes of sleepers. . . .

Both writers seem to be released from the bonds of earth and time. Melville: ". . . with all the past and present pouring in me, I roll down my billow from afar." Whitman: "I descend my western course, my sinews are flaccid,/Perfume and youth course through me and I am their wake."

In *Mardi*, too, Babbalanja seems consciously to tap the resources of wisdom which lie in the collective unconscious as he attunes himself to his mysterious interior "devil," Azzageddi. In his seizures by Azzageddi, Babbalanja always speaks with a more cryptic, profounder insight than he knows. Of all Melville's novels, however, *Pierre* seems most directly to anticipate modern psychology's theories of the unconscious. Its *Ambiguities* (the subtitle) are all of the mind, and in following the "endless, winding way,—the flowing river in the cave of man," Melville discovered complexities of motivation in the depths of the mind that Freud and Jung could have cited as the basis for their theories. But Melville's understanding of the depths of the psyche can best be suggested by a neglected passage from that novel of novels, *Moby Dick*, a passage with an intricate series of metaphors and symbols well worth close study:

This is much; yet Ahab's larger, darker, deeper part remains unhinted. But vain to popularize profundities, and all truth is profound. Winding far down from within the very heart of this spiked Hotel de Cluny where we here stand—however grand and wonderful, now quit it;—and take your way, ye nobler, sadder souls, to those vast Roman halls of Thermes; where far beneath the fantastic towers of man's upper earth, his root of grandeur, his whole awful essence sits in bearded state; an antique buried beneath antiquities, and throned on torsoes! So with a broken throne, the great gods mock that captive king; so like a Caryatid, he patient sits, upholding on his frozen brow the piled entablatures of ages. Wind ye down there, ye prouder, sadder souls! question that proud, sad king! A family likeness! aye, he did beget ye, ye young exiled royalties; and from your grim sire only will the old State-secret come.

The structure symbolism is reminiscent of Poe's houses of the mind, but Melville seems to conceive the structure of the psyche in more grandiose and awesome terms. And as we wind our way into the depths, we cannot help but feel that we are approaching, however obliquely and obscurely, the deepest and most ancient sources of being, out of space, out of time—a landscape that is all mankind's ("a family likeness") as much as Ahab's.

It is, of course, one thing to discover in the American Romantics some prophetic suggestions of modern psychological concepts; it is another to find patterns in these suggestions that might prove significant and illuminating in approaching individual works. It is, then, appropriate to sketch a tentative pattern here, offered more as hypothesis than as an inflexible formula. One characteristic of the monomyth (according to Joseph Campbell in *The Hero with a Thousand Faces*) is withdrawal and the journey, for which the self's retreat into and exploration of the unconscious is the paradigm. Departure and travel seem to constitute a major recurring metaphor in the work of all six of the American writers we have examined. In Emerson, the metaphor is not overt so much as everywhere implied, as in such sentences as: "Books are for the scholar's idle times. When he can read God directly, the hour is too precious to be wasted in other men's transcripts of their readings" ("The American Scholar"). Emerson's call to communion with the "aboriginal self," in "Self-Reliance," is clearly the call to a spiritual exploration. Thoreau's trip to Walden pond, however short the distance, may yet prove the longest in America; and in his chapter on "Solitude" he asked: "Why should I feel lonely? is not our planet in the Milky Way?" Whitman said, in "Song of Myself": "I tramp a perpetual journey, (come listen all!)/My signs are a rain-proof coat, good shoes, and a staff cut from the woods." Poe's narrators in "The Fall of the House of Usher" and "Ulalume" tell us in their opening sentences that they are journeying over strange landscapes; and Arthur Gordon Pym voyages forth in exploration of places never before seen by man. Hawthorne's "Young Goodman Brown" and Robin (in "My Kinsman, Major Molineaux") withdraw from home and venture forth on journeys that subtly merge nightmare and reality. And Melville's Ishmael, with the "damp, drizzly November" in his soul, accounts it "high time to get to sea" as soon as he can.

Clearly all of these journeys are in some sense symbolic journeys, and represent to some degree a descent into the depths of the "aboriginal Self." The discoveries are diverse, but are they as antithetical as we have always assumed? The psyche in its labyrinthine maze contains many truths; to emerge with one is not to deny others. Thoreau as he sets off for Walden has much in common with Ishmael as he sets off on the *Pequod*. As Thoreau goes about making the familiar exotic, and Melville the exotic familiar, we begin to detect a subterranean identity in the substance of their explorations. Similarly, the dreamworlds explored by Whitman in "The Sleepers" and by Hawthorne in "Young Goodman Brown" have much in common, however different the ultimate effects on the mature poet and the young man. Emerson's prose poem *Nature* shares much in the contours of its landscape with Poe's prose poem, *Eureka.* Isolated sentences, flashing forth from the deepest intuition, might well win the signature of both.

To suggest connections is not to deny differences. Genius by definition is unique. But it is true that scholarly ways of thinking may drift into rigidity, and what was originally brilliance of insight may in the repetition become exhausted cliché. The differences among these six American Romantics are clear, detectable, permanent. We would not want it otherwise. But as readers in depth, we might well want to ponder some compelling likenesses as we journey with them through uncharted interiors and view the remarkable continents they have discovered.

INDEX

INDEX

Absurd: in the contemporary novel, 5; in Faulkner, 49, 64–65; in Hawthorne, 203; Theater of the, influence on contemporary novel, 11

Age of Anxiety, 78–79

Albee, Edward, *The American Dream*, 11

Aldrich, Thomas Bailey, rewriting Dickinson, 151–52

Aldridge, John W., *After the Lost Generation*, 8

Alienation: in contemporary novel, 13; of Faulkner's heroes, 56–59; in Edith Wharton's world, 86

Anderson, Charles R., *Emily Dickinson's Poetry: The Stairway of Surprise:* discussed, 141; described, 145 n. 1; mentioned, 138

Anderson, Maxwell, mentioned, 77

Anderson, Sherwood, mentioned, 77

Angry Young Men: influence on contemporary novel, 10; mentioned, 80, 96

Austen, Jane, compared to Edith Wharton, 86

Baldwin, James: *Another Country*, 13; critical estimate, 19; quest for identity, 14; mentioned, 20

Barth, John: *The Floating Opera*, 13; critical estimate, 24–25

Beat Generation: defined, 80; influence on contemporary novel, 10

Beatniks: quest for identity, 96; and Whitman, 105

Beckett, Samuel, *Waiting for Godot*, 11

Bellow, Saul: critical estimate, 20–22; mentioned, 13, 15, 65

Bhagavad-Gita, mentioned, 80

Black Humor: described, 15; novelists of, critical estimate, 24; *see also* Humor and Horror

Braswell, William, *Melville's Religious Thought*, 187

Brown, Edward K., *Willa Cather: A Critical Biography*, criticism of *My Ántonia*, 66

Buber, Martin, and the quest for identity, 96

Bucke, Richard M.: *Cosmic Consciousness*, Whitman's mysticism, 109–10; mentioned, 105

Bunyan, John, the unpardonable sin, influence on Hawthorne, 213–14 (n. 3)

Burroughs, John, *Notes on Walt Whitman as Poet and Person*, on Whitman's mysticism, 109

Burroughs, William: *Naked Lunch*, 10; critical estimate, 19–20; mentioned, 16

Caldwell, Erskine, *God's Little Acre, Tobacco Road*, literature of the '30's, 78

Campbell, Joseph: *The Hero with a Thousand Faces*, on the personal unconscious, 251; metaphor of the journey, 258–59

Camus, Albert: Faulkner's views of, 48; mentioned, 65

Capote, Truman: critical estimate, 18; mentioned, 12

Cather, Willa: in the modern literary context, 81; literary reputation, 81; themes: struggle,

Index

Eliot, T. S. (*Continued*)
Four Quartets: compared with "Song of Myself," 112–36; emotional impact of, 124–25; fusing of images, 132; as music, 115–16; mystical experience as dramatic frame, 135–36; mystical experience as journey, 133–34; as mysticism dramatized, 119–24; paradox in, 129–30; prophetic tone in, 127–28; the role of the poet in, 125–27; theme of humility as key to mystical illumination, 124–25; theme of love, 134–35; theme of time, 128–29; water imagery in, 132–33

Ellison, Ralph: *Invisible Man*, quest for identity, 14; critical estimate, 20

Emerson, Ralph Waldo: "Friendship" and Melville, 171–72; and the metaphor of the journey, 258–59; and the oversoul, 252–53; and modern psychological thought, 252–53; and the quest for identity, 96; and Whitman's mysticism, 109; and Whitman, the oversoul, 101–2; mentioned, 249

Existentialism: and Faulkner, 48–49; as influence on the contemporary novel, 10; and the quest for identity, 96; mentioned, 80

Faulkner, John, *My Brother Bill*, 42

Faulkner, William: on art, in letter to Cowley, 47; and black humor, 15; characters created by, 56–64; dehumanized characters, 59–62; enduring characters, 63–64; circular imagery, 51–52; letters to Cowley, 43, 44; critical survey, 44–46; descent into the vortex as technique, 53–55; fact and legend, 41–43; his human sympathy, 50–52; his humor, 46; and Henry James, 54–55; literary

influence of, 9–10, 12, 21; his literary reputation, 65; moral judgment in, 62; philosophy of, in letter to Cowley, 47; place in literary history, 78; technique in, 52–53

Absalom, Absalom!: circle image in, 52; Clytemnestra as enduring character in, 63, 64; comment on by Faulkner, 51; key event in, 55; Henry Sutpen as alienated hero in, 56, 59; Thomas Sutpen as dehumanized character in, 59, 61–62; mentioned, 45

As I Lay Dying: Addie Bundren as dehumanized character in, 59, 60; Cash as enduring character in, 63; Darl Bundren as alienated hero in, 56, 57–58; humor and horror, 49–50; key event, 54; mentioned, 45

The Fable, critical estimate, 46
Go Down, Moses, 45
The Hamlet, 45, 62
Intruder in the Dust, critical estimate, 46

Light in August: comment on by Faulkner, 51; Joe Christmas as dehumanized character in, 59, 61; Lena Grove as enduring character in, 63; Gail Hightower as alienated hero in, 56, 58–59; humor and horror, 50; key event in, 54–55; "wheel of thinking," 51–52; mentioned, 45, 62

The Mansion, 46, 62
Mosquitoes, mentioned, 45
Pylon, mentioned, 45
The Reivers, 46
Requiem for a Nun: critical estimate, 46; mentioned, 62

Sanctuary: Horace Benbow as alienated hero in, 56, 58; comment on by Faulkner, 51; humor and horror, 50; key event in, 54; Ruby La Marr as enduring character in, 63; moral

265